CW01238766

AN ATLAS OF THE PENINSULAR WAR

By the same author:

Wellington at War in the Peninsula:
An Overview and Guide

*

Wellington Invades France:
The Final Phase of the Peninsular War, 1813–1814

*

A Commanding Presence
Wellington in the Peninsula: Logistics · Strategy · Survival

*

Los Curiosos Impertinentes:
Viajeros Ingleses por España; 1760–1855

*

Richard Ford, 1796–1858:
Hispanophile, Connoisseur and Critic

IAN ROBERTSON
AN ATLAS OF THE PENINSULAR WAR
1808–1814

CARTOGRAPHY BY MARTIN BROWN

YALE UNIVERSITY PRESS
NEW HAVEN AND LONDON

Published with assistance from the Annie Burr Lewis Fund

Copyright © 2010 by Ian Robertson

Original cartography derived either from out of copyright material or from Data Spain (© Data Spain).
www.data-spain.com

All rights reserved. This book may not be reproduced in whole or in part, in any form
(beyond that copying permitted by Sections 107 and 108 of the U.S, Copyright Law and
except by reviewers for the public press), without written permission from the publishers.

For information about this and other Yale University Press publications please contact:

U.S. Office: sales.press@yale.edu yalebooks.com
Europe Office: sales@yaleup.co.uk www.yalebooks.co.uk

Designed and set in Perpetua by Martin Brown
Printed in China through Worldprint

Library of Congress Cataloging-in-Publication Data

Robertson, Ian.
　An atlas of the Peninsular War 1808-1814 / cartography by Martin Brown.
　　p. cm.
　ISBN 978-0-300-14869-5
1. Peninsular War, 1807-1814—Maps. 2. Peninsular War, 1807-1814—Battlefields—Maps. 3.
Peninsular War, 1807-1814—Campaigns. 4. Atlases. I. Title.
　G1797.S1.R6 2010
　940.2'70223—dc22
　　　　　　　　　　　　　　　　　　　　　　　　　　　　　　2010027096

A catalogue record for this book is available from the British Library

10 9 8 7 6 5 4 3 2 1

Contents

List of Illustrations		vii
Preface and Acknowledgements		ix
Chronology		xi
Key to Cartographic Symbols		xvi
Introduction		1
The Historical Context		16

Atlas Section

1	Physical Map of the Peninsula	20
2	Catalonia, Aragon and the Levante Coast: insets of the Battle of Castalla, and the Siege of Tarragona	22
3	Central and Western Andalucia: inset of Cadiz area	24
4	The Portuguese Coast: from the Mouth of the Mondego to Lisbon	26
5	The Combat at Roliça	28
6	The Battle of Vimeiro	30
7	Moore's Campaign: inset of the combat at Sahagún	32
8	The Battle of Corunna	34
9	Wellesley's Advance on Oporto and Pursuit of Soult	36
10	The Passage of the Douro at Oporto	38
11	Wellesley's Advance into the Tagus Valley, and Retirement to Portugal	40
12	The Battle of Talavera I	42
13	The Battle of Talavera II	44
14	Combats on the Agueda and the Côa	46
15	Masséna's Invasion	48
16	The Battle of Busaco: insets of Ney's and Reynier's attacks	50
17	The Lines of Torres Vedras: inset of their position	52
18	Masséna Isolated and in Retreat: inset of the combat at Sabugal	54
19	The Battle of Barrosa: inset of the Barrosa Campaign	56
20	The Battle of Fuentes de Oñoro I	58
21	The Battle of Fuentes de Oñoro II	60
22	South-west Spain	62
23	The Battle of Albuera I	64
24	The Battle of Albuera II: and 2 details	66
25	Combats of El Bodón, and Arroyomolinos de Montánchez: inset of Winter Cantonments, 1811–12	68
26	The Siege of Ciudad Rodrigo: cross-section of Greater Breach	70
27	The Final Siege of Badajoz: inset of breached walls, and cross-section	72
28	The Almaraz Expedition	74
29	Manoeuvring prior to Salamanca: inset of the Fall of the Forts	76
30	The Battle of Salamanca I	78
31	The Battle of Salamanca II: 4 details: inset of the Combat at Garcihernández	80
32	The Advance on Madrid and Burgos, and Retirement to Portugal	82
33	The Siege of Burgos	84
34	Winter Cantonments, and Preparing for the Spring	86
35	The Advance on Vitoria	88
36	The Battle of Vitoria	91
37	The Pyrenean Quadrilateral	94
38	Soult's Counter-offensive, and Retreat	96
39	The Combats at Roncesvalles, and Maya	98
40	The Battles of Sorauren	100
41	The Siege of San Sebastian	102

42	The Frontier Triangle	104
43	The Combats at San Marcial, and Vera	106
44	The Passage of the Bidasoa and the Ascent of La Rhune	108
45	The Battle of the Nivelle	110
46	The Battle of the Nive	112
47	The Battle of St Pierre	114
48	Bayonne: the Investment; and the Sortie (14 April 1814)	116
49	The Advance on Orthez: inset of the Combat at Garris	118
50	The Battle of Orthez	120
51	The Advance on Bordeaux, Tarbes, and Toulouse	122
52	The Combats at Aire, and Tarbes	124
53	Manoeuvres on the Garonne, and the Battle of Toulouse	126

Dispersal, and Epilogue	129
Glossary	132
Selective Bibliography	140
Index to Actions	143

Illustrations

Thomas Lawrence, *Portrait of Sir George Murray.*	4
A mountain road west of Fundão, similar to the 'Estrada Nova'.	4
Anon. *Portrait of Sir Thomas Livingstone Mitchell c.1839.*	5
Thomas St Clair, *Troops bivouacked near Vila Velha.*	8
Contour depicted on a contemporary map of the area between Almeida and Coimbra compared to that on a modern map.	9
Detail of a contemporary map of the Bayonne area by Tomás Lopéz, dated 1793.	10
Edward Orme, *View of Elvas with the Forte de Gracia in the foreground, and to the right, the Amoreira aqueduct.*	12
Distant view (centre) of the Seminary at Oporto, with the Serra convent (right).	12
Aerial view of the fortress of Almeida.	12
Thomas St Clair, *British troops fording the Mondego.*	12
The Dos Casas stream at Fuentes de Oñoro, in 1960.	13
Wellington's Headquarters at Freineda during two winters.	13
William Bradford, *Crossing the Tagus at Vila Velha.*	13
Ciudad Rodrigo seen from the Greater Teson, in c. 1960.	13
Anon. *Anchorage at Pasajes, vital for the provisioning of Allied troops at San Sebastian.*	13
Edward Orme, *Allied artillery firing from the summit of Monte Ulia, San Sebastian.*	14
Plan of the Bidasoa estuary at low tide, dated 1779.	14
Edward Orme, *Distant view of Bayonne from sandhills to the west, near the site of the bridge of boats (detail).*	15
Robert Batty, *Wellington's Headquarters (right) at St Jean-de-Luz.*	15
Robert Batty, *Looking south from St Etienne towards the Citadel and Bayonne, with the distinctive silhouette of La Rhune (left), and the Peñas de Haya (in the distance beyond the cathedral).*	15
A corner of the Coldstream Guards Cemetery, Bayonne.	15
The Château de Larraldea, near Villefranque, when last seen by the author.	15
Detail of a contemporary map of Copenhagen.	16
Henri L'Evêque, *Disembarkation at Mondego Bay (detail).*	26
The embarkation at Corunna.	34
J. J. Forrester, *Watercolour of the Serra Convent from the north bank of the Douro.*	38
A contemporary plan of the Tagus at Almaraz	74
George Hennell, *Sketch of Fort San Vicente, Salamanca, made the day after its surrender.*	78
François-Joseph Heim, *The French besieged at Burgos.*	84
The bridge of Tres Puentes, Vitoria.	91
The ridge of the Lesser Rhune seen from the summit of La Rhune.	108
Edmund Wheatley, *Sketch of the damaged church of St Etienne, seen from the Jewish Cemetery, Bayonne.*	116
Anon. *Contemporary sketch of the battlefield of Toulouse from east of the Hers.*	128
Robert Batty, *Bridge of Boats across the Adour at Bayonne.*	133
The rambla, *or dry bed of the river Ponsul at Idanha-a-Velha.*	137

Illustrations | vii

Preface and Acknowledgements

My interest in the Peninsular War was prompted by my marriage to a Basque. At that time – now over fifty years ago – I started to collect the narratives of earlier English travellers to Spain and Portugal, together with contemporary memoirs of the war, which could still be acquired inexpensively and with comparative ease. There was little in print, and circumstances allowed me to commission, edit – indeed largely rewrite – Jac Weller's *Wellington in the Peninsula*, and the subject has engaged my attention ever since. That I had made Spain my base during the 1970s and '80s, when compiling the 'Blue Guide' to the country (followed by those to Portugal, and France, among others), also gave me many opportunities to explore the Peninsular War battlefields. It is only by visiting such sites that one can have any proper appreciation of the terrain, without suggesting that one need follow the precise track of retreat from Cacabelos to Lugo in a blizzard, or from Talavera to Trujillo under a blistering summer sun: let imagination run riot.

When adverting to guides – the uncritical ones – Aldous Huxley once remarked that 'For every traveller who has any taste of his own, the only useful guide-book will be the one he himself has written. All others are an exasperation – they make him travel long miles to see a mound of rubbish; they go into ecstasies over mere antiquity …' etc.; and I promised myself to avoid, whenever possible, misleading the traveller in such ways. Later, when writing on the Peninsular War, I became increasingly aware that the maps and plans included in almost all newly published books on that war were thoroughly unsatisfactory, a sorry situation which – with the necessary collaboration of a professional cartographer – I resolved to remedy as best I could, should the opportunity occur at some future date. I can only hope that this atlas will neither exasperate the fastidious perfectionist or professed expert, nor lead the unprejudiced reader too far astray from the often devious paths of the Peninsula, for I am only too well aware of the manifold hazards incidental to any compilation of this complexity.

The illustrations included have been accumulated over many years, and although the sources are indicated after their captions in several instances, I have not been able to establish these in every case. While every effort has been made to obtain permission to use what may be copyright material, the author and publishers apologise for any errors or omissions, and would be grateful to be notified of any corrections that should be incorporated in future editions.

Indeed, while not inviting controversy or being drawn into quibbling correspondence, I would welcome my attention being drawn to any untoward errors which – unwittingly, but inevitably – this first edition will contain, together with any positive suggestions for its improvement.

To list all those who have gone out of their way to provide advice or to assist me otherwise during the long gestation of the atlas, would extend these paragraphs inordinately. I have not attempted to incorporate all recommendations, and thus remain responsible for any number of minor inexactitudes, imprecisions, omissions, inconsistencies, and deficiencies – both in the text and the cartography – that will, inevitably, remain. Not every combat is described and depicted, nor is the probable position traced of every skirmishing line, battery, or cavalry outpost, for instance, any more than the location of all bogs, woods, or hamlets in existence two centuries ago.

Firstly, I must thank Rory Muir, and Andrew Hewson, without whose tenacity in persuading Robert Baldock to accept my proposal, it would have remained a mirage. Secondly, Martin Brown, who has so well displayed his technical virtuosity in creating a comprehensive and coherent series of maps and plans of Peninsular terrain, animating its frequently skeletal structure by depicting clearly and graphically the course of various campaigns and actions fought by Allied armies under Wellington's command during the ebb and flow of that long war. Throughout – and at some distance, geographically – in our joint struggle to approximate accuracy, he has worked indefatigably, tolerating with exemplary patience my constant interruptions over matters of detail, etc.

It may be invidious to refer to a few only by name when expressing my obligation, but I cannot leave the following unacknowledged, all of whom – in a variety of ways – have provided encouragement, facilities, or information, ploughed similar furrows in military or cartographic fields, and shared their knowledge and enthusiasm: Michael Ayrton, Andrew Bamford, Peter Barnes, Robert Burnham, George Caldwell, Christopher Chilcott, Robert Cooper, Mark Corby, Andrew Cormack, Michael Crumplin, Huw Davies, Guy Dempsey, Maria Helena Dias (Lisbon), Peter Edwards, Gareth Glover, Yolande Hodson, Martin Howard, John Hussey, Claude Larronde, Alicia Laspra (Oviedo), John H. Lewis, Nicholas Lipscombe, Claude Louvigné, Miguel Martin Mas (Salamanca), Augusto Morillo, Howie Muir, Gerald Napier, John Peaty, Victor Powell, Pedro Prieto (Romangordo), Derwent Renshaw, Carlos Sanchez Rubio (Badajoz), Richard Tennant, Mark Thompson, Jamie Wilson, and Christopher Woolgar.

In comparison to the open-handed co-operation of private individuals, when applied to for help or advice, the response by some institutions can only be described as perfunctory. Nevertheless, Taylor, Fladgate & Yeatman in Oporto must be thanked for permission to reproduce the illustration by Joseph James Forrester; William Heinemann Ltd for George Hennell's sketch on p.78, and Pearson Educational for Edmund Wheatley's on p.116. Jon Parker of Data-Spain has generously provided a deal of cartographical support. I am much obliged to Lucy Isenberg for suggesting several judicious amendments to the text and bringing a number of solecisms to my attention. I remain responsible for all lingering errors and infelicities, and entirely so for any that may still lurk in the mapping.

I am very grateful also for the moral support of many old friends, though few of them may have understood quite why I have found the subject of the Peninsular War so absorbing; while my wife Marie-Thérèse has not only patiently indulged my interest for at least five decades, but tolerated the sight of a paper-littered library far too long. Although assured that this description of the battlefields we have explored together is likely to be 'my parting shot', it remains to be seen – should I survive the inevitable 'flak' its publication will attract from those who profess to know better – whether I can keep to my promise to 'clear up'. Nevertheless, if this atlas is instrumental in pointing out further paths to be pursued, or in inciting younger students to undertake the chase of any hares it may start, it will have realised in part its purpose.

My impertinence must be excused for adapting to *Military Historians*, *Cartographers* and *Atlas*-projectors the wry comment made by Jonathan Swift towards the conclusion of *Gulliver's Travels*:

Writers of Travels, like *Dictionary*-Makers, are sunk into Oblivion by the Weight and Bulk of those who come last, and therefore lie uppermost. And it is highly probable, that such Travellers who shall hereafter visit the Countries described in this Work of mine, may by detecting my Errors, (if there be any) and by adding many new Discoveries of their own, jostle me out of Vogue, and stand in my Place; making the World forget that ever I was an Author. This indeed would be too great a Mortification if I wrote for Fame: But, as my sole intention was the PUBLICK GOOD, I cannot be altogether disappointed.

Arles, 8 March 2010

Chronology

The majority of Allied actions or movements are printed in bold. To emphasise the spread of time, some months are deliberately left vacant, being those in which little fighting of any consequence took place.

1807
31 July–30 Sept.		Copenhagen expedition
18 Oct.		French troops, commanded by Junot, enter Spain to attack Portugal
30 Nov.		French vanguard enters Lisbon
Dec.		

1808
8 Jan.		Another French army invades Spain to occupy several towns in Biscay and Navarre
10 Feb.		French troops enter Catalonia; Barcelona occupied on 29th
23 Mar.		Madrid occupied by the French under Murat
Apr.		
2 May		(El Dos de Mayo): insurrection in Madrid, followed by uprisings in many parts of Spain
15 June–13 Aug.		First French siege of Zaragoza
12 July		Wellesley in temporary command of expeditionary force to the Peninsula
14		Spanish defeated at Medina de Rioseco (north-east of Valladolid)
19		Dupont, discomforted at Bailén, surrenders to the Spanish under Castaños on the 22nd
24–16 Aug.		Second French siege of Gerona
1 Aug.		British expeditionary force starts landing at the mouth of the Mondego
17		Combat of **Roliça** (south of Obidos)
21 Aug.		Junot defeated at **Vimeiro** (north-west of Torres Vedras)
30		*Convention of Cintra* signed, by which French forces in Portugal are to be repatriated
20 Sept.		Wellesley, recalled, sails for England
6 Oct.		Sir John Moore in command at Lisbon. Moore's troops start their advance towards the Spanish frontier
29		Spanish under Blake dispersed at Zornosa (between Durango and Bilbao)
6 Nov.		Napoleon reaches Vitoria on his march towards Madrid
10–11		Blake defeated at Espinosa de los Monteros (north of Medina de Pomar)
13		Moore's vanguard enters Salamanca
22		Baird's units from Corunna reach Astorga (west of León)
23		Moore concentrated at Salamanca; Spanish defeated at Tudela (north-west of Zaragoza)
30		Spaniards scattered by Polish cavalry at the Puerto de Somosierra (north of Madrid)
3 Dec.		Hope's units join up with Moore's
4		Napoleon occupies Madrid
20–20 Feb.		Second French siege of Zaragoza
21 Dec.		British cavalry combat at **Sahagún** (south-east of León)
22		Napoleon leads troops across the Guadarrama range north-west of Madrid in an attempt to encircle Moore
24		Moore commences his retreat into Galicia
27		Minor cavalry action near **Mayorga** (north-east of Benavente)
29		Delaying action near **Benavente** (north of Zamora)

1809	1 Jan.	Soult left in pursuit of Moore, while Napoleon returns to France		18	French discomforted by the Spanish at Tamames (east of Ciudad Rodrigo)
	11	Moore's vanguard reaches Corunna		19 Nov.	Spanish defeated at Ocaña (south-east of Aranjuez)
	13	Spanish defeated at Uclés (south-east of Tarancón)		28	Spanish defeated at Alba de Tormes (south-east of Salamanca)
	16	Moore mortally wounded at **Corunna**; British army evacuated		Dec.	
	20 Feb.	Zaragoza capitulates to the French	**1810**	Jan.	
	29 Mar.	Spanish defeated at Medellín (east of Mérida); Soult occupies Oporto		1 Feb.	Seville occupied by the French
				5	Cadiz invested by the French
	23 Apr.	Wellesley again commanding in Portugal		19–20 Mar.	Skirmish at Barba del Puerco (east of Almeida)
	11 May	Action at Grijó, on approaching Oporto		21	French invest Astorga
	12	**Passage of the Douro** at Oporto		22 Apr.	Astorga surrenders
	21–3	Battle of Aspern–Essling, forcing Napoleon to withdraw from Vienna		28 May	Masséna enters Salamanca
				June	French invest Ciudad Rodrigo
	23	Spanish repulse Suchet at Alcañiz (south-east of Zaragosa)		10 July	Masséna takes Ciudad Rodrigo, and advances on Portugal
	24–11 Dec.	Third, and main, siege of Gerona		16	Combat near Barquilla and Villar de Ciervo
	10 June	Bridge at Alcantara broken. Victor retires up the Tagus valley		21	Fort Conception blown up
				24	Combats on the Côa (west of Ciudad Rodrigo)
	15	Spanish, under Blake, beaten at Maria, and at Belchite (18th), both south of Zaragoza		26	The French commence investment of Almeida
	3 July	Wellesley enters Spain at Zarza la Mayor (west of Plasencia)		15 Aug.	Masséna'commences bombardment of Almeida
	5–6	Napoleon defeats the Austrians at Wagram		22	Cavalry action at Ladoeiro (east of Castelo Branco)
	27–8	Major confrontation at **Talavera**, after which the British are forced to retire towards Portugal. Wellesley is created Viscount Wellington shortly afterwards		26	Explosion of Almeida's magazine, the fortress capitulating next day
				19 Sept.	French vanguard enters Viseu
				27	Masséna defeated at **Busaco**
				10 Oct.	Masséna approaches and is frustrated by The Lines of Torres Vedras
	28–9 Dec.	Walcheren Expedition (at mouth of Scheldt)		17 Nov.	Masséna withdraws to Santarém and its vicinity
	11 Aug.	Spanish defeated at Almonacid (south-east of Toledo)		Dec.	
	Sept. Oct.	Construction commences of defensive works north of Lisbon, later known as 'The Lines of Torres Vedras'	**1811**	11–23 Jan.	Soult besieges and takes Olivenza, and invests Badajoz

xii AN ATLAS OF THE PENINSULAR WAR

1811 (cont.)	19 Feb	Spanish defeated at the Gebora (just north of Badajoz)		Nov. 21 Dec.–	
	3 Mar.	Masséna's army starts its retreat from Santarém		4 Jan.	French ineffectually besiege Tarifa (south-west of Algeciras)
	5	Graham defeats Victor at **Barrosa**, near Chiclana (south-east of Cadiz)		26 Dec.	Spanish defeated at Valencia: Blake surrenders to Suchet on 8 Jan.
	10	Soult captures Badajoz Action at **Pombal** (north-east of Leiria)	**1812**	8 Jan– 19 Feb.	Wellington invests and recaptures **Ciudad Rodrigo**
	12	Action at **Redinha** (north of Pombal)		19 Mar.	Wellington again besieges Badajoz
	14	Action at **Casal Novo** (west of Miranda do Corvo)		6 Apr.	**Badajos** successfully stormed
	15	Action at **Foz de Arouce** (south-east of Coimbra)		11	Cavalry affair at **Villagarcía** (north-west of Llerena)
	25	Cavalry affair at **Campo Maior** (north-west of Badajoz)		19 May	Hill's successful raid at **Almaraz** (north-east of Trujillo)
	3 Apr.	Combat at **Sabugal** (south-east of Guarda)		1 June	Spanish defeated at Bornos (north-east of Arcos de la Frontera)
	22–3	Wellington reconnoitres Badajoz, and orders Beresford to prepare to besiege the fortress		11	Cavalry affair at **Maguilla** (north-west of Llerena)
				14	Napoleon invades Russia
				17	America declares war on Britain
	3–5 May	Wellington repulses Masséna at **Fuentes de Oñoro** (west of Ciudad Rodrigo)		17–18 July	Confrontations on the Guarena: Castrejon and Castrillo (some distance north-east of Salamanca)
	6–12	Badajoz invested, but the siege is raised		22	Marmont defeated at **Salamanca**
	10–11	Escape via Barba del Puerco of the garrison from Almeida		23	Cavalry affair at **Garcihernández** (north-east of Alba de Tormes)
	16	Soult is frustrated by Beresford at **La Albuera** (south-east of Badajoz)		11 Aug.	Combat at Majadahonda (west of Madrid) during the advance on Madrid
	25	Cavalry affair at **Usagre** (north-west of Llerena)		12	The Allies enter Madrid; Wellington declared Marquess on 18th
	27	Badajoz re-invested and besieged		24	Siege of Cadiz raised
	10 June	Failure of assault determined Wellington to turn siege into blockade		27	Soult evacuates Seville, which is occupied by Skerrett
	13	Wellington offers battle on the Caia (east of Elvas)		31	Leaving Madrid, Wellington advances on Burgos
	28 July	Tarragona falls to Suchet		19 Sept.	**Burgos** besieged
	19 Aug.	Figueras falls to the French		30	Hill's troops enter Toledo
	25 Sept.	Action at **El Bodón** (south of Ciudad Rodrigo)		4 Oct.	Soult and Joseph Bonaparte converge west of Hellín (south of Albacete)
	28	Wellington offers battle on the upper Côa		12	Napoleon retreats from Moscow
	25 Oct.	Spanish under Blake defeated at Sagunto (north of Valencia)		22	Raising the siege of Burgos, Wellington retires south-west
	28	French surprised and scattered by Hill at **Arroyomolinos** de Montánchez (north-east of Mérida)			

1812 (cont.)	23 Oct.	Cavalry affair at **Venta del Pozo** (south-west of Burgos)		22	Soult commences his counter-offensive in the Pyrenees
	27	Hill receives Wellington's order to join him north of the Guadarrama		25	First assault on San Sebastian fails; simultaneous actions at **Maya**, and **Roncesvalles**
	2 Nov.	The French re-occupy Madrid after it is evacuated by Hill's rearguard		28–30	Soult defeated at **Sorauren** (north of Pamplona) and near Lizaso (further north-west)
	8	Allies concentrated near Salamanca			
	17	Combat at San Muñoz on the Huebra		30 July–	
	19	Allied columns re-enter Ciudad Rodrigo		15 Aug.	Bentinck blockades Tarragona
	Dec.			1–2 Aug.	Soult retreats down the Bidasoa valley: actions at Sumbilla, the bridge of Yanci, and Echalar
1813	Jan.				
	14 Feb.	Joseph first hears of the débâcle in Russia		12	Austria declares war on France, news of which reaches Wellington on 3 Sept.
	20	Foy's raid on Béjar foiled			
	23 Mar.	Joseph sets up Headquarters in Valladolid, having evacuated Madrid; Soult is recalled to France		26–27	Napoleon defeats the Allies at Dresden
				30	French under Vandamme defeated at Kulm, report of which reached Wellington on 15 Sept.
	13 Apr.	French dispersed by Sir John Murray at **Castalla**		31	Spanish troops repulse Soult at **San Marcial**. **San Sebastián** stormed, the citadel surrendering on 8 Sept.
	22 May	Wellington commences offensive operations			
	30	Passage of the Esla, north-west of Zamora			
	2 June	Cavalry affair at **Morales** (east of Toro)		3 Sept.	Wellington hears of the rupture of the Armistice of Pleiswitz
	3–12	Sir John Murray's abortive siege of **Tarragona**		13	Action at Ordal between Bentinck and Suchet
	4	*Armistice of Pleiswitz* signed between the Northern Allies and Napoleon, extending the truce until 20 July		7 Oct.	The **Passage of the Bidasoa**: Wellington sets foot in France
				16–19	Napoleon defeated at Leipzig
	21	Joseph and Jourdan defeated at **Vitoria**		10 Nov.	General advance into France at the battle of the **Nivelle**
	25	Pamplona blockaded, surrendering on 31 Oct.		8 Dec.	Wellington receives confirmation of French defeat at Leipzig
	26	Action at **Tolosa** (south of San Sebastian)		9–10	Soult's counter-offensive thwarted at the battle of the **Nive**
	28	San Sebastian invested		11	Fernando VII signs the Treaty of Valençay, and re-enters Spain via Catalonia on 24 March
	29	*Treaty of Reichenbach*: Austria agrees to re-enter the war if Napoleon does not agree to peace terms			
	1 July	Napoleon, at Dresden, learns of the defeat at Vitoria		13	Hill defeats Soult at **St Pierre**, south-east of Bayonne, which is invested
	5	Suchet evacuates Valencia			
	11	Soult returns to command French forces facing Wellington		17	Graham's expeditionary force lands in Holland

1814	Jan.			30	*The Treaty of Paris* signed
	15 Feb.	Combat at **Garris** (north-west of St Palais)		June	Start of dispersal of Allied troops in south-west France
	26	Hope crosses the bridge of boats west of Bayonne, now surrounded		13	Wellington resigns command of Spanish forces
	27	Soult defeated at **Orthez**		14	Wellington's Farewell to his troops near Bordeaux
	2 Mar.	Combat at **Aire**		23	Wellington reaches Dover after five years and two months absence from Britain
	8	Beresford detached towards Bordeaux, occupied on the 12th			
	8–9	British failure at Bergen-op-Zoom		July	
	20	Combat at **Tarbes**		8 Aug.	Wellington leaves for Paris as ambassador
	24	Soult's troops enter Toulouse			
	25	Marmont and Mortier defeated at Fère-Champenoise (east of Sézanne)		Sept.	Last British troops in the vicinity of Bayonne and the Spanish frontier sail for England
	31	Marmont signs *Capitulation of Paris* and Allied troops enter the city			
				Oct.	
	10 Apr.	The battle of **Toulouse**, Soult retreating east during the ensuing night		Nov.	
				24 Dec.	End of the American War
	12	Wellington receives news of Napoleon's abdication (on the 6th)	1815	24 Jan.	Wellington leaves Paris to attend *Congress of Vienna*
	14	Sortie from **Bayonne**		26 Feb.	Napoleon escapes from Elba
	15	*Treaty of Fontainebleau* signed. Napoleon leaves for Elba on the 28th		7 Mar.	News of the escape reaches Vienna
				20	Napoleon enters Paris
	27	Bayonne formally surrenders		29	Wellington leaves Vienna
	30	Wellington leaves Toulouse for Paris		5 Apr.	Wellington reaches Brussels
	3 May	Wellington created Duke		May	
	14	Wellington returns to Toulouse		16 June	Battles of Quatre Bras, and Ligny
	17	Wellington leaves Toulouse for Madrid, remaining there from the 24th until 8 June		18	Napoleon defeated at Waterloo

Key to Cartographic Symbols

National Colours (arrow/unit/symbol)

- British and Allied
- French
- Portuguese
- Spanish

Military Units

- artillery batteries in position or motion (brigade, troop, company)
- cavalry in position (brigade, regiment, squadron)
- cavalry in column
- infantry formed in line
- infantry without indicating formation
- infantry in column of march
- infantry formed in square
- skirmishers
- baggage train park

Military Formations

- *xxx* COMMANDER — Corps
- *xx(1st)* COMMANDER — Division
- *x* COMMANDER — Brigade

General Military Symbols

- advance
- retreat
- trench or parallels
- redoubt
- lines of fortification
- battlefield

General Cartographic Symbols

- village/town/city
- built-up area
- main road
- track
- national boundary
- river/stream (sometimes with dry river bed)
- direction of river flow
- bridge
- mountain pass
- mountain peak
- contours (with heights in metric and with the contour value facing downhill)
- swamp/marsh
- woodland/scrubland
- rocky cliffline
- sand

An Atlas of the Peninsular War

Introduction

The many battles fought by Wellington have always excited interest and controversy, and always will. It is still not generally realised that, apart from the brief Waterloo campaign, a very high proportion – indeed virtually all the fighting on land between British and French troops during the Napoleonic period in Europe, and which formed a significant element of the eventual defeat of the emperor – took place in Portugal and Spain, and this conflict is thus known in England as the Peninsular War, and in Spain as La Guerra de la Independencia. Among other confrontations were those at Maida (1806); the disastrous Walcheren Expedition during the summer of 1809; and that at Bergen-op-Zoom in March 1814, not to mention landings at Naples in 1805, at Copenhagen in 1807, and in Sicily. Napoleon himself spent a mere two months in the Peninsula – November and December 1808. Nevertheless, the war exacted an immense commitment of imperial manpower and resources, and extended over a period of almost six years, from August 1808, when, provisionally commanded by Sir Arthur Wellesley, a British expeditionary force was landed on the Portuguese coast, until the culminating bloodbath at Toulouse in April 1814.

It was not until after the battle of Talavera, when created viscount, that Wellesley was known as Lord Wellington, or The Peer. He had served his apprenticeship in India, where he had landed early in 1797 as Colonel of the King's 33rd Foot, which had given him invaluable experience in the field: his successes at Seringapatam, Assaye, Argaum, and Gawilghur had already added lustre to his name, even if these campaigns seemed remote and peripheral to the contest taking place in Europe. Since his return to England in 1805, and partly due to family influence, he had held the post of Chief Secretary for Ireland. In August 1807 he had commanded a brigade during the Copenhagen expedition, and Parliament had thanked him for his part in bringing the recalcitrant Danes to heel.

The Peninsular War is a large subject, magisterially described in Sir Charles Oman's seven-volume *History*, also in the five relevant volumes of Sir John Fortescue's *History of the British Army*, and it has been written about repeatedly since both these works were completed eighty years ago.

Political developments which affected Wellington's strategic decisions are mentioned only *en passant* in the Historical Context that follows, for their complexities have been admirably explained in Rory Muir's *Britain and the Defeat of Napoleon*, while both Richard Glover's *Peninsular Preparation* and S.G.P. Ward's *Wellington's Headquarters* provide a great deal of invaluable information concerning the British army at the time, and the ramifications of its organisation and administration.[1]

Whilst historians of the Peninsular War in particular are grateful that both Oman and Fortescue have been reprinted in recent years,[2] the complement of maps and plans they contained were not reproduced satisfactorily and, in many cases, were reduced in size. Although superior in quality to most others printed in later studies, neither set of maps was entirely reliable. As far as the Peninsular War is concerned, compilations of contemporary maps and plans have been inadequate, and almost all the mapping in books published in recent decades has provided only very perfunctory representations of terrain.

The present atlas, concentrating on those campaigns in which Wellington commanded Allied armies in the successful prosecution of that war, sets out to provide a visual exposition of the ebb and flow of that long-drawn-out struggle which will satisfy both the professional and amateur.

In *Salamanca 1812* – Rory Muir's meticulous study of that action alone – when referring to maps of the battlefield, the author states that while Fortescue's map is 'the one which appears the most detailed and authoritative', the contour lines (marking every 10-foot change in elevation) give the impression that the terrain is more rugged than is the case; also, when compared closely to the modern Spanish ordnance survey map, significant differences in the distances between points are revealed. Muir refers to a number of other discrepancies, of which the most important is that Fortescue 'shows the Teso de San Miguel lying directly behind the village [of Los Arapiles], while the ordnance map (confirmed by personal observation) places its highest point further east, filling part of the gap between the village and the Lesser Arapile. Nor do the gradient lines always appear accurate when compared to the terrain on the spot.' Muir commented also that while in some respects Oman's maps may be more accurate, his depiction of hills was not always entirely convincing.

As far as the movement of troops on maps and their position on battle-plans is concerned, I can only reiterate Rory Muir's cautionary observation, that in many cases they can only be approximate or conjectural. Both depend on the same uncertain, partial, and often contradictory sources, and cannot pretend to be absolutely exact or definitive, nor should the information displayed visually in this way be accorded greater authority than that provided by those participating in an action or by later military historians: a measure of imprecision is inevitable, and the compiler of this atlas is the first to admit that no positions are, or can be, set in stone. What source, one wonders – whether historical or cartographical – can be relied on as being accurate? Memories are fallible or descriptions are incomplete. Lord Hatherton recorded that on 19 May 1820, when quizzed at dinner on the subject, the Duke of Wellington 'declared he had never seen the truth printed about public matters in the course of his participation in public affairs. All men seemed to be liars. Someone asked him if he did not except his own dispatches, upon which he observed: "I never told a falsehood in them, but I never told the whole truth, nor anything like it. Either one or the other would have been contradicted by 5,000 officers in my army in their letters to their mothers, wives, brothers and sisters and cousins, all of whom imagined they as well understood what they saw as I did."'

Among the many problems encountered – and by no means all have been properly resolved – have been the precise course and condition of roads and tracks (frequently little more than *caminos de herradura* or bridle-paths at the time) and also the amount, quantity and density of ground cover in the way of thickets and woods, etc., which may have obscured the position of enemy units or delayed the rapid movement of troops, for example. Likewise, although comparatively accurate contemporary town plans have been found helpful, the size of villages must have varied very considerably; and some have barely survived the passing of two centuries.

In the majority of cases, the plans that follow depict the probable position of confronting units at the commencement or at a crucial juncture in the battle. In many cases, it is uncertain also at what precise time an engagement or separate operation may have begun or how long it lasted: rarely did ranks remain static for long. If the disposition of troops altered to any great extent during a particular action (as at Fuentes de Oñoro or Albuera, for example), two plans – more in the case of Salamanca – are provided; but while the second should provide sufficient idea of its progress, admittedly this may not be always entirely adequate. Occasionally, the advance of separate bodies of troops at different times is detailed in an inset. In Wellington's words, the history of a battle was 'not unlike the history of a ball. Some individuals may recollect all the little events of which the great result is the battle won or lost; but no individual can recollect the order in which, or the exact moment in which, they occurred, which makes all the difference as to their value or importance.'

***

Very little in the way of large-scale maps of the Peninsula was available in the early years of the nineteenth century except for the grossly inadequate provincial maps issued in Madrid after 1765 by Tomás Lopéz (1730–1802). Nor could Cassini's extensive series covering France (at 1: 86,400, up-dated between 1798 and 1812), be relied on, any more than those issued by the French État-Major. Among others at hand were Thomas Jefferys' *Map of Portugal* (the 2nd edition of which was published by William Faden in 1790); E. Mentelle and P.G. Chanlaire's map of the Peninsula, published by John Stockdale on 13 October 1808, which gave only a very rough representation of its terrain; Aaron Arrowsmith's map of 1809, based on Roussel and La Blottière's *Map of the Pyrenees and Adjacent Provinces* (1730), with additions from Lopéz and Vincent Tofiño de San Miguel; and that by Jasper Nantiat, also published by Faden (1 January 1810). Nantiat's, in the opinion of Gen. Graham, deserved 'to be burned by the public hangman'.

Unfortunately, the hydrographer Tofiño de San Miguel's *Atlas Maritimo de España* (1789; translated by John Dougall and published by Faden in 1812 under the title *España Maritima or Spanish Coasting Pilot*), depicting the coast of the Peninsula, petered out at the French frontier: St Jean-de-Luz and Bayonne are ignored. However, it did provide a chart of the bay of San Sebastian and the narrow entrance to the harbour of Pasajes, vital as a port of supply during the later stages of the war. Arrowsmith had also published a chart of the Atlantic coast in the previous year, that by Marino Miguel Franzini (1779–1861).

At least, when first landing in Mondego Bay, Wellesley had at hand 'an excellent map and topographical accounts' of the country. Several maps had been made by Portuguese military cartographers, and were probably acquired by Gen. Sir Charles Stewart (1753–1801) when in Lisbon in the late 1790s. His eldest son, also Charles (later Baron Stuart de Rothesay; 1779–1845), when *chargé d'affaires* in Madrid in 1808, would have acquired other maps and plans. Robert Brownrigg (1759–1833), QMG in 1803, had expanded what had been a small department to one with a library and a 'drawing room for copying plans and containing a collection of the best plans and maps', and a deal of military information had been collated from the manuscripts of officers occupying, or formerly holding staff positions, 'or who may have been employed upon foreign service'.

It is unlikely that the 'topographical accounts' would have included many of the descriptions published during the previous half century by English travellers, or translated into English. Many of them – had they been heeded – could have provided insight into conditions within Spain and Portugal: the character and idiosyncrasies of the inhabitants; the lack of good communications, etc., and much other information, even if not always reliable. Wellington referred later to Gen. Charles-François Dumouriez's *Account of Portugal* (1797) as containing 'a great many unfounded notions', remarking to Stanhope that while the author seemed to be under the impression that the mountains beyond Castelo Branco 'were impassable… our troops and the French also marched through them twenty times. He thought too that the Tagus could not be forded below Abrantes. Now, almost the first thing I found when I came to Portugal was that the Tagus could be forded in twenty places, even as low as Villa Franca.'

Among other descriptions, those by Edward Clarke (1763), Joseph Baretti (1770), William Dalrymple (1777), Henry Swinburne (1779), Alexander Jardine (1788), J.-F. Bourgoing (1789), J. F. Peyron (1789), Joseph Townsend (1791), Robert Southey (1797), Richard Croker (1799), H.F. Link (1801), C.A. Fischer (1802), and Robert Semple (1807) may be mentioned,[3] while *A View of Spain*, being a translation of Alexandre de Laborde's five-volume survey, was published in 1809.

An early reference to the task of accumulating topographical information on the ground may be found in *The Peninsular Journal of Major-General Sir Benjamin D'Urban*, who had disembarked in mid October 1808 at Corunna as AQMG to Sir David Baird. On reaching Almeida, D'Urban was instructed by Gen. Anstruther 'to reconnoitre the Country for some distance in front and rear of the Coa', for should that area become the army's winter quarters, it was necessary that 'its resources, Roads of communication both with Portugal and Spain, and its natural features of defence should be at least generally known to him'. On the 20 November, together with Capt. Pierrepont, D'Urban set out on the assignment, returning after eight days, having ridden some 240 miles, to give Anstruther a 'Report and Sketch of which the Field Book and Rough Sketch are the basis', adding that of this 'he was kind enough to express his approbation'. It would appear that during most of the following month D'Urban was similarly occupied, riding on an average 40 miles in a day of ten hours. Eventually, on 14 April, he joined Beresford at Tomar, on being appointed Colonel and QMG of the Portuguese Army, having travelled since 1 November, according to his computation, 'some 2,168 English miles!'

After previous experience as a deputy QMG, Col. George Murray (1772–1846) was sent to the Peninsula in August 1808, and remained there under Moore. In the following March he was appointed QMG under Wellesley, a position he held (with a year's interval in 1812) until the end of the war. In late September 1809 Murray had directed several of his officers to start compiling appropriate topographical information, from which a skeleton map of the Alemtejo and Estremadura might be prepared. This, which would be compiled and drawn at Headquarters at the scale of 4 English miles to an inch, would run from the Tagus to a line from Juromenha (on the Guadiana south of Elvas) to Setúbal, including both Evora and Alcácer de Sal.

Thomas Lawrence, *Portrait of Lieut-Gen. Sir George Murray*.

A mountain road west of Fundão, similar to the 'Estrada Nova'.

In November, Lieut. William Stavely and Richard Henry Sturgeon of the Royal Staff Corps were sent to Talavera to 'sketch' the former battlefield. As Murray admired Sturgeon's capacity to depict relief and his highly finished drawings, he was later instructed to compile a plan of the Allied positions at Busaco, 'to which everybody was to contribute, that is to say each assistant was to send a sketch of his part of the line, and Sturgeon was to put it together in his own style…' Sturgeon had entered the Royal Military Academy at Woolwich in May 1795, where the chief drawing master from 1768 until 1796, when he retired, was the artist Paul Sandby (1731–1809). In 1747 Sandby had submitted specimens of his work to the Board of Ordnance and, soon after the establishment later that year of the Military Survey of Scotland, he was appointed draughtsman to the Survey, with which he remained for five years. Robert Dawson (1771–1860) was also influential in improving the quality of cartography, having designed in 1803 a curriculum for the cadets attached to the developing Ordnance Survey, and written a *Course of Instruction* which enabled them to become proficient in the practical aspects of surveying and map drawing within six months or so.

Among others thus employed were Capt. Alexander Todd, and Lieutenants James Freeth (Royal Staff Corps), and Georg Balck (Deputy AQMG). Other names referred to frequently in this respect were Philip Bainbrigge, João Carlos de Tamm (dismissed after a year for 'becoming negligent'), James Colleton, William de Willermin, and F.M. Read. In April 1813, Bainbrigge, and Charles Broke (later Broke Vere) were reporting on the state of the roads in Portugal north of the Douro, while Thomas Mitchell was exploring further north-east, west of the Esla; in addition, four officers were examining the Douro crossings in advance of the massive movement of troops into the Trás-os-Montes prior to the advance on Vitoria.

They were briefed to note positions, defiles, size of villages, the condition of roads, the amount of corn-land available, to provide warnings as to unhealthy spots, data on the depth of rivers and the practicability of fords, etc., while on reconnaissance. However, urgency was essential. As the map was intended chiefly to show the situation of roads and rivers, towns and principal villages, woods (providing shelter) might also be inserted as long as this did not cause any delay.

The state of roads – if any – was of particular importance, not only for establishing routes for the transport of artillery (and later, of pontoons), but also for the movement of essential *matériel* and supplies (including food and forage, ammunition, medical equipment, etc.) provided by long trains of heavily-laden bullock-carts or pack-mules. It should be emphasised that the usual speed of travel of the latter was 4 leagues a day, or approximately 12 or 13 miles (*c.* 20–21km), although this would vary considerably, depending on the nature of the ground to be covered.

This was no great problem as long as the infantry marched at its usual pace of about 15 miles a day, with occasional halts, for the divisional mules could catch up with them, but sustained marches of 20 miles or more a day stretched the system beyond its limits. In mid June 1813, for example, the abnormal speed of the advance on Vitoria caused a severe strain on the Commissariat. Allied troops, having outrun their supplies, were obliged, unusually, to subsist as well as they could off the country, a situation which accounts to some extent for their fatigued state, and the slowness of the ensuing pursuit. They were evidently exhausted by the 15th, when, as Lieut. George Woodberry (18th Light Dragoons) commented, his heart ached for the unfortunate infantry, for such numbers were 'laying on the Roadside unable to stir a step further, it is impossible for the poor fellows to march 35 to 40 miles two days running…'

It was not until November 1810 that all members of Murray's staff were issued with a concise manual entitled *Instructions for the officers in the department of the Quartermaster-General*, to which was annexed a model report of the road from Trujillo to Mérida, which did much to ensure some uniformity in the supply of information and mapping (or 'sketching', as this simple form of cartography was often called). In the following October, Pierrepont was instructed to sketch sections of the route followed by Masséna's retreat earlier that year, 'for the purpose of shewing the several Affairs with the Enemy', as part of a systematic undertaking, not only in case they might come in useful later, but that some such topographical record be retained for posterity. Many such maps and plans were pasted on linen to preserve them better, and eventually sent to the Horse Guards in London.[4]

In 1812 Murray was promoted major-general, and he was knighted after Vitoria. He accepted a lieutenant-general's command in Canada in 1814 and, although unable to take part in the Waterloo campaign, was appointed Wellington's chief of staff of the allied army of occupation and QMG of the British contingent. He was governor of the Royal Military College, Sandhurst, from 1819 to 1824, and held a number of civil and military posts during ensuing years, including that of colonial secretary between 1828 and 1830, which precluded his intention of writing a history of the Peninsular War as a counter-balance to Napier's. In 1836 and 1838 he had criticised Napier's *History* in four

Anon. *Portrait of Sir Thomas Livingstone Mitchell c. 1839.*

unsigned articles in *The Quarterly Review*, not only for the errors of fact it contained, but also, and deservedly, for its grossly inadequate cartography. The anonymity of these articles was penetrated with little difficulty by Napier, an unforgiving antagonist. Murray later prepared an edition of his own operation orders, published in 1841 in the form of a '*Memoir*' of 200 pages annexed to Wyld's *Atlas*.[5] After the war, Murray had received government approval that a compilation of maps and plans of Allied operations be made. Thomas Mitchell, who had already sketched several in 1812, was sent back to the Peninsula where, with the permission of the Portuguese and Spanish governments, he continued the task, starting with Fuentes de Oñoro. Regrettably, he was recalled in 1819 due to the Government's financial support being withdrawn, but by then he had surveyed numerous other sites between there and the Pyrenees, although a few remained unfinished.

It was not until 1840, by which time Napier's *History of the War* had been completed, that a substantial atlas of the war was eventually issued in the format of an elephant folio by James Wyld under the title *Maps and Plans Showing the*

Principal Movements, Battles and Sieges in which the British Army Was Engaged during the War from 1808 to 1814 in the Spanish Peninsula and the South of France. It is usually referred to as 'Wyld's *Atlas*' after its publisher, although very largely the work of Sir Thomas Livingstone Mitchell.

Mitchell had joined the army in July 1811 as lieutenant in the 95th, being seconded soon after to George Murray's department as a military surveyor. In 1827, when his *Outline of a System of Surveying for Geographical and Military Purposes* was published, Mitchell sailed for New South Wales as deputy to the surveyor-general, whom he succeeded in the following year, a position retained until his death in 1855. He had visited England in 1836 to publish (in 1838) the results of his first three expeditions into the interior of the continent, and a knighthood was conferred on him in the following year. He returned to Australia in 1841, after completing 'Wyld's *Atlas*'. Anyone who has perused this elaborate and visually impressive work in any detail will agree that it is a magnificent example of military cartography at its finest period, however cumbersome it may be. To reproduce such a *tour de force* today is hardly a viable undertaking.

As Sir George Murray admitted in his *Memoir*, entitled 'War of the Spanish Peninsula', referring to the first map (Operations from Mondego Bay to Lisbon), when ordering the comprehensive cartographic survey to be made, he had 'contemplated having similar sketches done of the whole of the daily marches of the army, and annexing to them the instructions for each movement'; but unfortunately 'the strength of the department being found inadequate to so large an undertaking, it was only partially executed'.

***

The appended historical synopsis will continue to reflect an Anglo-centric point of view, despite the cavilling of some historians, who have claimed that a derivative litany of Wellington's victories is merely a combination of cultural prejudice, political partisanship, and national myth, written with no proper understanding of the wider historical issues, and ignoring recent historiography, and thus belittling the contributions of his allies. Certainly, the participation of substantial numbers of Portuguese troops, having once been properly trained and commanded by British officers seconded to their army, was materially invaluable. This was very largely due to Beresford's efforts to reorganise their military establishment, having first cut out a deal of dead wood, for little had been done in this respect since the 1760s, when taken in hand by the English-born Hanoverian general, Wilhelm Graf von Schaumburg-Lippe (1724–77) during the Seven Years' War.

In contrast, Spanish armies and their commanders could rarely be relied on, either when offering to co-operate militarily, or when promising transport and provisions. It is no great surprise to find Wellington later asserting: 'I have fished in troubled waters, but in Spanish troubled waters, never again'.

Their fortuitous success in July 1808 at Bailén gave the Spaniards a grossly inflated idea of their military strength, with the result that in almost every ensuing confrontation with the French – other than at the battles of Alcañiz in May 1808 and Tamames in October 1809 – they were routed. It should be emphasised that, of the 20,000 troops at Gen. Dupont's disposal at Bailén, only one battalion consisted of veterans. Many of his units were made up of undrilled conscripts: Swiss mercenaries in the Spanish service who had been compelled to transfer their allegiance, Paris municipal guards, etc., certainly not the 'picked men' referred to by Napoleon on learning of the disaster.

As Wellington once observed concerning Spanish generals: '… nothing will answer excepting to fight great battles in plains, in which their defeat is as certain as the commencement of the battle'. They had shown, when besieged at both Gerona and Zaragoza, that they were able to put up a stubborn resistance. Their rank and file, when encouraged by the presence of British troops, could fight with courage, as at Albuera or San Marcial, and were of value as auxiliaries in the subsequent invasion of France, and at Toulouse. While Wellington could rely on generals such as Giron, Longa, Morillo, and Mina, he was justifiably reluctant to lead too many Spaniards into France where, inevitably, they would plunder and take their revenge. Those units that did so were ordered back across the frontier to avoid setting the whole country against the Allies, a situation to be avoided at all costs.

The activities of partisans or *guerrilleros*, in active or passive opposition to the invader, have survived as part of a hazy folk memory, but while their contribution to the outcome of the war should not be slighted, neither should it be exaggerated, any more than the exploits of their regular armies. A certain lack of proportion is evident in the flurry of Spanish publications, many of parochial interest, issued to coincide with the bicentenary of the war, in which it would appear that the intervention of Wellington's army was inconsequential, as reflected also in some local memorial events held in the Peninsula.

It should be emphasised that the several peripheral actions between regular or irregular Spanish troops and the French, which occurred spasmodically in Cataluña and along the Levant coast, are not described in this atlas, even if, admittedly, they tied down substantial numbers of the enemy over a long period.

It might be mentioned here that small maps included in some books concerning the Spanish resistance to the invader, in depicting the war's territorial progression over the years, are misleading in as much as they suggest that extensive areas of the country were entirely dominated by the French. This was never so in reality. Indeed, although their armies may have thrust along certain highways, and ostensibly occupied a number of larger towns, rarely were they able to retain any tight hold over more than a restricted area under their immediate command, and with large numbers of troops at hand. Very often, the moment these units moved elsewhere to forage, or further along intervening stretches of road between settlements, the ground previously held would revert to Spanish control until recovered in the uncertain tide of war.

Scarcely any first-hand accounts by Spaniards or Portuguese survive of their military participation in that war, perhaps due to their having witnessed comparatively few actions which deserved to be recorded; and yet the published narratives and 'letters from the Peninsula' by British participants run into hundreds, and additional ones still occasionally surface.[6] Such graphic descriptions, the majority of which were composed by officers, should be treated with caution, for although writing with immediacy, and giving first-hand evidence of what was taking place around them, many were unable to appreciate the importance of the part they were playing in the events they were experiencing. Capt. Thomas Henry Browne, although on Wellington's staff at Headquarters, when compiling his *Journal*, was the first to admit that his observations had been 'confined to what could be picked up in the hurry and bustle of continued marching and counter marching …' Comparatively few works stemmed from the rank and file, for very many of them were illiterate, could neither pen their recollections of the dramatic events in which they had been engaged, nor pillage from books already published. Many narratives were composed in later years, when dulled memories were jolted by the publication of Napier's great *History*, providing a mine of information from which authors could pad out their own 'memoirs'.[7] As Oman was well aware, the strength of men's memories differs: indeed, 'every year that elapses between the event and the setting down of its narrative on paper decreases progressively the value of the record.' A failing memory, the love of a well-rounded tale, a spice of autolatry, the inclusion of a picturesque anecdote, will have impaired the value of many a veteran's reminiscences, while even the most readable occasionally mix up the chronology of events, or give contradictory evidence to that supplied by another. Oman reiterated that while they may provide an admirable record 'of the way in which the rank and file looked on a battle, a forced march, or a prolonged shortage of rations … we must not trust them overmuch as authorities on the greater matter of war'. Although I have drawn on many of the more reliable of these descriptions elsewhere when providing a picture of 'campaigning', this *Atlas* is not the place to include quotations from such narratives unless particularly apt.

As far as the French were concerned, the contest in the Peninsula was considered of secondary interest and importance to the exploits of their invincible Emperor. Richard Ford, the author of *A Hand-Book for Travellers in Spain*,[8] when commenting on their military authorities, opined that 'The generality of French authors on the war in Spain desire to palliate the injustice of the invasion, the terrorism with which it was carried out, and to explain away defeats sustained; they seem to be written solely to conciliate French readers at the expense of truth and history, nay facts are occasionally so de-naturalized that an Englishman often supposes that the accounts must have reference to some totally distinct campaign and results.' A rare exception was Foy's *History*, which gave a more balanced narrative of events than most.

Wellington's experience in India had emphasised the importance of having a reliable supply system. As he later admitted: 'I made a computation of all the men I lost in Spain – killed, prisoners, deserters, everything – it amounted to 36,000 men in six years', and conceded that it would have been infinitely greater had not sufficient attention been given to the army's 'regular subsistence',

Thomas St Clair, *Troops bivouacked near Vila Velha.*

a vital contribution to his eventual success which has not yet been adequately examined. The Commissariat Department was faced with immense practical difficulties in their perennial struggle to provision and sustain the Allied army as an effectual fighting force. Imposed on him by the physical features and climatic conditions peculiar to the Peninsula, substantial logistical problems which materially affected strategic decisions had to be resolved. Very rarely was Wellington caught off his guard, or found in a precarious situation, due to an error of judgement.[9]

It is not often realised that fighting actual battles took up *less than 10 per cent* of the army's time. The struggle against the elements during an often bitterly cold winter was such that few encounters could take place during those interminable months of *inaction*, in which Wellington's men – both his officers and the rank and file – occupied themselves in a variety of sports and pastimes when not repairing their equipment, recuperating from the last campaign, or training and preparing for the next. One may aptly repeat here what Wellington told his friend Samuel Rogers: that when one visitor to Headquarters asked to see the army, directions were given that 'he should be conducted through ours. When he returned, he said, "I have seen nothing – nothing but here and there little clusters of men in confusion; some cooking, some washing, and some sleeping." "Then you have seen our Army," I said.'

By the spring of 1814, a high proportion of Wellington's troops, whether British, Portuguese, or members of the King's German Legion, apart from several Spanish units and other auxiliaries, had been exposed to several years of marching and fighting under a blistering sun, or lashed by driving rain and freezing winds. Having personal experience of the extremes and vagaries of the climate of the Peninsula over two decades, I can only confirm that the harsh physical conditions which the contesting armies had to endure should never be underestimated. The imagination must be well stretched in this enervated twenty-first century to appreciate properly the stamina and fortitude essential to survival: officers and men had to be very tough, both physically and mentally, whether it be fighting for their lives under a scorching summer sun or supporting the tedium of long, bleak, and bitter winters.

***

The maps provided have been drawn to emphasise contour in the often rugged and convoluted regions traversed by the confronting armies, a vital factor too frequently neglected by cartographers commissioned to show the terrain over which combatants were manoeuvring, fighting, or merely subsisting. Too often, when these isolating mountain ranges have been indicated in any way, they have resembled furry

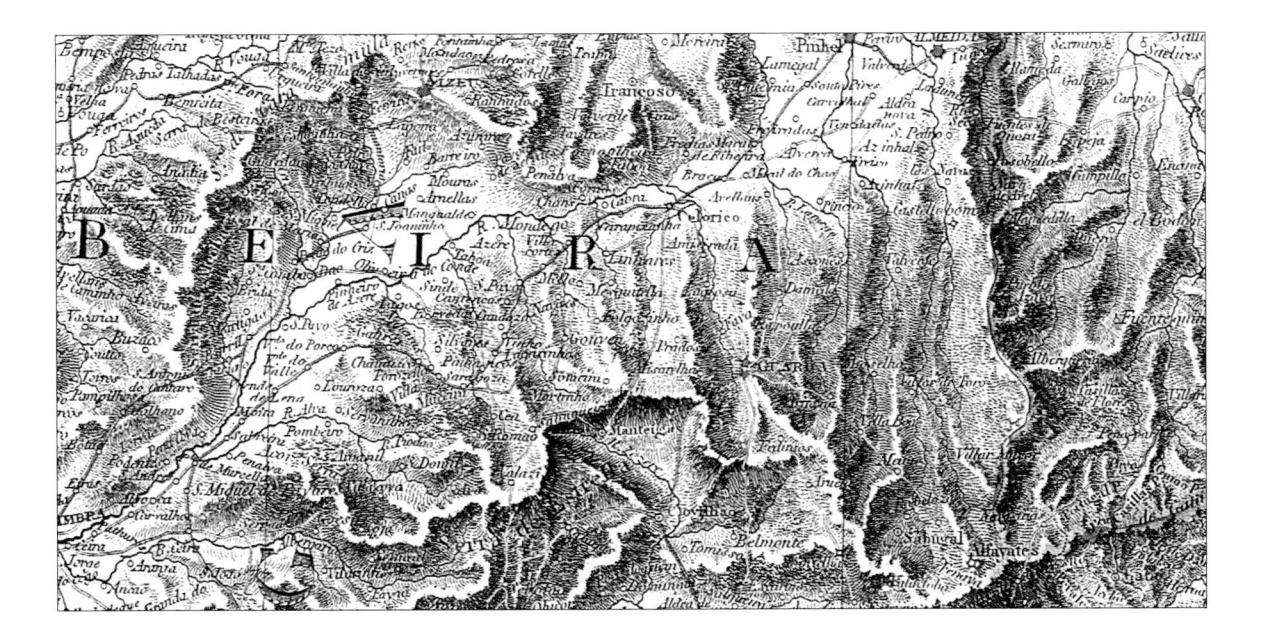

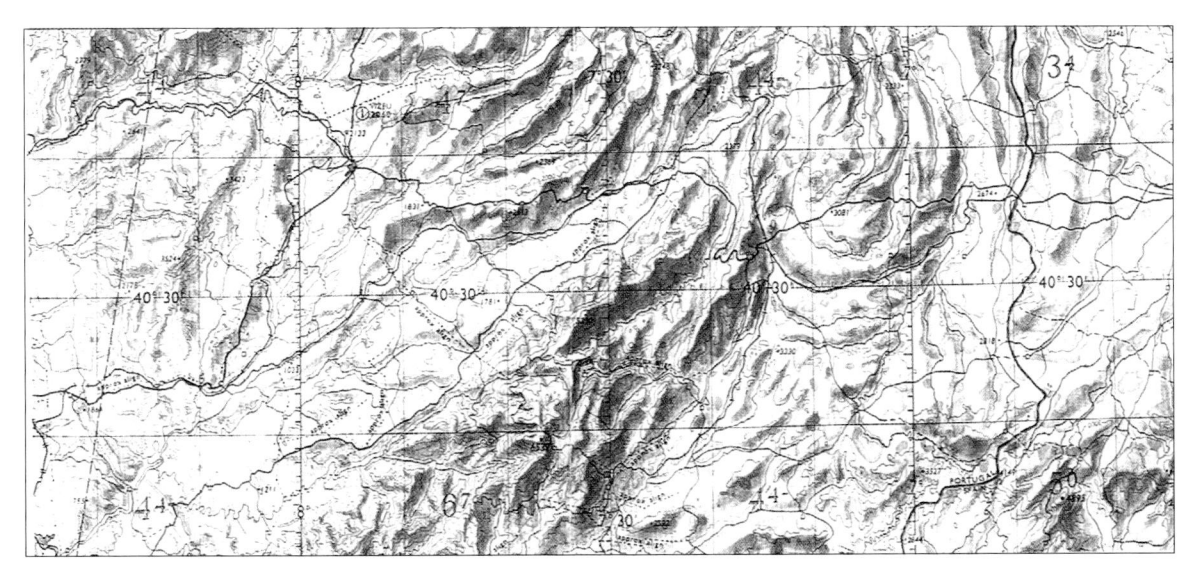

Contour depicted on a contemporary map of the area between Almeida and Coimbra compared to that on a modern map.

caterpillars. Sections of some contemporary maps are reproduced if only as examples of what was available at the time and of how unreliable many of them were. Readers requiring greater detail should find it depicted on recent maps published by the National Geographical Institutes of Spain, Portugal, and France, although not every place mentioned in narratives of the war will be marked: many villages and hamlets will not have survived the passing of time.[10] Some place-names have changed: Barba del Puerco (of the pigs) is now Puerto Seguro; Punhete is now Constância.

Most topographical names in the text are spelt in the form printed in these modern maps, except when occurring in quotations: thus inconsistencies will be found, although an attempt has been made to standardise them.

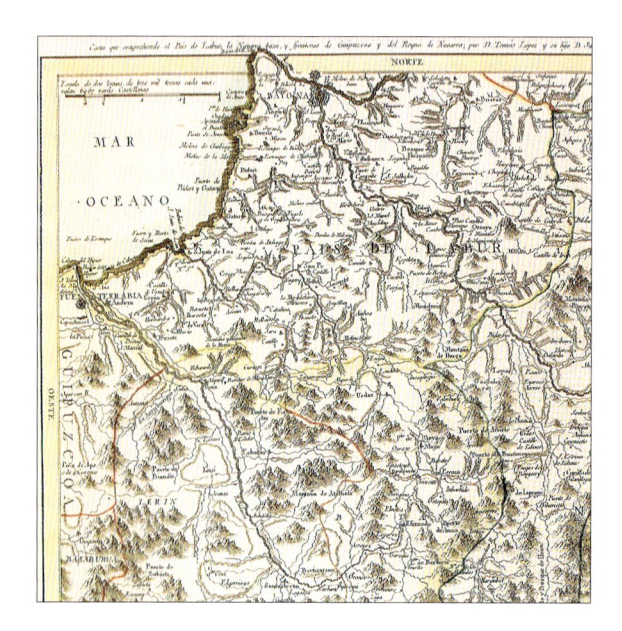

Detail of a map of the Bayonne area by Tomás López, dated 1793.

Most anglicisations have been retained (Corunna rather than La Coruña; Busaco rather than Bussaco or the Portuguese Buçaco, for example), but I have preferred Zaragoza to Saragossa. Vitoria, San Sebastian, and Pamplona remain thus: not Gasteiz, Donostia, and Iruñea, as they may be referred to locally; but as Oman warned his readers in 1930, 'Certain names of Basque villages are never written with the same letters by any two persons who have occasion to mention them', and they have proliferated in recent decades, many reverting to what are claimed to be earlier place-names.

While the accompanying maps and plans may be relied on to display the present lie of the land, the construction of a dam will have caused changes in the channel, rapidity, and levels of rivers, and an attempt has been made to depict their widths and the position of their former beds accurately. Likewise, the course of modern main roads rarely follows precisely the tracks once traversed by Wellington's troops, and it is often virtually impossible to trace their paths with certainty.[11] In many cases, notably during the early stages of the advance on Vitoria, and before traversing intricate mountain country, the Allied columns marched directly north-east across country, cutting wide swathes through the wheat-belt of the Tierra de Campos. William Tomkinson (16th Light Dragoons) refers to the cavalry being 'fed on green barley nearly the whole march, and got fat', and that the army had 'trampled down twenty yards of corn on each side of the road (forty in all) by which several columns have passed. In many places much more, from the baggage going on the side of the columns, and so spreading further into the wheat.'

The rough surface of the very few highways traversing the Peninsula two centuries ago might be compared with those rugged minor roads encountered by the present author when travelling off the beaten tracks of the Peninsula in the late 1950s, since when a high proportion of them have been substantially improved.

Population. The civilian population of Bayonne and Toulouse (ie. *not* including their garrisons) may have amounted to 13,000 and 51,000 respectively at that period. It has been estimated that the total population of the Iberian Peninsula in the first few years of the nineteenth century was less than 13 million, of which between 10 and 11 million were Spanish (including Basques and Catalans): the rest being Portuguese. There were few large towns: hardly half a dozen with more than 100,000 inhabitants.

The population of Madrid was c.175,000; Barcelona, 120,000; Seville, 100,000; Valencia, 100,000; and by late 1808 the number in Cadiz may have increased to 75,000, despite deaths from Yellow Fever in 1800; while Granada had some 60,000. But the number of inhabitants in many of the towns referred to frequently in these pages was comparatively few: for instance Badajoz (16,000), Burgos (9,000), Ciudad Rodrigo (3,000), Pamplona (3,000), and Valladolid (20,000).

In Portugal, despite the loss of life in the Great Earthquake of 1755, Lisbon had some 200,000, over 10 per cent of the country's population. Among other towns with significant populations were Abrantes (2,500), Almeida (2,000), Guarda (2,300), Castelo Branco (5,000), Coimbra (20,000), Elvas (12,000), Leiria (5,000), Oporto (30,000), Portalegre (7,000), Torres Vedras (3,000), and Viseu (3,000).

These very approximate figures should be taken into account when speculating on the amount of resistance offered to the invading French by the two countries.

A high proportion of the total – perhaps 80 per cent – was a rural population, sparsely distributed in small towns or large villages, isolated from each other, and at a considerable distance from any urban centre. There were also several extensive tracts of land which were either left as pasture unbroken by permanent habitation, or virtually deserted. There were already over 900 deserted towns (*despoblados*) listed in the Spanish census of 1797.

Recent changes. Although a few of the Peninsular War battlefields have changed out of all recognition during the last two centuries, many areas traversed by the Allied armies have remained untouched, to the extent that it is not too difficult to imagine fairly precisely what they may have been like at the time. In certain cases – as along the ridge of Busaco – there has been extensive reafforestation but, in many, the landscape remains virtually the same. Although numerous villages have increased in size, several – Fuentes de Oñoro and Sorauren come to mind – have seen little change other than the erection of a few new houses, while others referred to in memoirs may now be little more than a cluster of cottages. A number of towns (or at least their ancient nuclei) still preserve their individual character: Ciudad Rodrigo and Elvas in particular. Wellington's Headquarter villages of Freineda and Fuenteguinaldo still retain a distinct atmosphere, as does Lesaca, while the surviving fortifications of Almeida, and of Fort Conception (near Aldea del Obispo) deserve inspection, as do several forts, surviving or restored, along the Lines of Torres Vedras, despite the blight of wind turbines.

Wellington's residence and Headquarter building at St Jean-de-Luz still stand. The 'Mayor's House' at Barroilhet and the church and churchyard at Arcangues; and also the sad relics of the Château Larraldea (south-west and south-east respectively of Bayonne) are among those memorable sites where the Spirit of Place clings tenaciously, as it does likewise at Cadoux's Bridge at Vera. The Miserela bridge in the remote Cávado valley, and the Tagus crossings at Alcántara, and Vila Velha, are only a few of many other dramatic sites providing a vivid idea of the physical obstacles encountered in the Peninsula.

In certain cases, the area fought over has been left more or less undisturbed (as at Salamanca, Fuentes de Oñoro, Sorauren and elsewhere in the Pyrenees, at the Nivelle, and at Orthez). However, at Talavera, Albuera, Vitoria, and Aire-sur-l'Adour, the battlefields are now straddled by motorways or bypasses; while reservoirs have inundated certain features at Talavera, Albuera, and Sabugal. Although Vitoria itself has grown very considerably, the western and northern approaches to its wide valley remain comparatively unscathed. At Oporto, despite the city's growth and the proliferation of high bridges, one may well picture the scramble up the steep right bank to the Seminary during the Passage of the Douro. Barossa, Badajoz, Corunna, San Sebastian (where are least Montes Urgull and Ulia are prominent), Bayonne, and Toulouse are all disfigured by urban sprawl, making it hard to envisage their appearance and extent two centuries ago. Notable are the cemeteries surviving at Elvas, and the two at Bayonne; but that at San Sebastian has been neglected. Few monuments, other than the obelisk at Salamanca, are memorable. They vary from simple and inconspicuous, as at Fuentes de Oñoro, to that at Talavera, both intrusive and incongruous.

In selecting the few illustrations included in this atlas, the emphasis has been on reproducing those drawings made by artists among the confronted armies. Far too many battle scenes that were depicted, both at the time and since, were the result of artistic licence in a most fanciful form, displaying imaginary scenes, idealised, attractive, and impressive as they may be. Such scenes are legion, and still frequently embellish what are professed to be historical studies, but, having little semblance to the reality, are entirely misleading.

1 Stephen George Peregrine Ward died on 6 October, 2008, aged 91.
2 Oxford University Press, 1902–1930 (reprinted by Greenhill Books, 1995–1997); and MacMillan, 1899–1930 (reprinted by the Naval and Military Press, 2004), but the maps and plans reproduced in both reprints compare unfavourably with the original cartography.
3 Together with later travels in Spain, they have been the subject of a study by the present author, entitled *Los Curiosos Impertinentes: Viajeros Ingleses por España, 1760–1855* (1977; 2nd ed. 1988).
4 Those retained by Murray are now preserved in the National Library of Scotland.
5 A brief biography of Murray by S.G.P. Ward may be found in the *ODNB*, and in the *JSAHR*, vol. LVIII, no. 236 (1980).
6 Very few British narratives have been translated into Spanish, an exception being *The Recollections of Rifleman Harris*, as *Recuerdos de este Fusilero Benjamin Harris* (Reino de Redonda, 2008), edited by the present author.
7 The first of the six volumes was published in 1828; the last in 1840.
8 This masterpiece, first published in 1845, was reprinted in 1966, edited and with an Introduction by the present author.
9 Several problems of the Commissariat have been described by S.G.P. Ward in *Wellington's Headquarters* (1957), in his article 'The Peninsular Commissary' in the *JSAHR*, vol. LXXV, no. 304, 1997, and in *Wellington invades France: the Final Phase of the Peninsular War, 1813–1814* (2003), and *A Commanding Presence: Wellington in the Peninsula, 1808–1814: Logistics · Strategy · Survival* (2008), both by the present author.
10 The French IGN maps at 1:100,000, and 1:25,000 are invaluable.
11 With the technical resource of Google Earth, the exploration of the 'seat of war' may be greatly extended; and, by 'zooming', evidence of earlier tracks or buildings may be discovered, though not apparent on a modern map.

1. Edward Orme, *View of Elvas with the Forte de Gracia in the foreground and, to the right, the Amoreira aqueduct.*

2. Anon. *Distant view (centre) of the Seminary at Oporto, with the Serra convent (right).*

3. *Aerial view of the fortress of Almeida.*

4. Thomas St Clair, *British troops fording the Mondego.*

12 | AN ATLAS OF THE PENINSULAR WAR

5. *The Dos Casas stream at Fuentes de Oñoro, in 1960.*
6. *Wellington's Headquarters at Freineda during two winters.*

7. William Bradford, *Crossing the Tagus at Vila Velha.*

8. *Ciudad Rodrigo seen from the Greater Teson, in 1960.*
9. *Anchorage at Pasajes, vital for the provisioning of Allied troops at San Sebastian.*

10. Edward Orme, *Allied artillery firing from the summit of Monte Ulia, San Sebastian.*

11. *Plan of the Bidasoa estuary at low tide, dated 1779. The fortress of Fuenterrabía is seen on the Spanish bank facing Hendaye.*

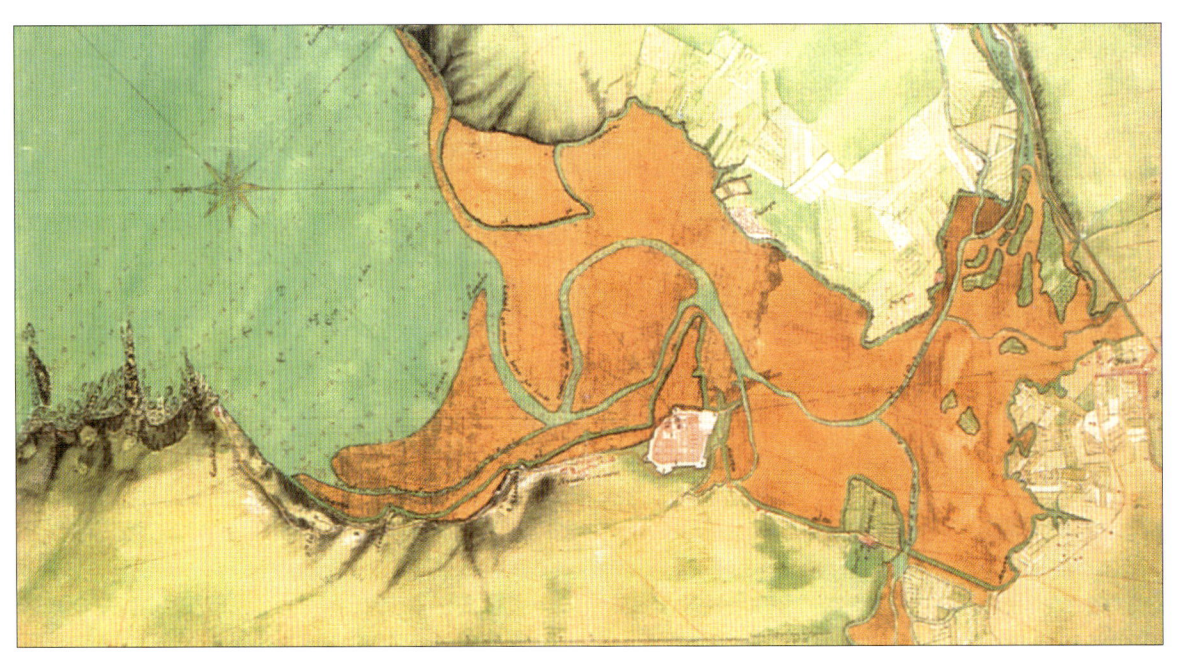

14 | An Atlas of the Peninsular War

12. Edward Orme, *Distant view of Bayonne from sandhills to the west, near the site of the bridge of boats (detail).*
13. Robert Batty, *Wellington's Headquarters (right) at St Jean-de-Luz.*
14. Robert Batty, *Looking south from St Etienne towards the Citadel and Bayonne, with the distinctive silhouette of La Rhune (left) and the Peñas de Haya (in the distance beyond the cathedral).*
15. *A corner of the Coldstream Guards Cemetery, Bayonne.*
16. *The Château de Larraldea, near Villefranque, when last seen by the author.*

The Historical Context

French armies, commanded by Napoleon and his marshals, had overrun extensive areas of mainland Europe during the first few years of the century, although Nelson's victory at Trafalgar in October 1805 had scuppered French pretensions to control the seas. In this disaster, the Spanish fleet had been largely destroyed also, for entangled in Napoleon's devious web of alliances, Spain had committed herself to France. Napoleon, no longer able to invade England, sought to weaken her economically by decreeing that continental ports be closed to British trade.

Soon after Russia's defeat at Friedland, and subsequent signing of a peace treaty at Tilsit on 25 June 1807, intelligence was received in London that Napoleon had proposed the formation of a maritime league against Britain. Rumours were circulating that the French were likely to make up for their shipping losses by invading neutral Denmark and seizing her fleet, which Britain was intent on preventing. Inevitably, Denmark would be unable to resist French military or diplomatic pressure to join their camp, so it was proposed that a British naval squadron be sent into Danish waters to their aid; an envoy would meanwhile bring them round to an alliance against France. In the event, as the Danes had no intention of resigning their fleet to any form of temporary protective custody, it was decided to make a pre-emptive strike, the morality of which was questionable. Lord Cathcart, already commanding a force collaborating with Swedish and Prussian armies on the Baltic coast, was instructed to transfer it to a position nearer the Danish capital, where additional units from England would land.

Among this contingent was a brigade commanded by Maj.-Gen. Sir Arthur Wellesley,[1] which disembarked near Copenhagen on 15 August, and at Koge defeated a Danish attempt to relieve the capital: indeed, their militia had little chance when confronted by disciplined troops. On 2 September, Cathcart's summons having been rejected, the city sustained a three-day bombardment before capitulating, soon after which the entire Danish fleet surrendered and was escorted to England, taking their accumulated naval stores with them, leaving only a few old ships and those on the stock to be destroyed.[2]

At the same time, Napoleon was attempting to intimidate Portugal into severing her connection with Britain, for – apart from Sweden – she was Britain's remaining continental ally, and a loophole in his design to bring his resilient adversary to heel. On 19 July, their minister in Paris was curtly informed that Portugal must close its ports to British shipping forthwith, with French and Spanish ambassadors in Lisbon stressing that if she failed to comply and more actively co-operate with France, this might well precipitate hostilities, although war was not

Detail of a contemporary map of Copenhagen.

declared formally. By late August the British government, on learning of Napoleon's threat, immediately agreed to send military aid, although this might take time: indeed, eleven months passed before any expeditionary force disembarked in the Peninsula. There was a better chance there than elsewhere of establishing a firm foothold on mainland Europe, a positive step which might revitalise militant opposition to Napoleonic aggression.

To thwart any such landing, the French would have to invade Portugal and occupy Lisbon, an objective facilitated by the Spanish agreeing to allow the transit of some 25,000 men. On 18 October 1807, Gen. Junot's vanguard, marching from Bayonne, crossed the frontier on the first stage of their gratuitous invasion, which met little resistance. Their progress south-west was leisurely, for they were discreetly taking note of all fortified places and defensible positions en route. On entering Portugal, they followed a road looking direct enough on a map, but in reality a track impassable to wheeled vehicles, and traversing a granitic wilderness without resources. In torrential rain, thousands scattered in the search for sustenance, suffered dreadful privations, and then 'went missing'. It was not until 30 November that the famished vanguard limped into and seized Lisbon virtually unopposed. Only hours earlier, the feckless royal family and court, together with several thousand of the administrative hierarchy and hangers-on, had set sail under British convoy for Brazil, leaving the capital to its fate.

It was several months before Junot had built up a creditable force, during which opposition gradually grew, notably in Oporto, where a provisional *junta* had been established under its patriotic bishop, Antonio de Castro. Before long, troops were being assembled to combat the invader, and envoys sent to London to enlist support. By mid June 1808, the capital was in ferment, making Junot's position increasingly uncomfortable. Leaving small garrisons in frontier fortresses, he withdrew most other detached corps to Lisbon and west of the lower reaches of the Tagus, where some 24,000 troops were soon concentrated, with the result that insurrectionary *juntas* were able to proliferate elsewhere.

Naïvely, Spain, when permitting their militant neighbours to traverse the highway to Portugal, never suspected that Napoleon had designs on itself; but with the door to the Peninsula open, French units had been infiltrating constantly, those commanded by Marshal Murat, Napoleon's brother-in-law, occupying Madrid on 23 March 1808. The king, Carlos IV, a pathetic figure dominated by his wife Maria Luisa and Manuel Godoy, was decoyed to Bayonne and forced to abdicate in favour of his son, Fernando (who remained in captivity at Valençay for the duration of the war then imminent). Joseph Bonaparte, Napoleon's elder brother, was proclaimed king in his stead.

On 2 May, once realising that they had been tricked, the Madrileños rose up in almost unanimous – and briefly energetic – revolt. Among them were many *afrancesados*, cultured and liberal-minded Spaniards sympathising with the French and their Revolutionary tenets, and anticipating an end to the blighting power of the Church and effete and parasitic nobility, although mere collaborators proliferated. While popular resistance was ruthlessly suppressed in the capital and a few other towns, within weeks much of the country was 'up in arms'. Many of the ill-equipped, badly-organised, and worse-led, individual Spanish armies sensibly avoided general actions with veteran French troops, but this was not always so, and the few that engaged in conventional combat suffered severely.

By 8 June, a group of patriotic deputies, sailing from the Asturias to seek British military intervention on their behalf, had reached London, their appeal buttressed by positive assurances that Spanish armies and supplies would be available with which to prosecute the war. It was agreed that British troops already assembled in Ireland to attack and occupy Spanish possessions in America – which might otherwise fall into French hands – would be diverted from their initial destination to make a landing on the north or west coast of the Peninsula.

Enjoying the confidence of Lord Castlereagh (then Secretary of State for War), Wellesley, now a lieutenant-general, was given temporary command of this small expeditionary force, with discretionary orders to land wherever seemed most favourable and take whatever action he thought fit; but he had been given only an imprecise idea of what the military situation might be on *terra firma*. The Spaniards had estimated Junot's army as numbering hardly 15,000 men (over 10,000 short of the total). Wellesley would soon discover to what extent he should rely on all unsubstantiated reports or fanciful figures his Allies chose to feed him.

On 20 July, with a fleet of transports in his wake, that had set sail from Ireland, Wellesley himself landed briefly at Corunna, the first port of call for British shipping on the Atlantic coast of Spain. Although the Galicians were unaware of it at the time, an Andalusian force commanded by Gen. Castaños had just engaged in battle at Bailén with Gen. Dupont's French army, which unexpectedly capitulated to them on the 22nd.

After this débâcle, the French were obliged to abandon Madrid and concentrate north of the river Ebro. They could no longer afford to ignore either the presence of other Spanish 'armies', or the more resourceful guerrilla bands by then roving the country. When they were not themselves pillaging the peasantry, the guerrillas stirred up the inhabitants to a more active resistance and opposition to the invader, harried the extended French lines of communication, effectively isolating smaller units, and interrupted the flow of supplies unless their convoys were provided with strong escorts, causing substantial numbers to be pinned down countering these activities. Later, they became adept at intercepting dispatches and supplying their allies with intelligence of enemy movements. The relentless war of attrition practised by the partisans bled the French white, and their importance in contributing to the eventual outcome of the war should not be underestimated. Meanwhile, in attempting to live off the country as they had done elsewhere in Europe, the French were soon to find that there was much truth in the old adage that 'In Spain large armies starved and small ones got beaten'.

For a concise summary of events following the disembarkation of the British expeditionary force, see the complementary text to Map 4. The atlas section describes the course of the war during the ensuing five and a half years, while Plan 53 is followed by a brief account of the Dispersal of Wellington's forces, and an Epilogue.

[1] The future Duke of Wellington is referred to as Wellesley in this Atlas until after the battle of Talavera, when he was raised to the peerage as Viscount Wellington of Talavera and Baron Douro.

[2] Well-described in Thomas Munch-Petersen's *Defying Napoleon* (2007).

ATLAS

1 Physical Map of the Peninsula

1808–14

What passed for paved highways in the Peninsula were very few and far between, the majority radiating from Madrid, and between one and another there were hardly any cross roads of consequence. Little had changed by the time, many years later, when in conversation with Stanhope, Wellington remarked that 'in Portugal the only road at all deserving of the name was from Lisbon to Pombal. From Lisbon to Elvas it was most detestable, often only the dry bed of a rivulet.' When asked what the Portuguese did when these were full, he replied: 'Stay at home, I believe … But I have been obliged more than once to give orders at the villages that the large stones and fragments might be picked out of the rivulets, so that the troops might march on these roads.' Certainly, what might have been a foaming torrent in winter might be transformed into a meandering stream in summer, forded with ease, or even providing a conveniently un-rutted sandy bed or *rambla*. Un-surfaced roads, too often little more than dusty dislocating tracks in summer, became quagmires in winter, and virtually impassable in wet weather.[1]

Had any notice been taken of the descriptions published during the previous half century by every single British traveller experiencing the lamentable condition of all forms of communication in the Peninsula, and also the virtual lack of transport – or even the reports of French prisoners, had they been cross-questioned – this would have come as no surprise.

But it was not only total ignorance of the condition of the roads that was apparent. Few officers seem to have appreciated the fact that the country through which their armies intended to march was one of the most fragmented in Europe, much of it a high-lying plateau or *meseta*, divided up by road-less mountain ranges and cleaved by fast-flowing rivers spanned by very few bridges. Naturally, the comparatively recent construction of dams has caused changes in the beds of several rivers, while variations in their levels and velocities have made it difficult to ascertain the exact position of former fords, which will be referred to when describing individual maps. With the exception of the valleys of the Ebro and Guadalquivir, down which ran roads of variable quality, many stretches of other important rivers – among them the Duero (Douro in Portugal), Tajo (anglicised as the Tagus), and Guadiana, and their tributaries – ran in deep and rocky gorges. No roads of any sort ran along their banks, while few could be used for transport by boat except near their mouths: they were more a hindrance to communication than a help.

As the French learned to their cost, once across the deeply furrowed and intricate terrain of the Pyrenees (passed less arduously only at either extremity), if making for Madrid, an invading army had to traverse several desolate mountain chains, isolating one province from another, by tracks threading tortuous defiles – perfect sites for guerrilla ambuscades – when not climbing steeply to easily defended passes or *puertos*. Whilst intervening plains, comparatively well populated – although towns remained isolated from each other – might be able to provide food and fodder for a ravenous army, little sustenance could be found in more mountainous areas, and it was a lengthy and laborious process, necessitating lumbering ox-drawn wagon-trains and immense convoys of pack-mules to transport accumulated supplies and forage over these ranges. On re-entering less remote or barren districts, the troops would be obliged to disperse yet again in their perennial search for provisions.

1 George Ticknor, the American historian of Spanish literature, when first visiting the country a decade after the war and before any form of 'diligence service' had been set up, remarked that 'There was no travelling in Spain. Between Barcelona and Madrid, in a journey of thirteen days, we met only a few muleteers, a few carts, and one single coach like our own, only half a dozen in all; and yet the road was the main highway between the capital and one of the principal cities of the kingdom'; but it had long been so. Major William Dalrymple, travelling in the Peninsula while on leave from the Gibraltar garrison in 1774, setting out from Ponferrada for Galicia – the route by which Moore was to retreat – had remarked on the road being 'very bad' after having 'travelled on a new road for about two miles, which is intended to be carried to the sea,' adding: 'And here I must observe, that except at La Carolina in the Sierra Morena, and for a few leagues about Madrid, I have never seen any made [i.e. surfaced] roads. There are no heavy carriages in the country I have passed, otherwise it would be impossible, particularly in winter, for them to travel. Left the Camino Real [the Royal Road], and came into an abominable road, but extremely pleasant on the banks of a most refreshing stream, the mountains rising on each side of us … began to ascend the mountain, the road like steps of stairs.'

PHYSICAL MAP OF THE PENINSULA | 21

2. CATALONIA, ARAGON, AND THE LEVANTE COAST

The Battle of Castalla, and the Siege of Tarragona

French brigades had invaded Catalonia in mid February 1808, and occupied Barcelona on the 29th. The Spaniards had shown vigorous resistance at Gerona (its third siege lasting from late May to mid December 1809), at Zaragoza (which held out until late February 1809), and at Figueras, for four months in 1811. Indeed, the eastern littoral and the Ebro valley were the site of numerous sporadic combats throughout the war between the Spanish armies or Catalan irregulars (*Somaten*) and isolated French units, to the extent that none were available to support their armies engaged elsewhere in the Peninsula.[1]

Among their generals commanding in Aragon, Catalonia, and Valencia were Moncey, Duhesme, St Cyr, Augereau, Decaen, Macdonald, Reille, with Suchet, by far the most successful, to whom the garrisons of Lerida, Tortosa, Tarragona, Saguntum, and Valencia had capitulated when besieged, the last in January 1812. The number of their effectives in north-eastern Spain and the Levante coast fluctuated between 35,000 (1808) and 60,000 (October 1812).

British units saw comparatively little activity in this part of Spain, with the exception of Gen. Sir John Murray's creditable action in defeating Suchet at Castalla on 13 April 1813,[2] his less creditable performance at Tarragona that June, and Sir William Bentinck's operations on that coast. These diversions, set in motion by Wellington prior to his advance on Vitoria in May 1813, kept Suchet amply occupied, and deterred him from sending any reinforcements to Joseph and Jourdan.

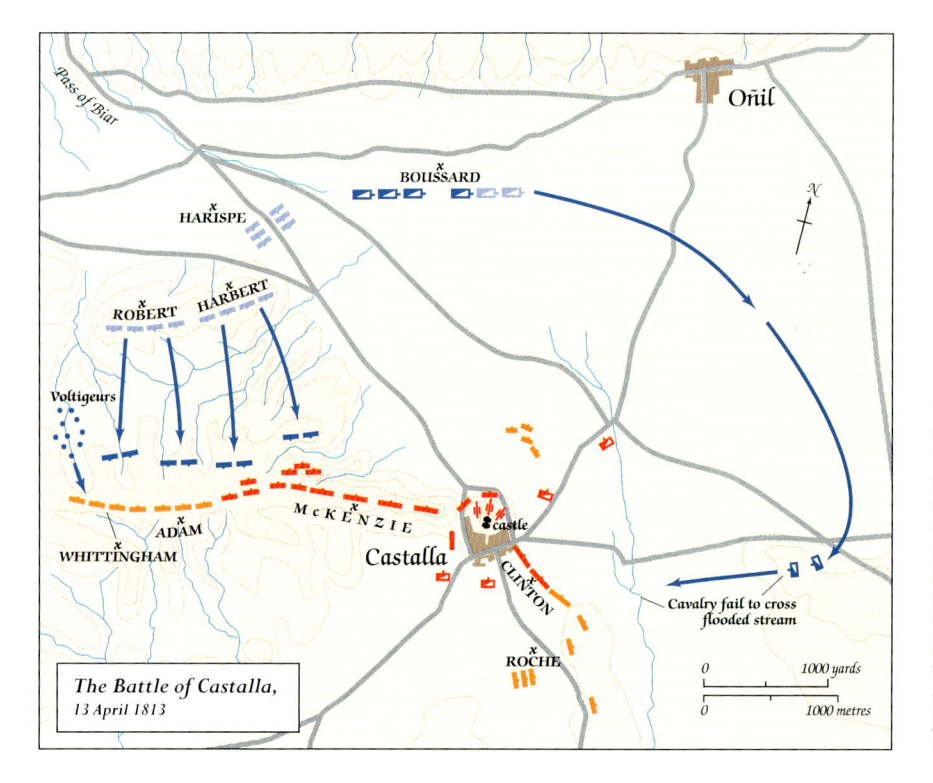

The Battle of Castalla, 13 April 1813

1 In an unsuccessful attempt to control the huge area, on 26 January 1812 Napoleon decreed the political union – virtually annexation – of several provinces to France, with which to form four *départements*.
2 Among commanders of this army of British, Sicilian, and Spanish units were Col. Frederic Adams, and Generals William Clinton, John Mackenzie, Philip Roche, and Samuel Ford Whittingham. The campaign has been well described in chapter XVIII of Jonathon Riley's *Napoleon and the World War of 1813* (2000).

CATALONIA, ARAGON AND THE LEVANTE COAST

3 Central and Western Andalucia

Late June to early September 1809

While comparatively little fighting took place here during the war between Wellington's troops and the French, it was the scene of Dupont's expedition to occupy the area, the combat at Alcolea (7 June 1808) prior to the sack of Cordoba, and his subsequent retreat and defeat at Bailén (19 July). Seville became the base of the Spanish Central *Junta* by the year's end, and remained so until it retired to the security of Cádiz in late January 1810,[1] in the face of another invasion of Andalucia. Having forced the passes of the Sierra Morena, an army commanded by Joseph Bonaparte and Soult entered Seville and invested Cadiz, which long remained a thorn in their flesh.

Soult, with 70,000 men, made Seville the base of operations throughout that summer, during which Victor, with c. 19,000, was tied down opposite Cadiz, and several raids were undertaken into Extremadura (by Mortier) and Murcia (by Sebastiani). For the next two years, Soult was virtually 'Viceroy of Andalusia'. The control of the larger towns under French occupation – among them Cordoba, Granada, Malaga, and Jaen – was as much a drain on his resources as the repressing of guerrilla activity in the mountains of Ronda and elsewhere, south-west

The Seige of Cádiz,
5 February 1810–24 August 1812

- outlying Spanish positions

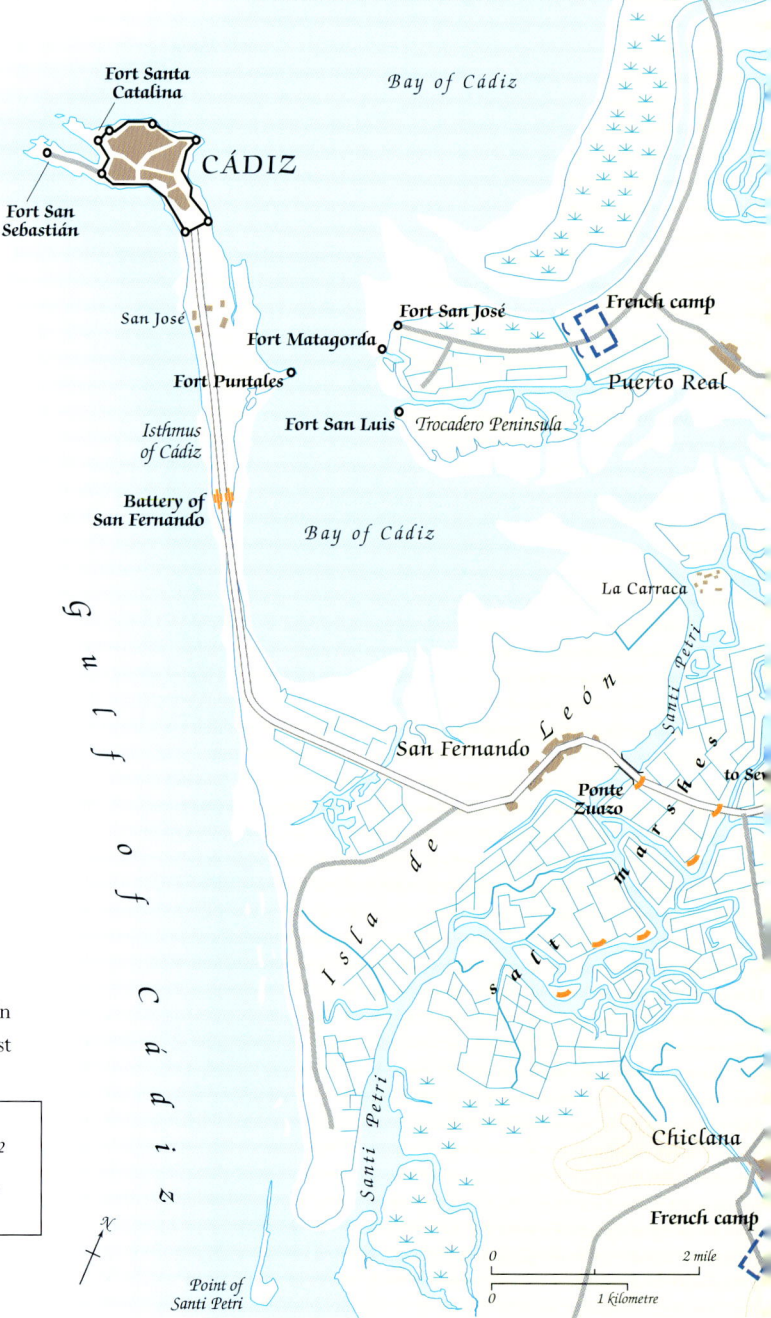

24 An Atlas of the Peninsular War

of which was the scene of the Tarifa campaign, and the battle of Barrosa (*see Plan 19*) in February and March 1811. It was from Seville that Soult marched to capture Badajoz, and to fight at Albuera that May. It was not until mid August 1812 that Soult commenced the evacuation of Andalucia, by withdrawing the garrison at Niebla, soon followed by the dismantling of the Lines facing Cádiz, and retreating from Seville to Cordoba. Within a month, Soult had concentrated 45,000 men at Granada before continuing his progress east via Baza, Huéscar, and Caravaca to converge with Suchet's force near Hellín.

1 The *Junta* had refused a British expeditionary force of 6,000 permission to land there in February 1809 to regain a foothold in Spain, although a contingent to reinforce the garrison was later accepted.

4 The Portuguese Coast: from the Mouth of the Mondego to Lisbon

August 1808

Support was not long in reaching the Peninsula. Sailing ahead of a fleet weighing anchor in the Cove of Cork on 12 July, Wellesley landed at La Coruña (better known to the British as Corunna) on the 20th. The Galicians asserted that, while grateful for any financial subsidy England might provide, they could defeat the French unaided: they had no need of auxiliary troops.[1] The first transports entering Vigo Bay awaited further orders while Wellesley sailed on to Oporto to meet the *Junta* there, conspicuous in Portugal in resisting the French occupation. After conferring with Adm. Sir Charles Cotton, commanding naval units off the coast, Mondego Bay was chosen as providing the most convenient beach at which the Expeditionary Force might disembark. It lay some 100 miles north of the Tagus estuary,[2] was guarded by a fort at Figueira da Foz, already in the hands of students from Coimbra, and had been occupied by British marines since 7 July.

British troops started to land during the first week of August: it was a slow process, with the men wading ashore through the pounding surf, while their mounts, long cooped up, were unceremoniously dropped overboard to swim for it. They were impressed by Portuguese hospitality, being presented with provisions in plenty both by the *Juntas* and the local peasantry. The first week was employed landing ammunition, equipment and stores. The small wagon train of the Commissariat Department which had accompanied them had to be supplemented by hiring bullocks, carts and carters, mules and muleteers. Eventually the army, 14,000 strong, leaving their heavy packs on board ship and, reinforced by Portuguese units, largely raw levies under the command of Col. Nicholas Trant, proceeded leisurely south through Leiria under a blistering sun, carrying with them four days' rations. Leach recorded his march as being 'over an uninterrupted plain of white sand, hot enough almost to have dressed a beef-steak, into which we sank ankle deep at every step'. The magnificent monasteries at Batalha and at Alcobaça were later skirted, but although scouts reported that enemy units under Delaborde lay ahead of them, and another larger force under Loison was approaching from Abrantes, to the east, it was not until reaching Obidos that any skirmishing with the French took place. Wellesley determined to attack the former before the two generals could join forces.

Henri L'Evêque, *Disembarkation at Mondego Bay* (detail).

1 They downplayed as a minor setback what was a severe defeat at the hands of the French at Medina de Rioseco on 14 July. Nearer the truth was the welcome news, received by Wellesley on 1 August, that an entire corps under Dupont had capitulated to Castaños at Bailén nine days earlier.
2 It would have been hazardous to make an amphibious landing near Lisbon, as the Tagus estuary had been fortified, and several Russian warships anchored there could not be relied on to remain neutral.

THE PORTUGUESE COAST | 27

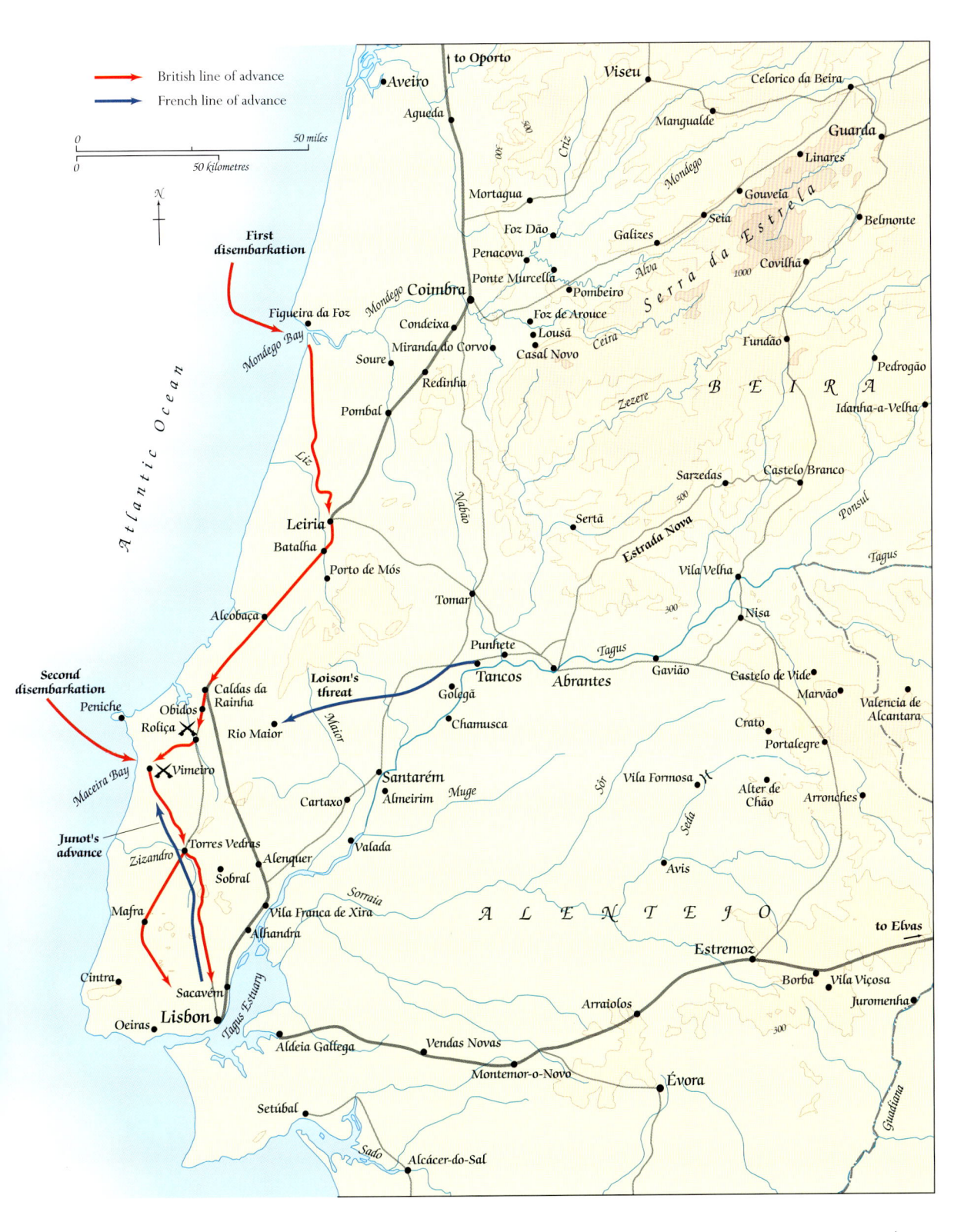

5. The Combat at Roliça

17 August 1808

French forces were stationed on the Lisbon road north of the village of Roliça, awaiting reinforcements from near Rio Maior. Behind them rose a horse-shoe shaped line of low hills, towards which Wellesley's force advanced, with Hill's brigade on the right, the central column (Nightingall's brigade followed by Craufurd's[1]), to the left of which were Fane's. Ferguson's brigade, supported by that of Bowes, was deployed further to the east, while Wellesley had sent Trant's Portuguese circling to the west as part of a wide pincer movement. As they approached the French, Wellesley's central columns opened out into battle array, their scarlet lines providing an impressive display.[2] But Delaborde (with some 4,350 men at hand) was too experienced and wary a general to take the bait, and sensibly retired behind a cavalry screen to a stronger defensive position along the main ridge of hills.

This was cleft by several steep-sided gullies, up one of which Col. Lake too impulsively led his unit (the 29th), to find themselves under a rain of fire from both flanks as they scrambled out of the ravine, Lake himself being one of the first casualties. Although the whole British line finally swarmed to the summit, beyond which Delaborde put up a stiff resistance, once his position becoming untenable, he skilfully withdrew. Pursuit of the French into more open country was not pressed by Wellesley's brigades, which bivouacked in line of battle facing south and east.

Next morning, they were marched south-west towards the estuary of the Maceira river, at the mouth of which was a sandy land-locked bay, conveniently sited for the disembarkation from approaching transports of 4,000 reinforcements. Prior to the impending arrival of Gen. Sir Hew Dalrymple, these reinforcements would be commanded by Sir Harry Burrard, a general senior in rank to Wellesley. An additional 15,000 troops, commanded by Sir John Moore, were expected later.

By the evening of the 20th, Wellesley had 16,500 British infantry and Trant's Portuguese at hand, but only 240 mounts, which, together with his guns, were deployed not far inland in the vicinity of Vimeiro, a village perched on a flat-topped hill between two higher ridges, the whole providing an eminently defensible position.

During the night, patrols reported that the French were approaching in force from Lisbon.

---

1 This was James Catlin Craufurd, not the better-known Robert Craufurd.

2 With the central column were the majority of the British and Portuguese cavalry, and 12 guns; another 6 guns were with Ferguson.

THE COMBAT AT ROLIÇA | 29

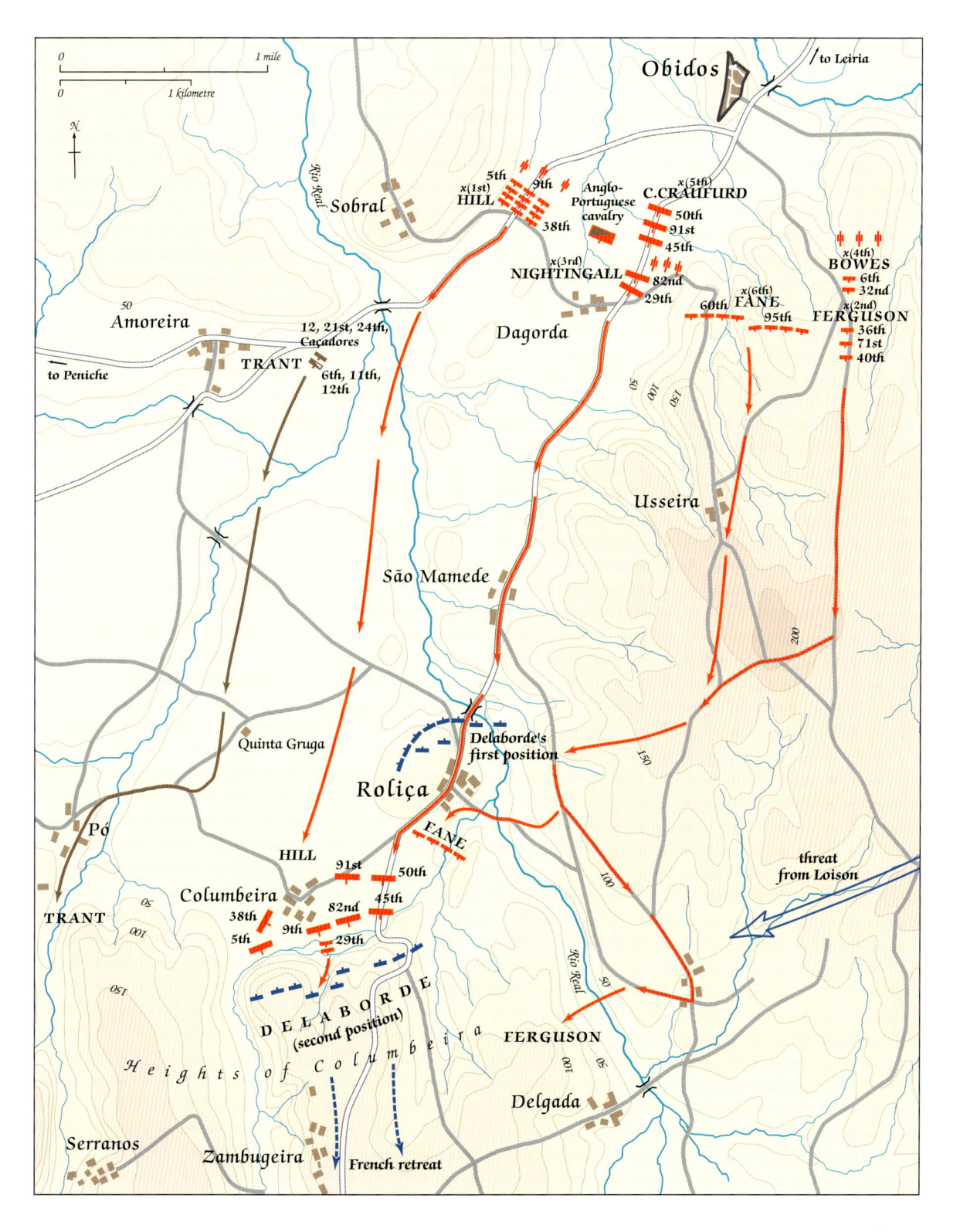

6 The Battle of Vimeiro

21 August 1808

Soon after dawn, Junot's approaching columns were seen far more to the east than south-east, necessitating an immediate change of front, the brigades on Vimeiro hill being redeployed, with three battalions disposed in a two-deep line along the reverse slope of its flat crest, behind which another two, with 12 guns, were placed in support. It was here that the French made their initial attack, surging uphill in two parallel columns, their flanks protected by cavalry,[1] but their compact masses met with repeated

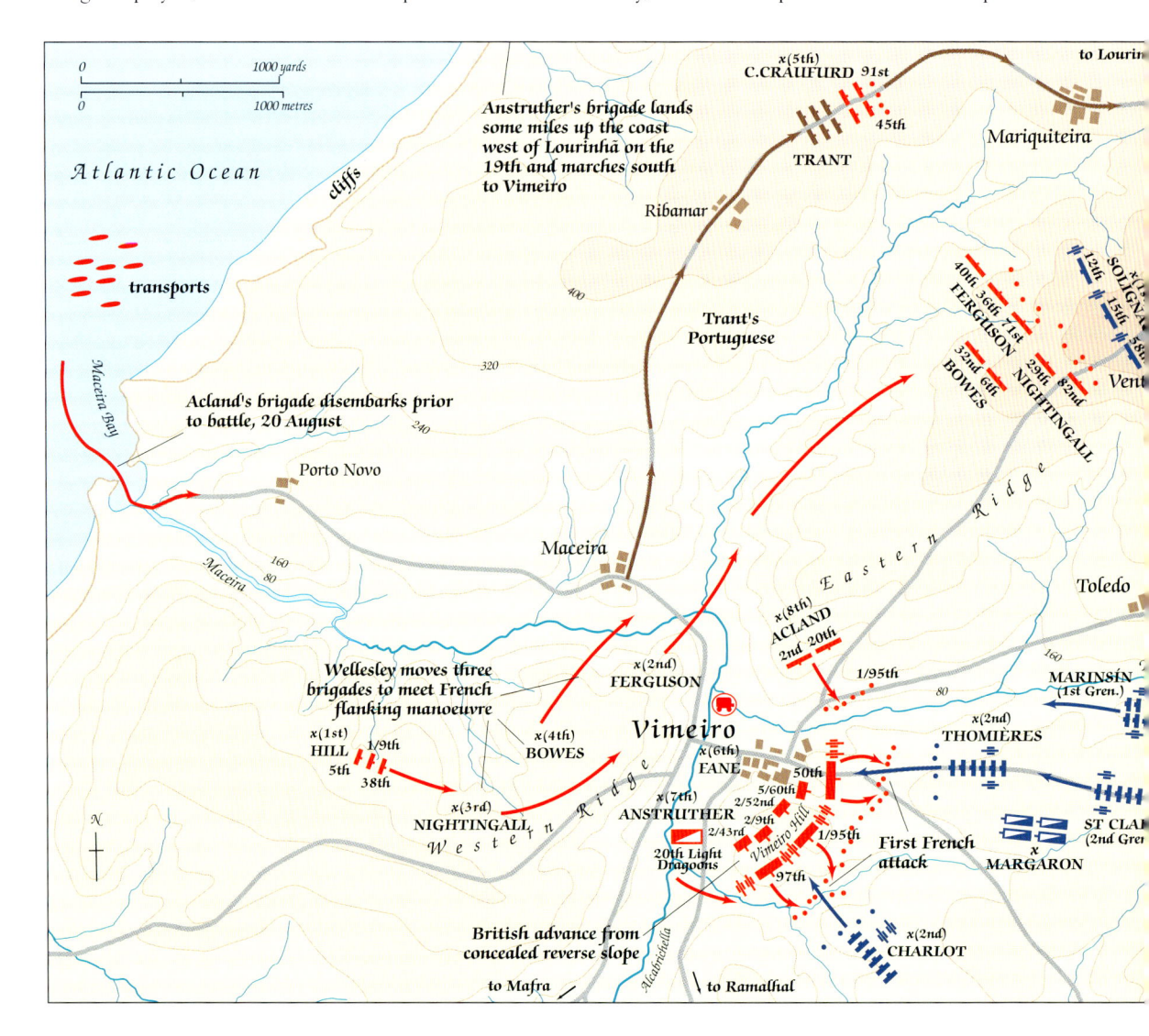

30 | AN ATLAS OF THE PENINSULAR WAR

murderous volleys from 900 muskets in line and devastating artillery salvoes, including that of howitzers firing shrapnel shells, followed by bayonet charges, at which they dissolved and broke. Meanwhile, several other columns ascending ridges further north, only to encounter similar disciplined volleys of converging fire, turned back and disintegrated likewise. Wellesley's few cavalry now went into action, attacking the retreating French, but galloping on out of control, and out of range of supporting artillery, they were themselves badly mauled by Junot's more disciplined dragoons, when these turned on them.

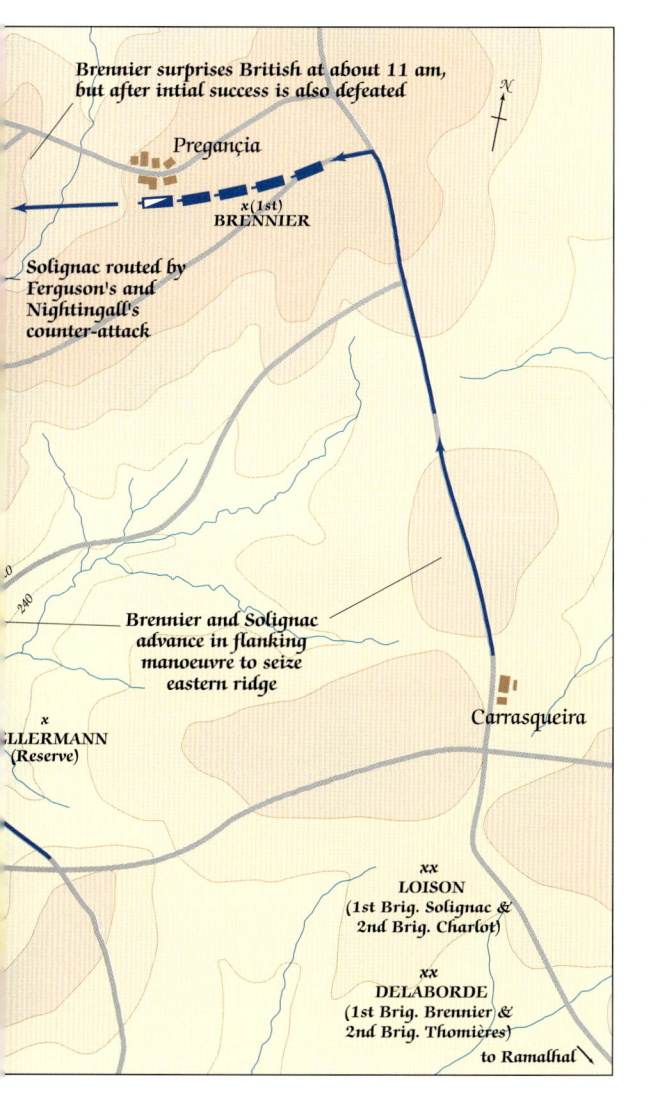

But by now the French had had enough. They would have been routed had not Gen. Burrard pulled rank on Wellesley and adamantly forbade further pursuit until additional reinforcements arrived, while Dalrymple, who landed next day, disparaged Wellesley's recommendation that a rapid thrust towards Santarém would intercept any French attempt to retreat to the north-east, confining them between the Tagus and the coast. Isolated garrisons at Almeida and Elvas were in no position to come to Junot's aid.

The French were thoroughly demoralised, and an unconditional surrender could have been enforced had not Dalrymple agreed to the armistice they proposed. Even in negotiating a document suspending hostilities previous to the Convention of Cintra, the senior generals displayed their pusillanimity by submitting to Junot's demands. Thus, in mid September, the first brigades of his army of 20,000, together with 3,500 wounded and the spoils of conquest, were evacuated to France in British ships. No clause was made restricting them from fighting again, not that this could have been enforced.[2]

Meanwhile, Moore's contingent, having landed at Mondego Bay on 21 August, entered Lisbon on 9 September.[3] Moore's assignment was to employ his troops in the North of Spain and 'to cooperate with Spanish armies in the expulsion of the French from that kingdom'. But before his troops could march against the common enemy, there were numerous problems to be resolved: he had found 'everything in the greatest confusion' in the wake of the French occupation.

---

1 Although Wellesley's infantry outnumbered Junot's 10,300, his 240 mounts were opposed by 1,950 French cavalry.

2 'Britannia sickened' when details of the disgraceful terms of the Convention reached London: the two generals acceding to these provisions were recalled soon after, having so 'honourably' ended their unedifying careers.

3 Wellesley returned to England on 20 September, after conferring with Moore, who took command of British forces in Portugal shortly after.

THE BATTLE OF VIMEIRO | 31

7 Moore's Campaign

October 1808 to mid January 1809

Leaving a force at Lisbon under Cradock, on 20 October Sir John Moore, now in command of the expeditionary force, commenced his advance towards the Spanish frontier with some 22,000 men, initially divided into four groups.[1] They were to converge at Salamanca with another 8,000 infantry and additional cavalry, landing at Corunna meanwhile under Baird and Henry Paget.[2] Of the four columns, Beresford's set out along the highway to Coimbra before veering up the Mondego valley through Celorico to Almeida; Moore himself proceeding via Abrantes, crossed the Tagus at Vila Velha for Guarda. A third column, commanded by Edward Paget, after crossing the Tagus at Alcántara, and then the pass of Perales, made for Ciudad Rodrigo. Hope's smaller column, with most of the artillery and 1,000 cavalry, took a roundabout route,[3] following the Madrid highway from Elvas and, after crossing the Tagus at Almaraz, continued up the valley almost to the gates of the capital before ascending north-west over the Guadarrama range to approach Salamanca.[4] It was not until 13 November that Moore's vanguard entered Salamanca (his rearguard catching up ten days later), while Hope's contingent had not traversed the Guadarrama until the 28th.

Moore's intention was to threaten French communications and strike at any additional units entering Spain, but he lacked any proper system of intelligence. Although a successful action against Soult's cavalry took place at Sahagún on 21 December, Moore was unaware of the fact that Napoleon himself was about to lead a numerically superior force over the then blizzard-lashed Guadarrama pass north-west of Madrid, intent on capturing the insignificant British army in its entirety.

On news of this unexpected turn of events reaching him on the evening of the 23rd, Moore had no compunction in ordering a rapid withdrawal to the coast to avoid being cut off: it was the only possible way in which to extricate his army from its perilous situation. Baird's contingent was ordered to retire across the Esla at Valencia de Don Juan.

After dispersing enemy cavalry at Mayorga, the bulk of the army crossed at Benavente, further south. Napoleon's plan of encirclement was frustrated. With the excuse that he had more urgent matters to attend to in Paris, Napoleon left the pursuit and mopping-up operations to Soult: never again did he set foot in the Peninsula.

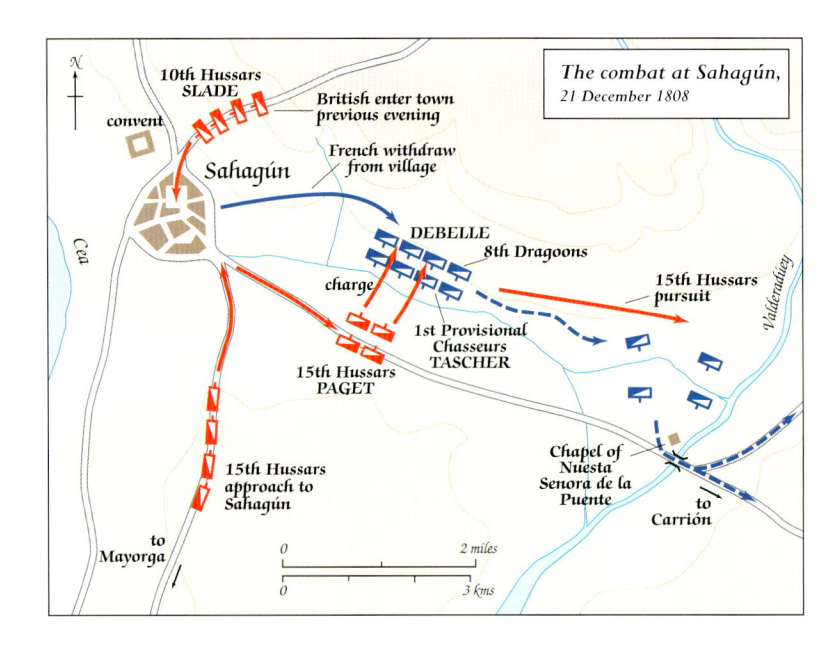

In increasingly atrocious weather, Moore's brigades commenced their retreat north-west towards Corunna, where the main fleet of transports was ordered to concentrate. On approaching Astorga, Robert Craufurd's Light Brigade peeled off from the main body and proceeded west across convoluted country towards Orense and Vigo Bay, where several vessels remained to pick them up.[5] A number of spirited rearguard actions took place, as at Cacabelos, but many units became undisciplined (and often drunk, as at Bembibre), with men and camp-followers falling by the wayside to freeze to death or be taken prisoner by Soult, hard on their heel. Beyond Villafranca del Bierzo began the arduous ascent of snow-clad and wind-blasted ranges into Galicia. From Lugo, entered by Henry Paget's rearguard on 6 January, and where a serious confrontation was avoided, the famished and demoralized army trudged on to approach Betanzos, their feet frost-bitten and bleeding. It was not until 11 January that the vanguard limped into Corunna, in the harbour of which transports were now anchoring.

- ······▶ Baird's advance from Corunna
- ⎯⎯▶ Moore's advance from Portugal
- ---▶ Moore's retreat to Corunna
- ⎯⎯▶ French advance

1 The itineraries are liable to vary in detail; certain units may have taken alternative tracks between towns, from Almeida via Lumbrales, Vitigudino, and Ledesma to approach Salamanca, for example.

2 The landing of Baird's contingent was delayed by the Galician junta until 26 October, and it was unable to join forces with Moore near Mayorga until 20 December.

3 Moore had been entirely misinformed about the state of the direct roads, assured that they could not be traversed by artillery. Although QMG George Murray's officers had been sent ahead to draw maps and examine road conditions between Lisbon and the frontier, it was not until 28 October that they had reported on those between Coimbra and Almeida.

4 Hope was unaware that, only two days earlier, Napoleon's vanguard had forced the Somosierra pass (a mere 40 miles further north-east as the crow flies), and scattered the 12,000 Spanish troops defending it. Napoleon himself had entered Madrid on 4 December.

5 Many of those 'missing the boat' eventually filtered south through northern Portugal.

MOORE'S CAMPAIGN | 33

8 THE BATTLE OF CORUNNA

16 January 1809

Moore still commanded 14,800 men, but few horses had survived the retreat. The wounded and those too prostrated to fight were embarked, and his effectives, when fed, re-shod, re-equipped, and re-animated, were deployed in defensive positions to await Soult's inevitable attack, one which it was unlikely could be mounted until the 16th. Meanwhile, stores and any *matériel* which could not be carried away were destroyed.

Moore surveyed the future battlefield on the 12th. Not having enough men to occupy the dominating heights of Peñasquedo further south, he had little alternative but to deploy them along a ridge of nearer hills, among them Monte Mero, strewn with boulders, which would provide protection to his skirmishers. Soult's intention was to contain the British left and centre with two divisions, while Mermet's division and the bulk of his cavalry would swing round and attack their right, but it took time to place them in a position to make this outflanking movement, and it was not until the early afternoon of that short winter day that Bentinck's brigade, defending the village of Elvina, was attacked. The French cavalry made little headway, hampered by the tangle of granite walls, and were held in check by Fraser's men on the Alto de Santa Margarita, defending the neck of the peninsula on which Corunna stood.

Edward Paget's Reserve division (which had rapidly countermarched from a position in the rear) reached the front in time to frustrate another cavalry thrust, and a second attack on Elvina had been driven back with the support of battalions of the Guards. Moore, while watching the progress of the battle as the sun was sinking, was hurled from his saddle by a round shot which shattered his left shoulder, and was carried to the rear. His wound was mortal, but he survived long enough to know that the enemy had been beaten at every point.

By 6 p.m., the firing had ceased. Unable to penetrate their centre or turn either of the British flanks, Soult had no desire to prolong the struggle into the night, and withdrew, allowing the British to reoccupy the ground they had previously held, and it was not until next morning that he was aware that the hill of Santa Lucía, commanding the harbour, had been evacuated. This enabled him to place a battery there, but the few random shots fired at long range caused only minor damage during the ensuing embarkation, which was covered by Beresford's rear guard. It was left to Hope, on whom the command had devolved, to spike his few remaining guns and station strong picquets while his brigades were progressively withdrawn from the battlefield. The last troops clambering aboard the waiting transports during the 18th were those of Fraser's division. Some 400 mounts had to be destroyed. It is estimated that battle casualties were about 900.

In what has been referred to as the 'Dunkirk' of its age, some 26,000 of the original expeditionary force of 33,000 were belatedly landed at harbours along the south coast of England – the convoys had been scattered by storms in which two transports were wrecked. Their fatigued and ragged condition aroused widespread controversy: but at least a high proportion of the British Army had been saved to fight another day, albeit 6,000 of the survivors were sick enough to require immediate medical treatment.

Anon. The embarkation at Corunna.

CORUNNA
Fort San Antonio
0 1000 yards
0 1000 metres
The last transports depart, 18 January
British transports
Corunna Bay
Fort San Diego
Santa Lucia
Heights of Santa Margarita
Position from which French fired upon British shipping, 17 January
BERESFORD
6th 2/23st 2/43rd 9th
(covering embarkation)
Fort d'Ossa
xx(3rd) FRASER
32nd 79th 38th
xx(4th) E.PAGET
Oza
Heights of Santa Lucia
Passage
Heights of Perillo
Monelos
San Cristóbal
Eiris
C.CRAUFURD
36th 71st 92nd
MERO
Perillo
DISNEY
52nd 91st
xx(1st) BAIRD
WARDE (Foot Guards)
xx(2nd) HOPE
Monte Mero
HILL
Heights of San Cristóbal
MANNINGHAM
LEITH
14th
59th
32nd
BENTINCK
4th
1st
81st
Piedralonga
50th
Elvina
1st Foot Guards
42nd
95th
ANSTRUTHER
20th
28th
Palavea
Palavea
Ortega
Portazgo
Monte de Mesoiro
Mesoiro
La HOUSSAYE
MERMET
DELABORDE
MERLE
LORGE
Heights of Peñasquedo
to Lugo

9 Wellesley's Advance on Oporto and Pursuit of Soult

May 1809

On 23 April, only twenty days after being formally nominated Commander-in-Chief in Portugal, Wellesley had disembarked at Lisbon, together with additional units.[1] Gen. Beresford, newly arrived in the Peninsula, was already undertaking the drastic reform and reanimation of the demoralised and undisciplined Portuguese army, a battalion of which, when trained, would be incorporated into each British brigade.

Soult still commanded over 20,000 men, with whom he had been attempting to cow the Galicians, before invading Portugal. On 29 March he assaulted and sacked Oporto,[2] from which some units cautiously extended further south, but although 10,000 infantry and 1,200 cavalry occupied the city, Soult had already decided to evacuate northern Portugal. He felt insecure, isolated, and in only fragile communication with Ney, who remained in Galicia with 17,000 men, where he endeavoured, unsuccessfully, to suppress subversives. While still keeping an eye on Cuesta, whose army he had scattered at Medellín, Victor was moving up and into the Tagus valley, but only in tenuous contact with Gen. Lapisse, who was operating in the vicinity of Ciudad Rodrigo with a smaller force. Together, they would outnumber Wellesley, who deduced that if he left Gen. Mackenzie near Abrantes with 12,000 men to prevent any flying column approaching from the east,[3] he might attack Soult and eject him from northern Portugal before turning on Victor. But as it had been stipulated in his brief that he should not extend his campaign into Spain, Wellesley applied to London, requesting them to modify his instruction and permit him to advance against Victor if it should prove to be expedient.

On 6 May Wellesley reviewed his assembled troops, reinforced by Portuguese units, at Coimbra. These increased his total infantry to 18,900, of which 5,800, a high proportion being Portuguese, then marched north-west towards Viseu under Beresford's command to prevent Soult from moving east from Oporto to unite with Lapisse.

From Lamego, Beresford crossed the Douro on the 10th, to enter Amarante (in mountainous country 30 miles east of Oporto) next day.

Meanwhile, the main body of Wellesley's troops had recommenced their progress up the highway to Oporto. With the intention of turning the flank of any hostile force impeding his advance, on approaching Aveiro, Hill's brigade was embarked on a small fleet of vessels and ferried north on the adjacent coastal lagoon to land at Ovar. A minor cavalry action took place after crossing the Vouga, but French units concentrated near Grijó, realising that they were likely to be outflanked, drew back. By the 12th, enemy forces (some 10,000 infantry and 1,200 cavalry at hand) were all across the Douro, then in spate. All lighters and river-boats had been withdrawn from the southern bank, beyond which Soult had neglected to leave any outposts, complacently assuming that the river provided sufficient defence, and that any attempt to dislodge him would be by an amphibious landing near its mouth: so his picquets were posted facing west. For Oporto, see Plan 10.

Soult's demoralised forces had no alternative but to retire north precipitately (the road to Amarante being cut), and united with other units before veering north-east through rugged terrain and in appalling weather. Wellesley followed on their heels, entering Braga on 15 May, but the rapidity of their retreat, in which all the French wheeled transport, baggage and artillery was destroyed or jettisoned, was such that it was impossible to catch up with them. They had crossed the Cávado at Salamonde before Silveira's Portuguese, sent across country by Beresford, were able to cut them off. Beresford himself had marched via Chaves to prevent them escaping east, but gave up the chase at Allariz and returned to Chaves on the 21st. Meanwhile, a rearguard action had taken place at a bridge spanning the Miserela on the 16th, before the French clambered pell-mell over the trackless frontier range towards Orense, having lost 4,000 men and virtually all their equipment and *matériel*.

Wellesley followed in their wake as far as Montalegre, before turning south, partly to reduce his over-extended communications, and be closer to his supplies. His casualties in the pursuit of Soult had been minimal, but his troops were exhausted. The majority marched south in easy stages via Braga, Oporto, Coimbra, and Tomar towards Abrantes, on which Beresford's men converged via Vila Real, Lamego, Guarda, and Castelo Branco.[4] Meanwhile, on 10 June, Col. Mayne had blown up a span of the Roman bridge at Alcántara, which made enemy communications hazardous along that stretch of the Tagus.

→ Wellesley's advance and withdrawal
→ Beresford's withdrawal
→ Soult's lines of retreat

1 Cradock, the ineffectual general commanding at Lisbon since 14 December, had withdrawn outlying troops from as far afield as Almeida and Oporto (the presence of which would have menaced Soult's inevitable advance into Portugal) and placed them in cantonments near the capital, where they had remained inactive, in expectation of an eventual evacuation.

2 He captured several vessels, British *matériel*, and much artillery. Portuguese militia suffered heavily, as did civilians, drowned when the bridge of boats across the Douro gave way.

3 Should Victor advance further south, Mackenzie could hold the line of the Tagus, then in flood.

4 In mid May, Victor had briefly occupied Alcántara, but his reconnaissance towards Castelo Branco had been exaggerated by Mackenzie.

10 The Passage of the Douro at Oporto

12 May 1809

Wellesley, on reaching the cliff-top convent of N.S. da Pilar,[1] behind which the main body of his troops remained hidden, inconspicuously surveyed the city rising steeply from the quays opposite him. He noticed that the eastern suburbs had been left virtually undefended and, also within artillery range, saw what appeared to be an unguarded and unoccupied building within a walled enclosure, which, if he could ferry sufficient troops across, would provide a secure foothold on the far bank. Due to the configuration of the ground, the bend in the river here was also probably out of sight of Soult's main position. While ordering forward his guns, Wellesley had been informed that at Avintes, some 4 miles upstream, a scuttled but only slightly damaged ferry-boat was being bailed out and repaired. It was here that Gen. Sir John Murray was ordered to cross with his KGL units and some light dragoons to oppose any attempt by Soult to escape east.

A barber, who had rowed across unnoticed during the previous night and hidden his skiff below Wellesley's post of vantage, was persuaded to collect, assisted by other boatmen, four wine barges left unguarded on the far bank.

John Waters, a colonel in the Portuguese service, but previously employed by Messrs Warre, the Port wine shippers and who knew the area intimately, supervised this delicate operation. He also confirmed that the building in question – a seminary – was indeed vacant. At about 10.30 a.m., once the barges had been unobtrusively brought over, the regular shuttling of troops – thirty men in each vessel – was commenced. Having scrambled up the steep bank to the propitiously-sited stronghold, they would fortify the enceinte by piling earth behind the walls to form a banquette. Within the next hour, and before any barge had been seen crossing, some 600 men had been transported over and a substantial foothold effected.

Once aware of the landing, Gen. Foy sent units to investigate, but the first gun to unlimber and direct its fire against the seminary was immediately put out of action and its gunners killed by a shrapnel shell from Wellesley's artillery, to which their advancing infantry provided a vulnerable target. A second attack was checked by effective musketry from the garden wall, windows, and roof of the seminary, which continued to receive reinforcements. In the ensuing confusion, several more now unguarded barges were ferried over by the locals, enabling additional troops to cross, who swarmed into the upper town to take in flank enemy units making a third attempt to impede egress from the seminary.

Before long, Soult sensed that the game was up: it would be impossible to make a leisurely withdrawal: the main body of his troops, thoroughly demoralised, were already streaming precipitately east in the direction of Amarante.

Joseph James Forrester, *Watercolour of the Serra convent seen from the north bank of the Douro.*

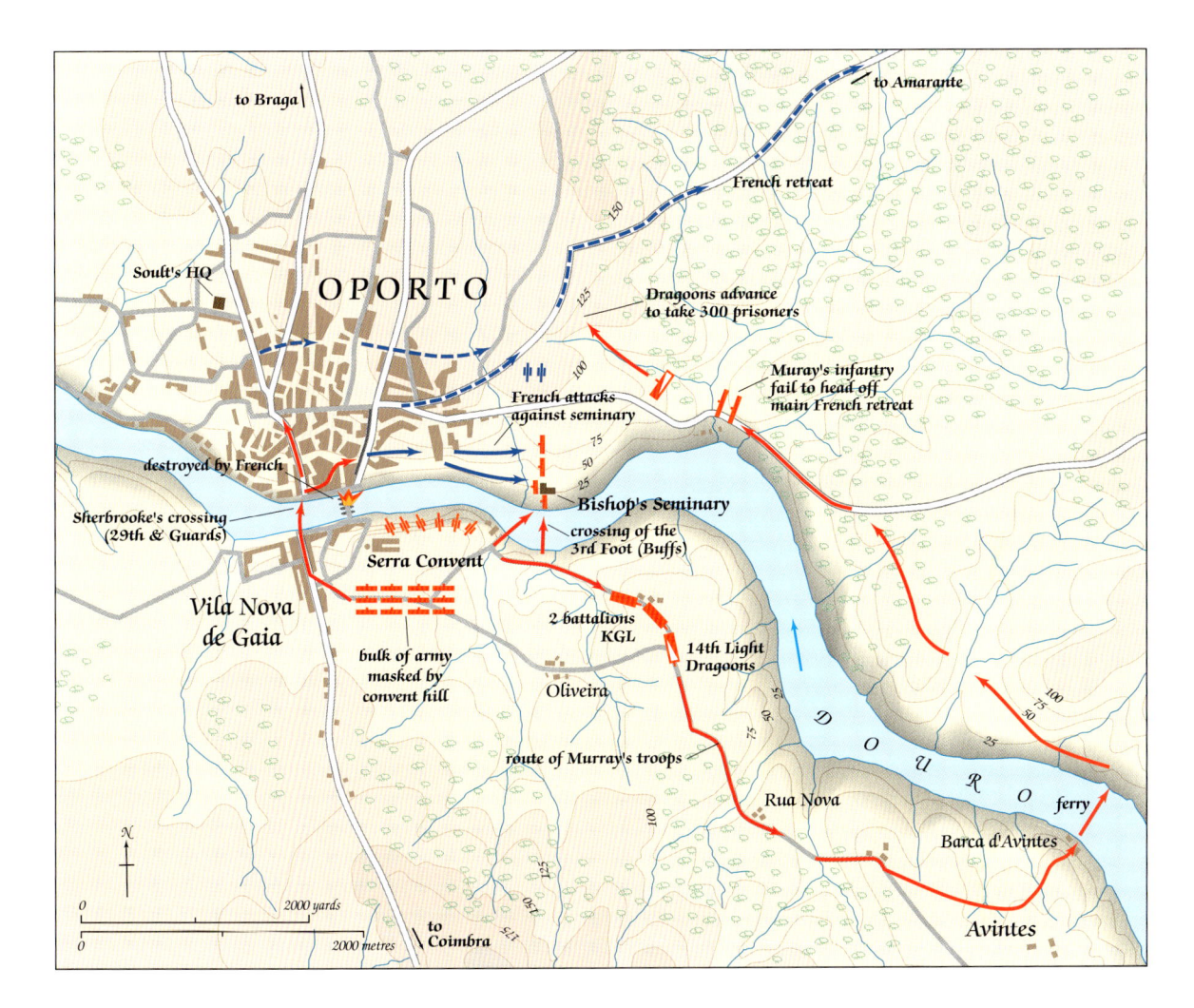

Murray had assumed that these flying troops were too strong to attack, and had remained passive, and it was not until Wellesley had sent Gen. Charles Stewart to lead forward his cavalry that an attempt was made to intercept the headlong retreat. Soult had hastened away with his rearguard, hospitably leaving his dinner in the Palácio das Carrancas for Wellesley and his staff, but had also abandoned some 1,500 men in Oporto's hospitals, and a deal of equipment, including no less than 70 guns. British casualties in this remarkable exploit were 23 killed, 2 missing, and 98 wounded (among them Edward Paget, commanding at the seminary, who lost an arm): enemy casualties were more than double.

Wellesley would now have to ferry over all his guns, ammunition, and provisions: a rapid pursuit was impossible.

As he later explained: 'If an army throws away all its cannon, equipments, and baggage, and everything which can strengthen it, and ... abandons all those who are entitled to its protection,[2] but add to its weight and impede its progress, it must be able to march by roads through which it cannot be followed, with any prospect of being overtaken, by an army which had not made the same sacrifice.'

---

1 The building is also frequently referred to as the Serra Convent.
2 Regrettably, at Talavera a few weeks later, but in different circumstances, Wellesley himself would also have to abandon his wounded.

11 Wellesley's advance into the Tagus Valley, and retirement to Portugal

Late June to early September 1809

On 28 June Wellesley's troops, rested, re-equipped and re-shod after their recent exhausting campaign, set out from his base at Abrantes on the first lap of their advance into Spain. Separated into four divisions, 16,600 infantry, almost 3,000 cavalry, and 5 batteries of artillery, followed by a train of bullock-carts carrying medical stores, ammunition, and a variety of stores, traversed divergent routes to Castelo Branco before crossing the frontier at Zarza la Mayor (north of Alcantara, where a span of the Roman bridge had been blown up by Col. Mayne earlier that month) to approach Plasencia via Coria.[1] Wellesley had been assured repeatedly by Gen. Cuesta, commanding the Spanish army in the Tagus valley, that all British forces co-operating with him would be well supplied with provisions, forage, and transport, none of which, in the event, was forthcoming.[2]

Proceeding from Plasencia, on 17 July British units started to cross the Río Tietar by a part trestle and part flying bridge rapidly erected at Bazagona,[3] near its confluence with the Tagus, to approach the highway to Madrid. On the 21st the British and Spanish armies converged on Oropesa, where they paraded for inspection by Wellesley before continuing their march east parallel to each other towards Talavera. The wide valley of the Tagus is here bounded to the north by the long line of the Sierra de Gredos, rising to almost 2,600m at the Pico Almanzor. Few could imagine that this barrier range, then shimmering in the heat, was capped by snow for much of the year.

In face of the Allied advance, French forces under Victor, at this time stationed no great distance east of Talavera, retired behind the Alberche to await developments. Although it had been agreed to make a concerted attack on the enemy, Cuesta perversely chose to 'drive Victor back to Madrid' on his own, but on finding that the French had been reinforced, he soon turned tail, his men swarming back precipitately to Talavera. Although Wellesley had initially sent two divisions across the Alberche to support them, he soon realised that the only way to stem Victor's advance would be by getting Cuesta's troops to defend a line of static field fortification immediately north of the town, while British units would extend this disposition to a height further north, aligned west of a small stream. For the impending confrontation, see Plan 12.

***

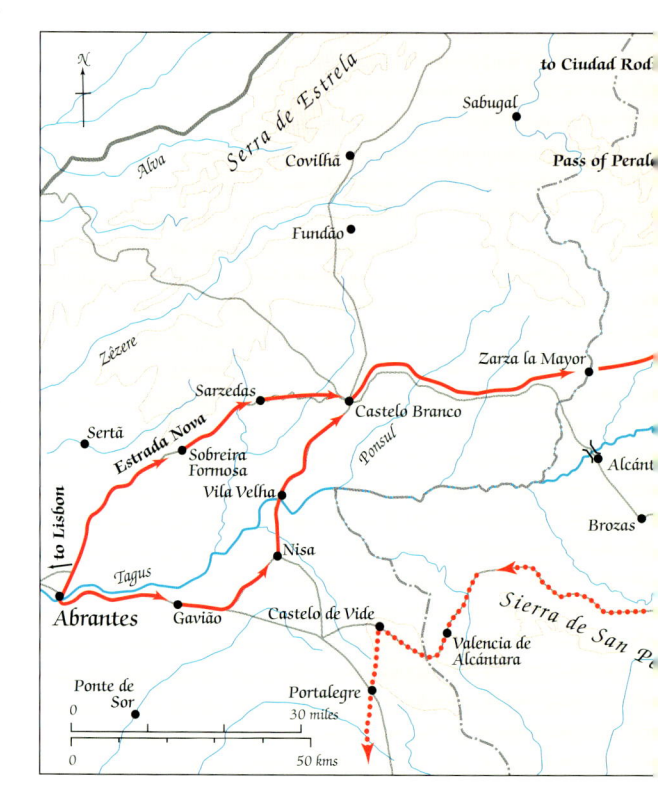

Although a few belated convoys of food had reached Talavera by the time the dust of battle had cleared, the British troops were almost starving; and left without any means of evacuating their wounded.[4] To be nearer his sources of supply, Wellesley was forced to retire. He would have preferred to have done so by the same route by which he had entered Spain, had not Spanish units allowed several brigades marching south from Salamanca under Soult's command to cross the Puerto de Baños, north of Plasencia, entered on 1 August, which seriously threatened to cut his line of retreat.

On 3 August, the British veered south from Oropesa to Puente de Arzobispo, there crossing the Tagus and traversing the trackless flank of the rugged sierra skirting the far bank: the river should secure them from an enemy crossing in force. Craufurd's brigade was sent ahead to secure the bridge at Almaraz. In the event, the Spanish rearguard holding the bridge at Arzobispo were surprised during their siesta and scattered by French cavalry; but by then their main force had already occupied an almost impregnable site near Mesas de Ibor.

By the 10th, Wellesley's debilitated troops were bivouacking in a strong position dominating the valley below the Puerto de Miravete, but the heat was grilling, and many suffered from malaria and dysentery, and they were still famished: Craufurd's rearguard, clambering south-west from Almaraz, had 'neither bread, meat, nor rations of any kind,' until lucky enough to stumble on a herd of pigs. Soult had long given up any attempt to trap them, and they later veered due west via Caceres to regain Portugal at Castelo de Vide before marching south towards Campo Maior. The main body of the army had proceeded south-west to enter the valley of the lazily flowing Guardiana at Mérida, and by 3 September had reached Badajoz. Wellesley had been granted the title of viscount on news of the battle reaching London; and on 16 September he was able to sign with the name by which he is renowned: Wellington.

1 Thus Wellesley's right flank was protected from possible attack across the Tagus, while Wilson's Lusitanian Legion and Portuguese units under Beresford protected their left.
2 Admittedly, some were supplied at Plasencia, but no means of transporting them.
3 Interesting details of bridge-building operations may be found in Robert Burnham's contribution to *Inside Wellington's Army*.
4 Of the more seriously wounded, 1,500 were left in the care of the hospitals and civilian population. Several surgeons remained with them, and they were well treated by the French on their re-occupation of Talavera.

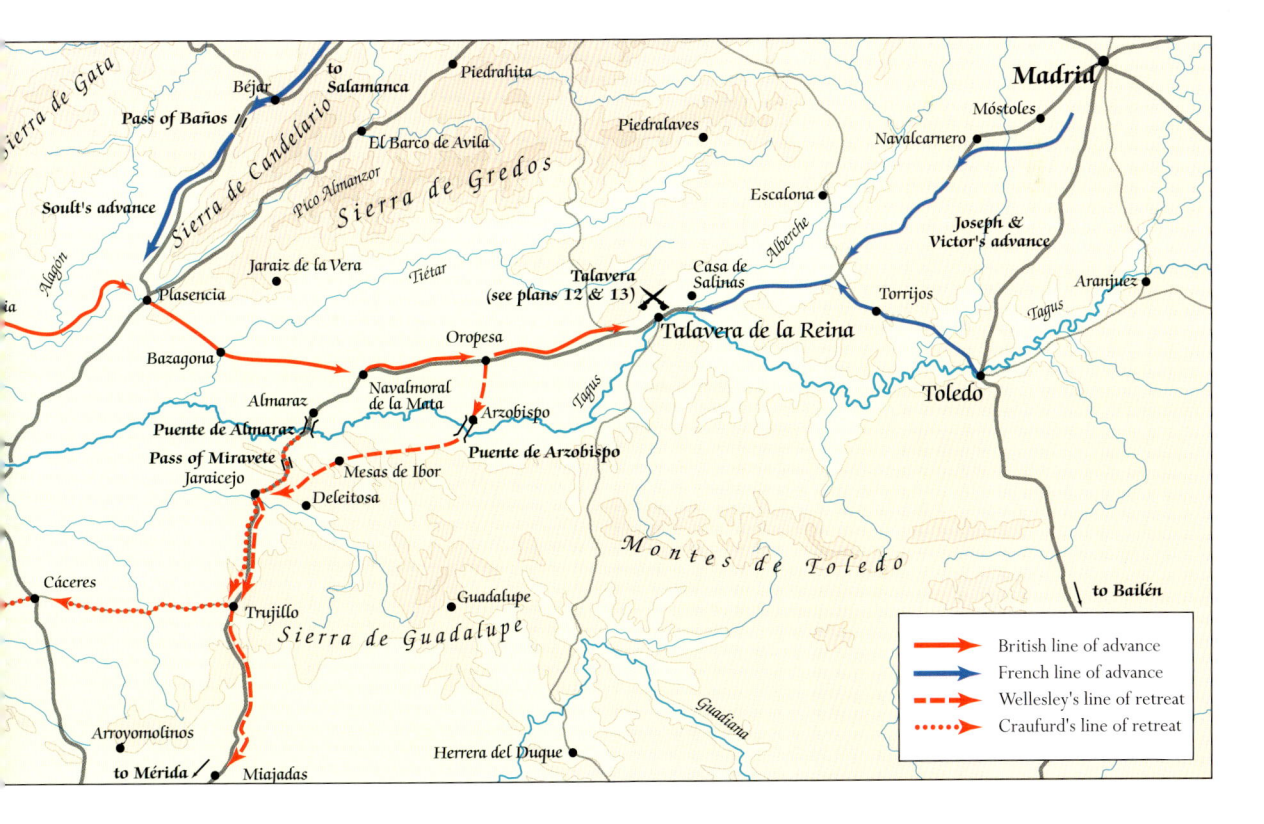

WELLESLEY'S ADVANCE INTO THE TAGUS VALLEY, AND RETIREMENT TO PORTUGAL

12 The Battle of Talavera I

27–28 July 1809

Although Wellesley had initially sent units across the Alberche to support the Spaniards' reckless advance, it was soon obvious to him that the only way to stem the enemy counter-thrust would be to persuade Cuesta to deploy his troops (c. 32,000) behind a line of strong field fortification immediately north of Talavera itself.[1] In withdrawing to this more defensible position, Wellesley's 3rd Division (the brigades of Mackenzie and Donkin), had briefly halted in the vicinity of the Casa de Salinas, standing among olive groves and evergreen oaks (*encinas*), and suffered unnecessary casualties when surprised by Lapisse's infantry columns advancing furtively through the trees after fording the Alberche.[2] Wellesley's other divisions had already retired behind the shallow Portiña stream. Although easily forded, it served to align them north from the hillock of the Pajar de Vergara – between which and Talavera itself the Spaniards were sprawled. On and abutting the redoubt of the Pajar stood the 4th Division (the brigades of Alexander Campbell and Kemmis), extended by the 1st (Sherbrooke's, including Langwerth's and Low's KGL brigades), and with the 3rd Division in support; while Hill with the 2nd Division, at first further south, was moved to a position slightly west of the crest of the higher-lying Cerro de Medellín. Wellesley's few guns were placed on the lower slopes, and on the Pajar.

The level area between the Pajar and the Medellín was without any shade or cover, while further north, between the latter and the Cerro de Cascajal, a slightly lower height extending the ridge to the east, the Portiña ran in a ravine.[3]

The heads of Victor's columns were the first to reach the future battlefield, and took up positions on the Cerro de Cascajal, leaving Sebastiani's Corps, together with Joseph Bonaparte, still some distance in the rear.[4] This was at about 7 p.m. on the evening of the 27th, soon after which Victor ordered his artillery to commence a harassing cannonade. Meanwhile, on the cautious approach of Latour-Mauburg's dragoons towards the Spanish positions, their entire line fired a deafening volley and turned tail. In his later dispatch, Wellesley thus described the scene he had witnessed: 'Nearly 2,000 ran off … who were neither attacked, nor threatened with an attack, and who were frightened only by their own fire; they left their arms and accoutrements on the ground, their officers went with them, and they … plundered the baggage of the British army which had been sent to the rear.'

At about 9pm that evening Victor impatiently mounted an attack on the Cerro de Medellín, knowing from his previous stay in Talavera that by seizing that commanding height he would be at a distinct advantage next morning. Hill himself was nearly taken prisoner when investigating the firing in his front, there thinly held by two battalions of the KGL, but with Richard Stewart's brigade being brought forward, the line held, although the rest of the night was spent uneasily.

---

1 A dilapidated 45-arched bridge spanned the Tagus here, providing the only crossing between Toledo and Puente de Arzobispo.
2 Wellesley's cavalry, which might have been used as vedettes, had already withdrawn to the rear, and infantry picquets must have been badly placed.
3 The ravine has been damned to form a reservoir north of the two Cerros, now straddled by a motorway, near which rises an incongruous monument; thus the valley between the Cerros and the Sierra de Segueilla, further north, in which the later cavalry action took place, is inundated.
4 In total, the army amounted to 37,500 infantry, 8,500 cavalry, and 80 guns.

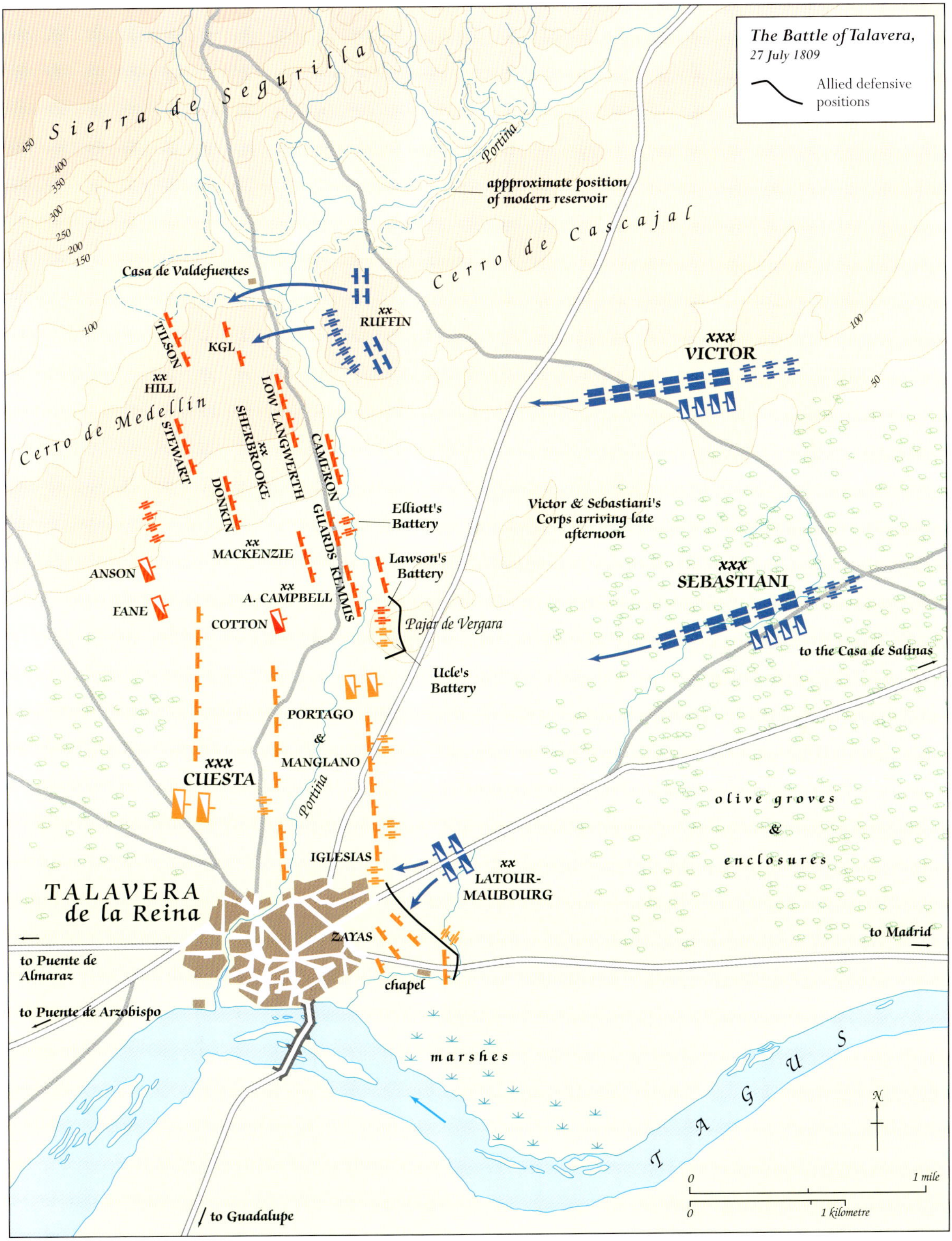
The Battle of Talavera,
27 July 1809
Allied defensive positions
Sierra de Segurilla
Portiña
appproximate position of modern reservoir
Cerro de Cascajal
Casa de Valdefuentes
RUFFIN
TILSON
KGL
HILL
VICTOR
Cerro de Medellín
STEWART
SHERBROOKE
LOW LANGWERTH
CAMERON
DONKIN
GUARDS
KEMMIS
Elliott's Battery
Victor & Sebastiani's Corps arriving late afternoon
MACKENZIE
Lawson's Battery
ANSON
SEBASTIANI
A. CAMPBELL
FANE
COTTON
Pajar de Vergara
to the Casa de Salinas
Ucle's Battery
PORTAGO
&
MANGLANO
CUESTA
Portiña
olive groves
&
enclosures
IGLESIAS
LATOUR-MAUBOURG
TALAVERA de la Reina
ZAYAS
to Madrid
to Puente de Almaraz
chapel
to Puente de Arzobispo
marshes
TAGUS
N
to Guadalupe
0
1 mile
0
1 kilometre
450
400
350
300
250
200
150
100
100
50

13 The Battle of Talavera II

27–28 July 1809

On the misty dawn of the 28th, the British positions on the Medellín were heavily bombarded. Wellesley ordered his men to lie flat behind the hill-crest, from which they were brought forward as Ruffin's columns advanced, the central one being met by 1,200 muskets of Stewart's two-deep line; the southern being taken in flank by part of Low's brigade: neither column could withstand their punishing fire, and made for the rear after suffering severe casualties. An artillery duel at long range was followed by a lull, in which an informal truce enabled the adversaries to collect their wounded and slake their thirst in the Portiña, for the blistering heat was suffocating.

Wellesley had meanwhile placed his 6-pounders on the Medellín to sweep any thrust against his left wing, reinforced by British and Spanish cavalry positioned in the (now water-filled) valley north of the Cerro de Medellín, beyond which, on the Sierra de Segurilla, a Spanish contingent under Bassecourt was deployed. Wellesley had also observed preparations for a massive attack further south, where 30,000 infantry were poised to advance, which they did after another cannonade at 1pm. Again, their columns – commanded by Ruffin, Lapisse, Sebastiani, and Leval, from north to south, with Milhaud's dragoons 'containing' the Spanish line – issuing from a thinly wooded area, advanced directly towards Wellesley's centre, between the lower slope of the Medellín and the Pajar de Vergara redoubt. Leval's troops, the first to come into collision with the British line, there held by Alexander Campbell, suffered severely, their flank being also bravely attacked by Spanish cavalry, and Leval lost several guns. Two powerful columns were brought to a standstill opposite Sherbrooke's Division, but it was badly mauled when too rashly pressing a counter-attack, which left a gap in the defensive line, promptly closed by units ordered up obliquely from either side. At the moment of crisis, the line held, with additional advancing columns being met by a succession of rolling volleys; but casualties were very heavy among the contenders.

Victor now attempted to push into the northern valley, but Allied cavalry was already in position to counter this. If threatened by a cavalry attack, the French infantry would form squares, making them vulnerable to Wellesley's artillery on the Cerro, but his Light Dragoons, rather than keeping to a controlled speed when still at a distance, impetuously increased their pace to a gallop and ran full tilt into a *barranco* – the precipitous bank of a *rambla*, the dry bed of a tributary of the Portiña (now covered by the reservoir) – concealed by high grass: naturally, several necks and limbs were broken. By the time the survivors had reformed and charged ahead, they found themselves outnumbered by a brigade of chasseurs, and lost half their strength. By now there was little evidence of any further assault on Wellesley's lines; but he was in no state to take the offensive, and the remaining hours of daylight were spent by both sides collecting their wounded, and saving them from being burnt by the fires started among the dry grass, caused by smouldering wadding fanned by the wind. Units were re-positioned and picquets posted, should Victor attempt to mount another night attack. But as day dawned, the plain to the east was found to be empty: under cover of darkness the French had discreetly retreated well beyond the Alberche.

The action was over by the time Craufurd's heavily equipped Light Brigade had reached the battlefield after a prodigious forced march under a blazing sun, the last 43 miles (70kms) being covered in about 22 hours. The next two days were spent burning the dead on huge piles or burying them in mass graves. As Wellesley's lines of communication were threatened, any pursuit of the French was out of the question: the only recourse was a rapid retirement. See Map 11.

For Wellesley, it had been a Pyrrhic victory: a 'murderous' engagement – 'two days of the hardest fighting I have ever been party to', in his own words. Having to take the brunt of the battle, his casualties had been particularly heavy: over 5,000 men, one quarter of the entire British force. French losses were heavier – over 7,000 – but were a lower proportion of the troops involved.

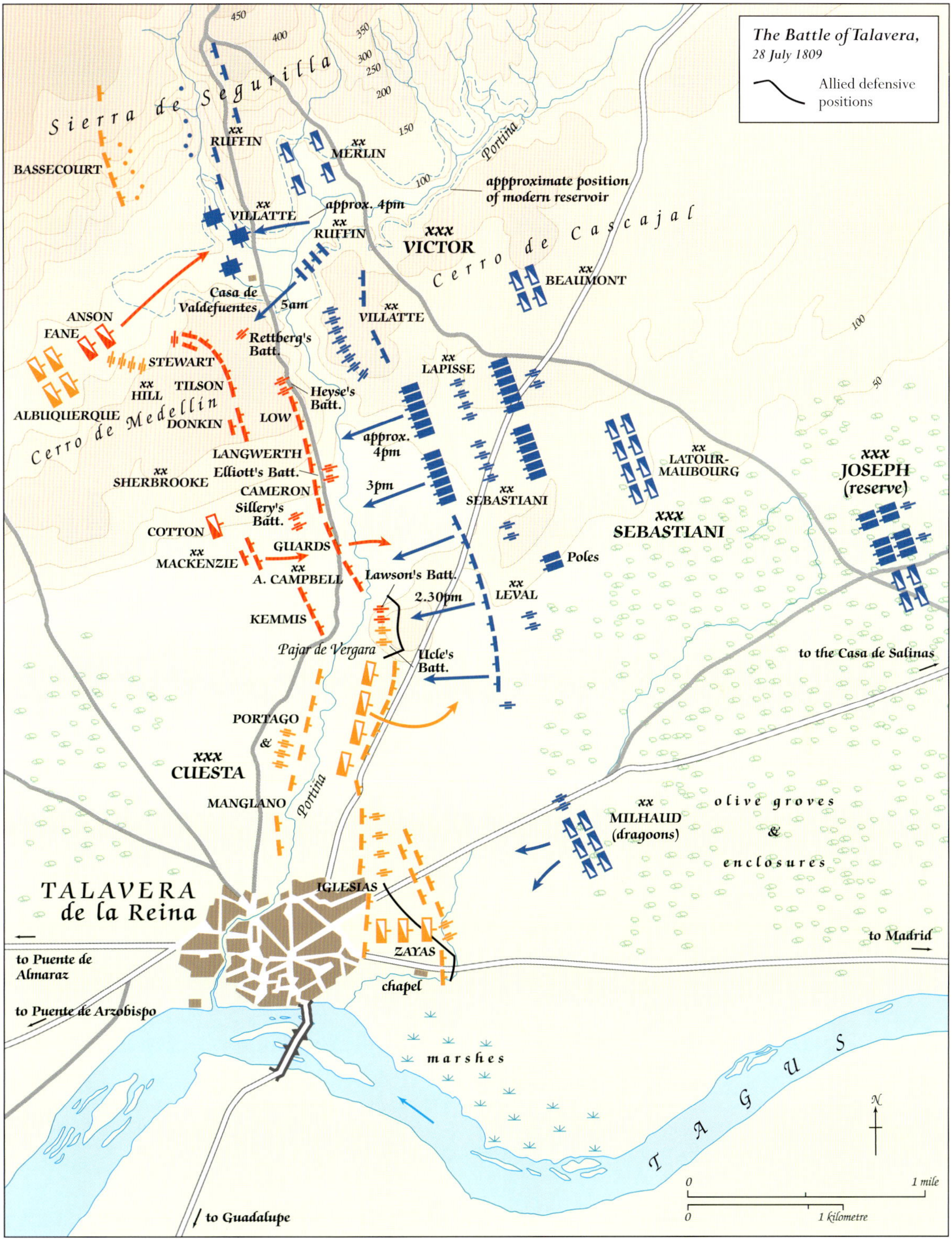
The Battle of Talavera,
28 July 1809
Allied defensive positions
Sierra de Segurilla
Cerro de Cascajal
Cerro de Medellin
Portina
approximate position of modern reservoir
BASSECOURT
RUFFIN
MERLIN
VILLATTE
approx. 4pm
VICTOR
BEAUMONT
Casa de Valdefuentes
5am
ANSON
FANE
STEWART
Rettberg's Batt.
TILSON
HILL
Heyse's Batt.
ALBUQUERQUE
DONKIN
LOW
LAPISSE
LANGWERTH
Elliott's Batt.
SHERBROOKE
CAMERON
Sillery's Batt.
3pm
SEBASTIANI
LATOUR-MAUBOURG
JOSEPH (reserve)
COTTON
GUARDS
MACKENZIE
A. CAMPBELL
Lawson's Batt.
Poles
2.30pm
LEVAL
KEMMIS
Pajar de Vergara
Ucle's Batt.
to the Casa de Salinas
PORTAGO & MANGLANO
CUESTA
MILHAUD (dragoons)
olive groves & enclosures
IGLESIAS
TALAVERA de la Reina
ZAYAS
chapel
to Madrid
to Puente de Almaraz
to Puente de Arzobispo
marshes
TAGUS
to Guadalupe
0 1 mile
0 1 kilometre
N
450
400
350
300
250
200
150
100
50

14 Combats on the Agueda and the Côa

March–July 1810

Malaria, endemic at Badajoz, in the mosquito-ridden valley of the Guadiana, and in the hospitals of neighbouring if higher-lying Elvas, took a further toll on Wellington's debilitated army;[1] but as winter approached, its health improved. During this period of comparative inaction, Beresford continued to train and discipline Portuguese troops. In addition, a militia was being established, together with an *Ordenança*, a form of 'Home Guard' of partially armed peasantry, who, knowing every goat-track throughout the country, would be invaluable in harassing the enemy, preventing marauding except by large detachments, and causing chaos along their lines of supply and communication.

Other than at Tamames (where the French were rebuffed in mid October), Ocaña, and Alba de Tormes (Spanish defeats; both in November), little fighting took place during the following few months in central Spain; but by February Soult had occupied Seville and invested Cádiz, by then the provisional seat of the Spanish government. Meanwhile, in October, anticipating the French would inevitably invade Portugal again in the spring, and that he would as inevitably be forced back towards Lisbon, which it was essential to retain at all costs as a vital base and foothold in the Peninsula, Wellington had ordered two chains of defensive bastions to be constructed at some distance north of the city, later referred to as 'The Lines of Torres Vedras'. See Map 17 (p.52). He also implemented a stringently enforced 'scorched earth' policy, which would deny the enemy all sustenance whenever the invasion took place. When this happened, the civilian population would be instructed to retire behind the defensive lines together with their livestock.

By mid March Wellington's improved intelligence system had given him notice that the French were massing in the vicinity of Salamanca. Headquarters of the 1st Division were moved forward to Celorico, the 2nd to Pinhel, and the 4th to Guarda, with Craufurd's Light Brigade together with other units being deployed not far west of the Agueda,[2] while Hill's Corps was later instructed to cross the Tagus at Vila Velha and to join him in the Mondego valley, leaving Portuguese units to watch the frontier near Elvas.

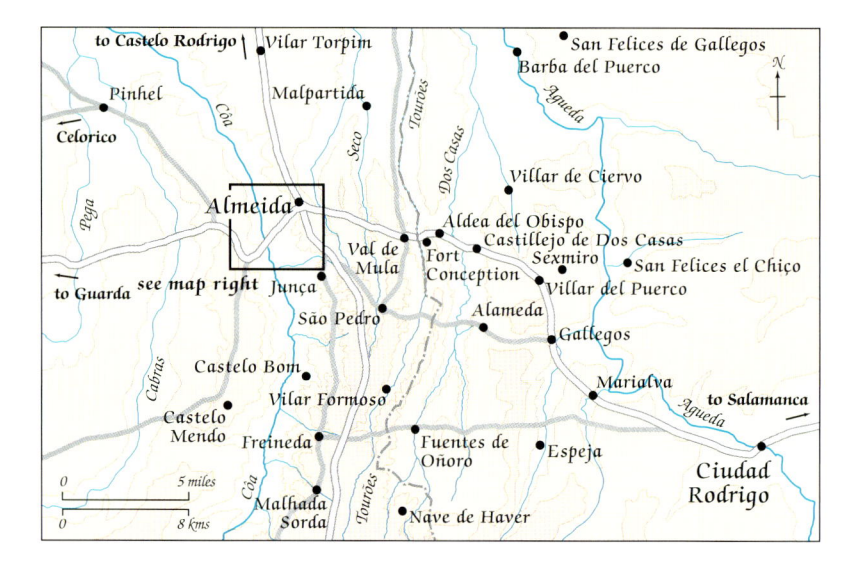

The Combat on the Côa,
24 July 1810

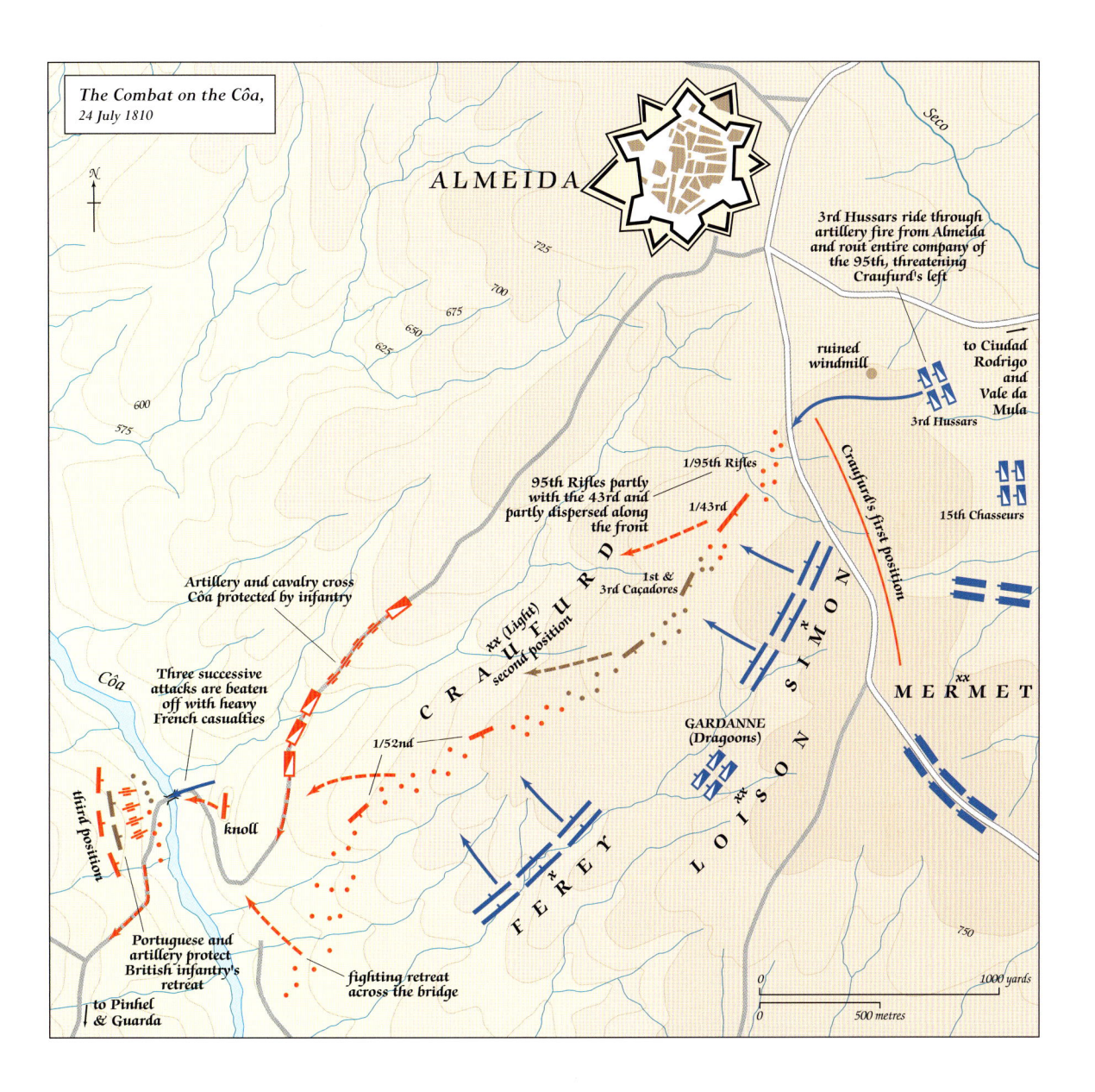

1   Malaria (in addition to typhus, enteric fever, dysentery, and hospital gangrene) made awesome inroads among the troops, not only here, but more so in the large-scale Walcheren Expedition (c. 44,000 men) taking place almost simultaneously on the insalubrious islands of the Schelte estuary, and undertaken to neutralise Napoleon's squadrons at Antwerp. Although Flushing surrendered on 16 August, malaria jeopardised the success of the expedition, for by late September 4,000 had died of the 'relapsing fever', and only 106 in combat. Although the troops were soon transported home, there were still 11,000 on the sick list in the following February, and many were left permanently incapacitated, to the extent that Wellington was later reluctant to receive reinforcements of units which had taken part in that expedition. The medical authorities were not yet aware of the cause of malaria, merely commenting that the buzzing noise made by the swarms of mosquitoes infesting the marshes was more alarming than the harm they inflicted.

2   It was at Barba del Puerco, on the Agueda, with its many fords, that Craufurd's men stemmed an attempted French thrust towards Almeida during the night of 19 March; they were less successful in holding the line of the Côa on 24 July.

THE COMBATS ON THE AGUEDA AND THE CÔA | 47

15 MASSÉNA'S INVASION

July–September 1810

Already, by mid January 1810, Wellington's HQ was at Viseu, with infantry units spread out over a wide area further east towards the Spanish frontier. It was his conviction that the predictable invasion of Portugal, with the capture of Lisbon as its target, most likely would be made down the Mondego valley; indeed, almost inevitably, for he had ordered the destruction of all alternative roads, even the tortuous 'Estrada Novo' (traversing the hills north of the Tagus between Castelo Branco and Abrantes).

By mid March, reports had been received of enemy forces massing at Salamanca. Beresford, commanding Allied troops at Abrantes, provisionally left there to defend the approach road from the crossing point of the Tagus at Vila Velha de Ródão, was ordered north via Tomar to join Wellington, who was concentrating his forces north-east of Coimbra.

By 24 June, Marshal Masséna, commanding the 'Army of Portugal', was supervising siege operations at Ciudad Rodrigo, which did not capitulate until 10 July. On the 21st, Fort Conception, guarding the frontier no great distance to the north-west, was blown up to make it untenable by the French.[1] The larger Vaubanesque stronghold of Almeida, although soon isolated, was expected to delay the French advance for several weeks, but the chance explosion of its main powder magazine on 26 August rendered it indefensible, and it capitulated after a brief siege. With the two main frontier fortresses in his hands, Masséna, with 65,000 men (including 8,400 cavalry, and with 114 guns) now descended into the upper Mondego valley.

Meanwhile, Wellington's advanced infantry units, screened by his cavalry, had retired at leisure down the valley towards the long hog's-back ridge of the Serra do Buçaco, which formed an ideal defensive position across the main approach road to Coimbra from the north-east.

Hill, stationed near Castelo Branco to counter a short-lived threat from Reynier units, was ordered to march north-west from Sarzedas, through intricate hilly country and to cross the Mondego below Penacova, where the river was abutted by the southern extremity of the Serra do Buçaco. From here, a lateral track running north immediately west of the summit had been repaired to ease communications on the ridge. It was along the southern two-thirds of this 'damned long hill' that Hill deployed his forces, extending the line of those taken up by Wellington. See Map 16.

From Almeida, the vanguard of Masséna's main force followed an execrable road west via Pinhel and Trancoso towards Viseu, entered on 19 September, while other units tramped west along an equally bad track via Freixedas, Celorico, and Mangualde to converge on Viseu,[2] but the progress of his veterans had been harassed ceaselessly by the Portuguese *Ordenança* or irregulars. In comparison, Spanish forces, which could have threatened Masséna's right flank, did nothing, as Gen. D'Urban had noted as early as mid December: 'During the whole campaign … the Galician Army, although furnished by England with clothing, Money, Arms, and Provisions, has made not one effort … to make a diversion or in any way give uneasiness to the Enemy.'

---

1 It would have required a garrison of 1,000, and, once surrounded, would have been difficult to relieve.
2 Apparently Masséna did not demean himself by referring either to the maps of central Portugal or to reports of road conditions collected previously by Junot.

Masséna's Invasion | 49

16 The Battle of Busaco (Buçaco)

27 September 1810

From Viseu, Masséna's vanguards advanced south-west in the direction of Coimbra, and driving back Craufurd's picquets near Mortágua, approached the steep heather-covered ridge of the Serra do Buçaco, below which his whole army later bivouacked. Little did he realise that almost the entire Anglo-Portuguese army – over 51,000 strong, together with 60 guns – lay in wait for him just behind the crest, from which Wellington had a very exact idea of his dispositions.[1] Undissuaded by the saner counsel of his subordinates – those who had fought at Vimeiro were well aware of the risk of making a frontal attack on British troops when deployed along such an eminently defensive position – Masséna then ordered his columns to assault the ridge, the first ascent being made through the early morning mist by a column from Reynier's Corps. This ran directly into part of Picton's Division, but raked by artillery fire and controlled volleys, it rapidly disintegrated and stumbled downhill, being only briefly pursued. Two further attacks by columns climbing up from the hamlet of San Antonio, further south, were likewise repulsed. Of Reynier's battalions, 23 had been broken by the 5 British and 6 Portuguese battalions engaged in these actions. Hill's units now closed towards the centre of the ridge, but the main confrontation took place further north, as Ney's troops advanced up the main road from Mortágua through the hamlets of Moura and Sula towards the ridgecrest, only to be met by Craufurd's riflemen, and by Ross's artillery, but their dense columns were unable to withstand such a concentrated fusillade at short range and, panic-stricken, streamed back to the valley floor. Another attack was likewise repulsed by Pack's Portuguese units, whose rate and accuracy of fire now equalled that of the British veterans.

The French had not expected such a punishing reception. Despite the fact that Masséna still had 20,000 fresh infantry with him – several battalions of both Reynier's and Ney's Corps, and not a single one of Junot's, had yet seen action – apart from minor skirmishing, the battle was virtually over, although it was not yet noon. Masséna had had enough:

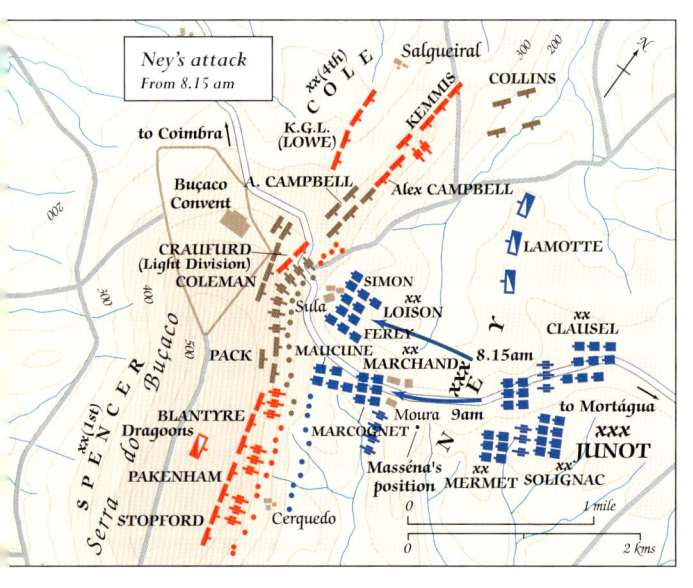

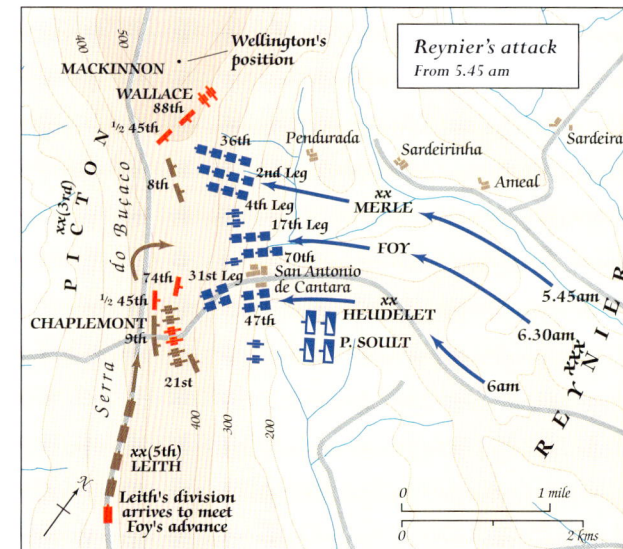

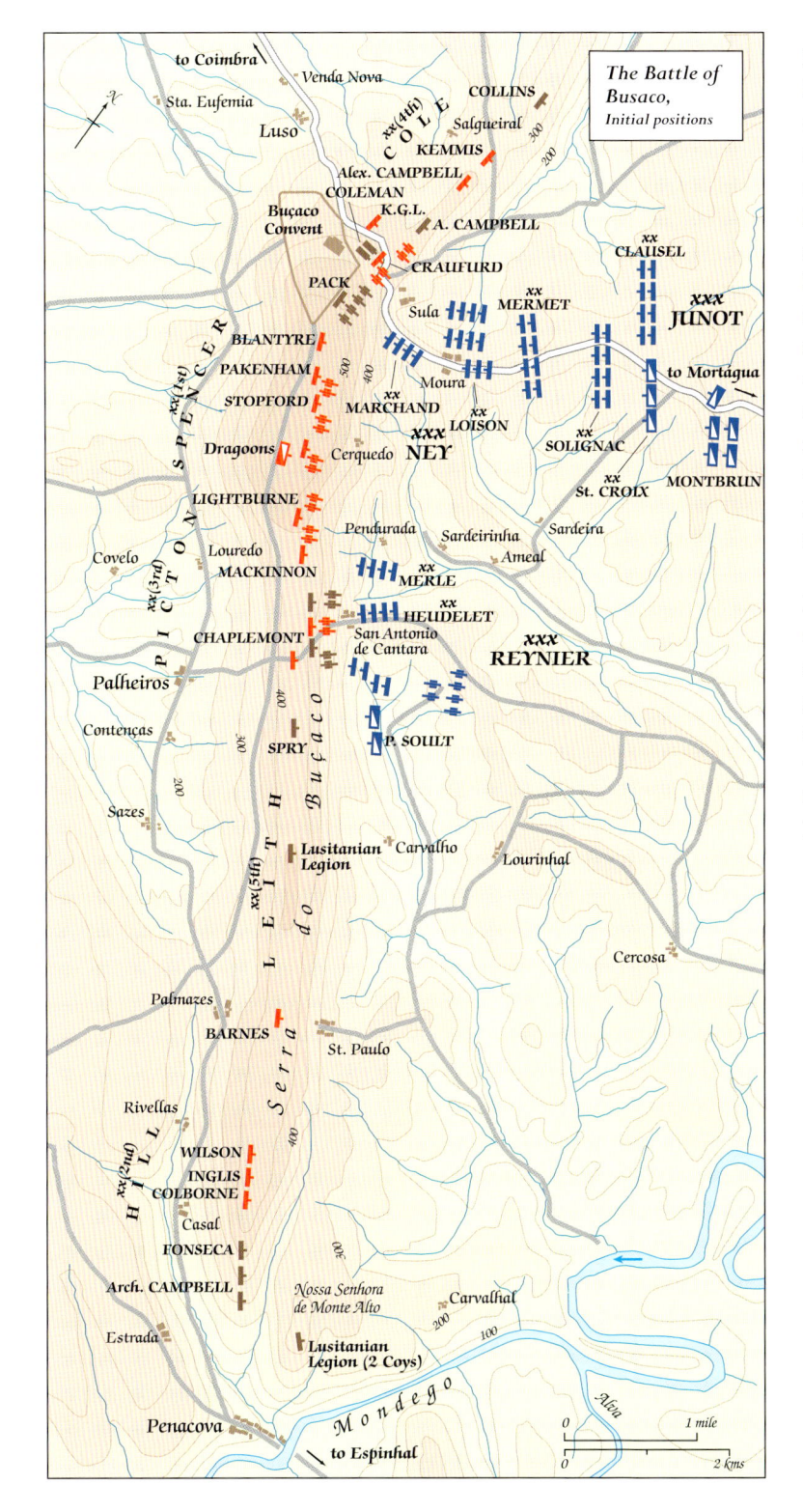

he could not afford to sustain such heavy losses.[2] The remaining hours of daylight was spent collecting their dead and wounded. Masséna now sent his cavalry to find ways in which the Allied line might be turned, and eventually some units were able to follow a track bearing north-west from Mortágua through Pala, Carvalhal, and Boialvo to meet the Oporto highway north of Coimbra. But Wellington had a head start, and the majority of the army retired south-west towards Coimbra, while Hill's Corps recrossed the Mondego at Penacova and marched south via Espinhal to Tomar.

Following in Wellington's wake, Masséna traversed and sacked Coimbra, where he left over 4,500 sick and wounded men inadequately guarded.[3] But by then, their cavalry acting as a rearguard, the Allies were well ahead on their march south through Leiria in the direction of Lisbon, as planned.

---

[1] Wellington's Headquarters prior to the battle were in conventual dependencies within an extensive walled enclosure towards the north end of the ridge.

[2] Over 4,000, including over 300 officers, a higher ratio of officers to men than was to occur in any battle of the war. Allied losses were c.1,250, half of whom were Portuguese; but 33,000 Allied troops had not even been engaged in the battle.

[3] These were made prisoner by Trant in a daring raid some ten days after the battle.

THE BATTLE OF BUSACO

17 The Lines of Torres Vedras

8 October to 14 November 1810

During the first few days of October Wellington's army tramped south, joining an exodus of some 200,000 people being herded, with their livestock, towards Lisbon, to which area – virtually an entrenched camp of over 500 square miles – they had been instructed to retire earlier.[1] The Allied columns started to enter the Lines on the 8th, just as the autumn rains commenced. The French followed in their wake, only to be brought up short by the Lines, the very existence of which Masséna was ignorant: anticipating a walk over, he had not even brought heavy artillery with him.

A year had passed since Wellington, recognising the potential of its natural features – well-described by Oman as 'a ganglion of mountains rather than a well-marked chain' – had ordered these two extensive lines of fortifications to be constructed across the intricate terrain of the peninsula between 20 and 30 miles north of the capital.

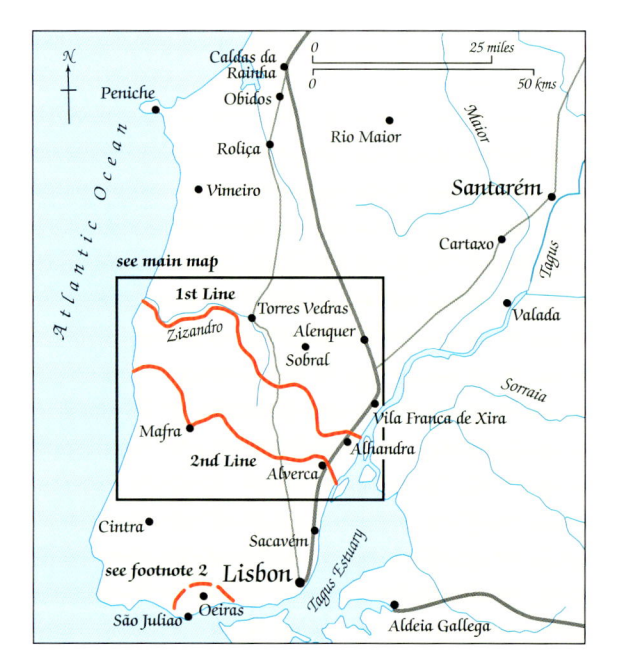

The northerly of the two roughly parallel chains of batteries and forts extended from the coast along the south bank of the Zizandro, and from Torres Vedras itself south-east to Alhandra on the Tagus, patrolled by gun-boats manned by British sailors, while men-of-war were anchored in the estuary.

The second line ran from the coast north-west of Mafra to Alverca.[2] Local peasant labour and the Lisbon militia, supervised by British engineers and officers, had fabricated 21,000 palisades and 10,000 fascines; hills were scarped, glacis levelled, walls and earthworks raised, lateral roads laid out, and lower-lying areas flooded. A system of semaphore was set up by which a message could be transmitted across the peninsula in seven minutes, while from his Headquarters at the central point of Pero Negro (south-west of Sobral, near which Monte Socorro, rising to almost 1,300 feet, provided a fine observation post) a written order from Wellington could reach any unit within an hour. Eventually, the 152 redoubts of the two lines held 534 guns, and were garrisoned by 25,000 militia, 11,000 *Ordenança*, and 8,000 Spanish troops, leaving the regular units free to move to the defence of any position attacked.

Although two attempts were made near Sobral shortly after reaching the Lines, there was no way in which Masséna could break through. Retiring to a more defensive position in the vicinity of Santarém in mid November, Masséna decided to sit it out: Wellington would surely make a false move, and he would then crush him.[3]

But Wellington was now in a better position to play a waiting game; his troops were under cover, he had provisions in plenty, and was expecting reinforcements to reach him during those wintery weeks. He was indeed impressed by the length of time Masséna's emaciated and entirely isolated troops were able to subsist in a countryside laid waste, for it was not until early March, with the prospect of impending starvation, that they commenced their hazardous retreat.

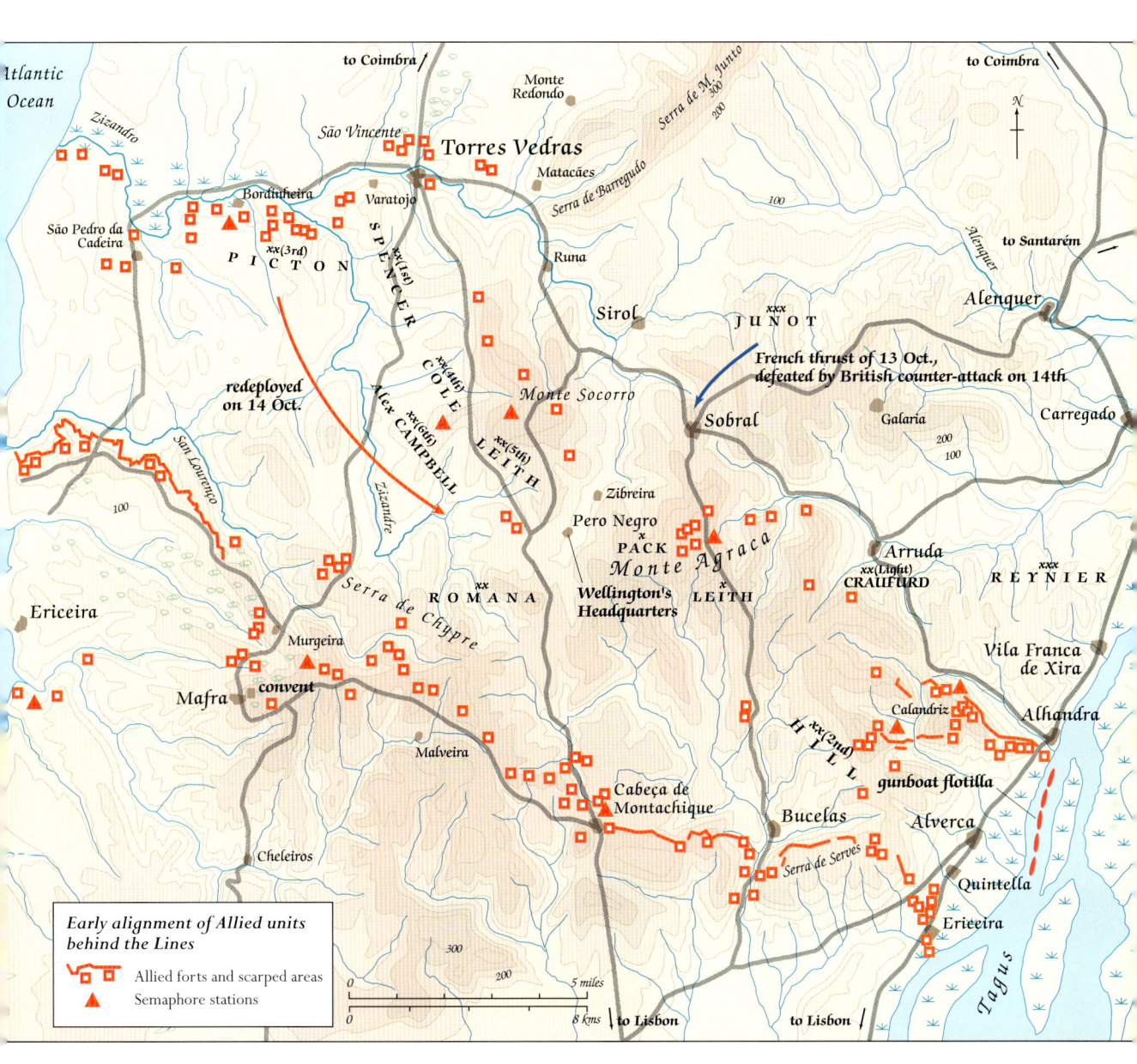

1 In spite of the congestion, the area, and Lisbon itself absorbed the influx of refugees, although many also crossed to the south bank of the Tagus estuary, from which supplies and provisions could be ferried with ease.
2 A short subsidiary line was also prepared on the Tagus estuary to provide a protected concentration area should it be necessary to embark the army. Forts were erected also on the opposite bank in the event of a possible thrust by Soult from the frontier, defended at Badajoz by Spaniards and at Elvas by Portuguese. Approaches to the port of Setúbal were also fortified.
3 The only reinforcements that managed to reach Masséna during the winter were some 8,000 from D'Erlon's Corps, which had set out from Almeida on 14 December.

THE LINES OF TORRES VEDRAS | 53

18 Masséna Isolated and in Retreat

14 November 1810–3 April 1811

Masséna maintained his position for a month only. On 14 November, in dense fog, he started to pull back towards Santarém, expecting to find more sustenance for his army further north and north-west. He also planned to bridge the Zezere and Tagus to improve communications with Castelo Branco and Spain and enable him to enter the Alentejo should food and forage run short. But no materials were at hand for the construction of pontoons: Masséna found himself cooped up and isolated, with his demoralised forces being inexorably depleted by desertion and death.

Wellington cautiously followed in Masséna's wake, redeployed his divisions in order to tighten the noose, and awaited developments: starvation would take its toll. Hill, with the 2nd Division and other units, was sent to defend the left bank of the Tagus, with his HQ at Chamusca.

On 19 February, his situation becoming desperate, Masséna held a council of war, at which it was decided that the most expedient solution would be to withdraw into the Mondego valley, still comparatively un-devastated and where they might subsist,[1] and which offered easier communication with Ciudad Rodrigo, from where provisions and reinforcements might reach them. On the night of 5 March, his troops precipitatedly decamped, leaving watchfires burning as they evacuated their positions and blowing up bridges behind them. Three Corps of his emaciated and shrunken army were converging on Leiria next day, their vanguard a full march ahead of their pursuers.[2] Reynier's units followed a separate road north via Tomar towards Espinhal.

While the bulk of the Allied army followed in Masséna's wake, Beresford was ordered to march to the relief of Badajoz, but was unable to reach the fortress before it capitulated to Soult on 10 March, news of which only reached Wellington late on the 13th.[3] See Map 20.

Few expected the harrowing scale of gratuitous destruction (as at Alcobaça, Batalha, and Tomar) and too frequent evidence of wanton cruelty which the Allies encountered, following hard on the heels of their adversaries. Several vigorous rearguard actions took place, notably at Pombal, Redinha, Condeixa, Casal Novo, and Foz de Arouce, as Masséna's army turned north-east, unable to cross the Mondego at Coimbra, its north bank being defended by Trant's forces. By the 26th, the Allied vanguard had entered Celorico. While D'Erlon's units pushed on past Almeida, into

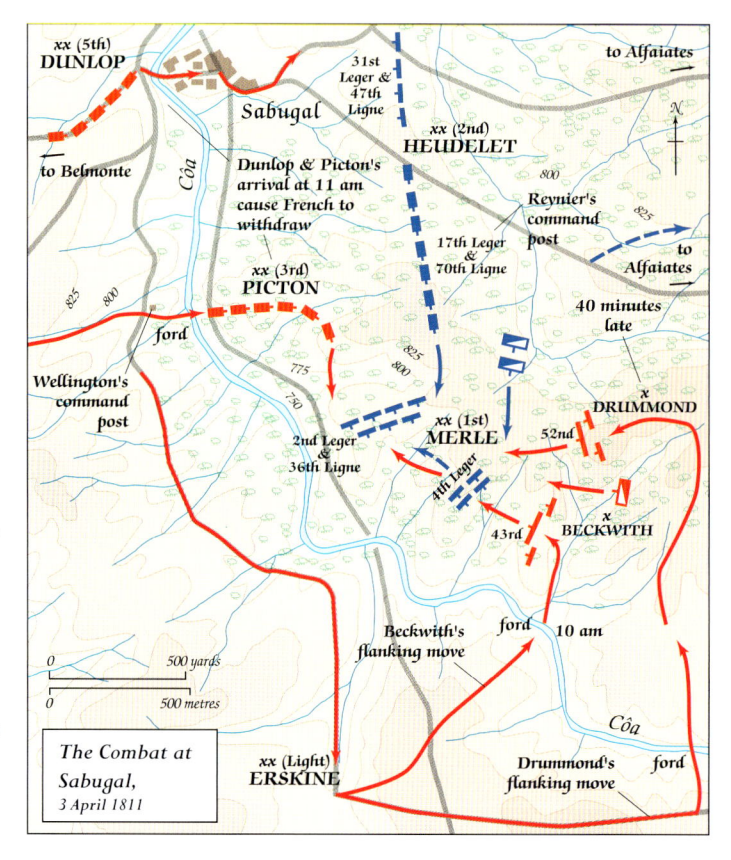

The Combat at Sabugal, 3 April 1811

which he threw a garrison, the bulk of Masséna's army, on ascending past Guarda, were out-manoeuvred and veered south towards Sabugal, which Reynier occupied in force.

Here, on a foggy 3 April, in the face of a spirited attack by the Light, 3rd, and 5th Divisions, the French gave way, but the cavalry missed the chance of taking them in the rear largely due to Erskine's incompetence.[4] The Allied vanguard pressed on through Alfaiates and Aldeia da Ponte to reach the frontier, while the Light Division formed a line of outposts at Fuentes de Oñoro on the 8th. The only body of enemy troops remaining on Portuguese soil was that at Almeida, invested by the 6th Division. By 11 April, Masséna was back at Salamanca, after an absence of almost ten months.[5]

1 Since November, his numbers had dwindled to 40,000, and he had lost over 5,000 mounts and draught horses.
2 Wellington, whose expected reinforcements had not all disembarked, was taken by surprise at the suddenness of this move, and unable immediately to catch up with Masséna's rearguard.
3 Soult had not been inactive during the winter. In late January, he had taken Olivenza and invested Badajoz, and on 19 February severely defeated Spanish forces near the Gebora (not far north of the fortress). On 16 March, the Spanish had surrendered Alburquerque.

Beresford's cavalry had botched an action at Campo Maior, north-west of Badajoz, on 25 March.
4 The sites of some fords crossed may now be submerged by a reservoir.
5 His total losses have been estimated at 25,000 men, of which only 2,000 were killed in battle; 8,000 had been taken prisoner; the rest had been picked off by Portuguese irregulars, had deserted, or died from malnutrition or actual starvation. Wellington's 'scorched earth' policy had paid off. In addition, Masséna had lost numerous guns, and virtually all his wagon train.

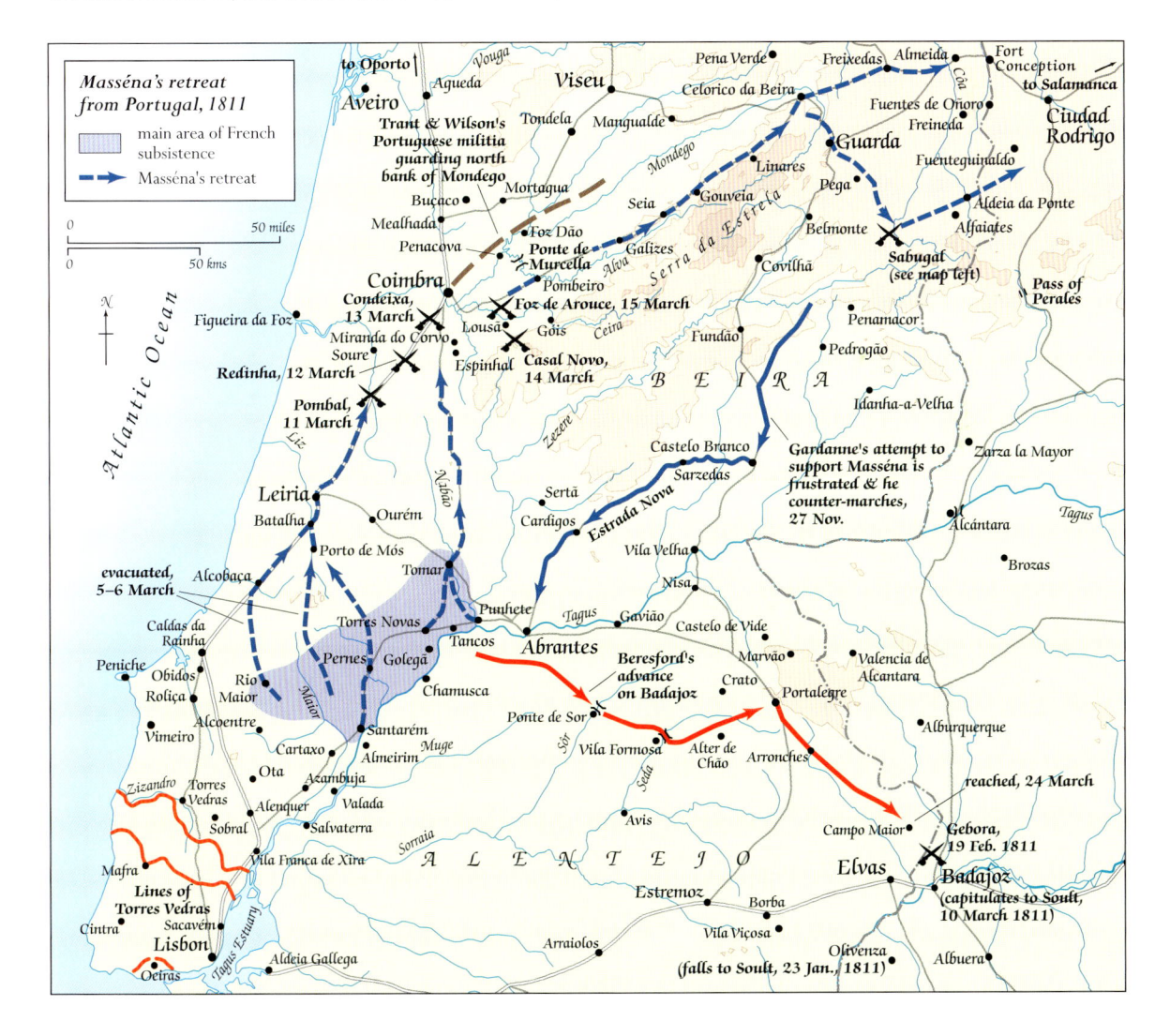

MASSÉNA ISOLATED AND IN RETREAT | 55

19 THE BATTLE OF BARROSA

5 March 1811

It was not until early in 1810 that the *Junta* at Cadiz (with a garrison of c. 18,000 men), blockaded by Victor, would accept Anglo-Portuguese reinforcements. In due course their number was increased to 8,000, commanded by Gen. Graham, of which some 3,000 were later withdrawn to Lisbon.

The following February – Soult having by then marched north from Seville to besiege Badajoz – was thought a propitious moment to undertake a diversionary expedition to lure Victor from before Cadiz. On 21 February, a force of 5,200 under Graham sailed from Cadiz to land at Algeciras. This was reinforced from Gibraltar before assembling at Tarifa.[1] Here they were met by La Peña's 9,600 Spaniards, and together they proceeded north past Vejér.[2]

After a deal of needless counter-marching, on approaching the San Petri river and finding it barred by a small force under Gen. Villatte, La Peña lost his nerve, and proposed retirement to the security of the Isla de León, but first it was necessary to disperse Villatte's troops. Gen. Zayas made a sortie from his position defending a bridge of boats to the Isla, still in Spanish hands, while Graham was ordered, against his better judgement, to descend from the Cerro de Puerco, a defensible ridge near the Torre Barrosa (a coastal *atalaya* or watch-tower), and take up a position in adjacent stone-pine woods, leaving only Col. Browne's battalion (28th) on the hill. Victor, now approaching from Chiclana, assuming this was unoccupied, sent Generals Ruffin and Laval, with 6,800 infantry, to take it. His cavalry would cut the coast road.

Learning that the Cerro was being attacked by the vanguard of a strong thrust, Graham faced about, with difficulty extracting his units from the wood, and raced to support Browne, now hard pressed. The ensuing struggle was very fierce and casualties heavy, but the French eventually broke and fled, with a squadron of KGL hussars charging their rearguard.

Graham retired to the Isla, disgusted by the pusillanimity of La Peña who, although promising support, had kept his troops immobile within earshot of the battle.[3] The Spaniard had then had the audacity to claim the victory.

---

1 It was at Tarifa, between 20 Dec. 1811 and 4 Jan. 1812 that a small garrison commanded by Skerrett was unsuccessfully besieged by Victor, as detailed in vol. 5 of Oman's *History*.

2 Graham had conceded overall command to the Spaniard, as disposing a higher proportion of the combined force.

3 Graham's losses were 1,238 (200 killed); those of Victor were 2,060: 244 killed, 1,684 wounded, including Villatte, and Ruffin (mortally).

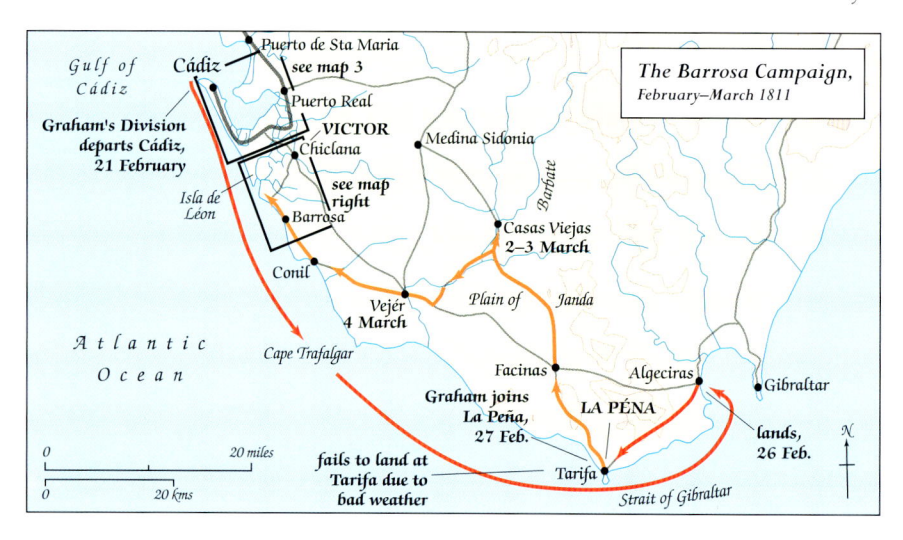

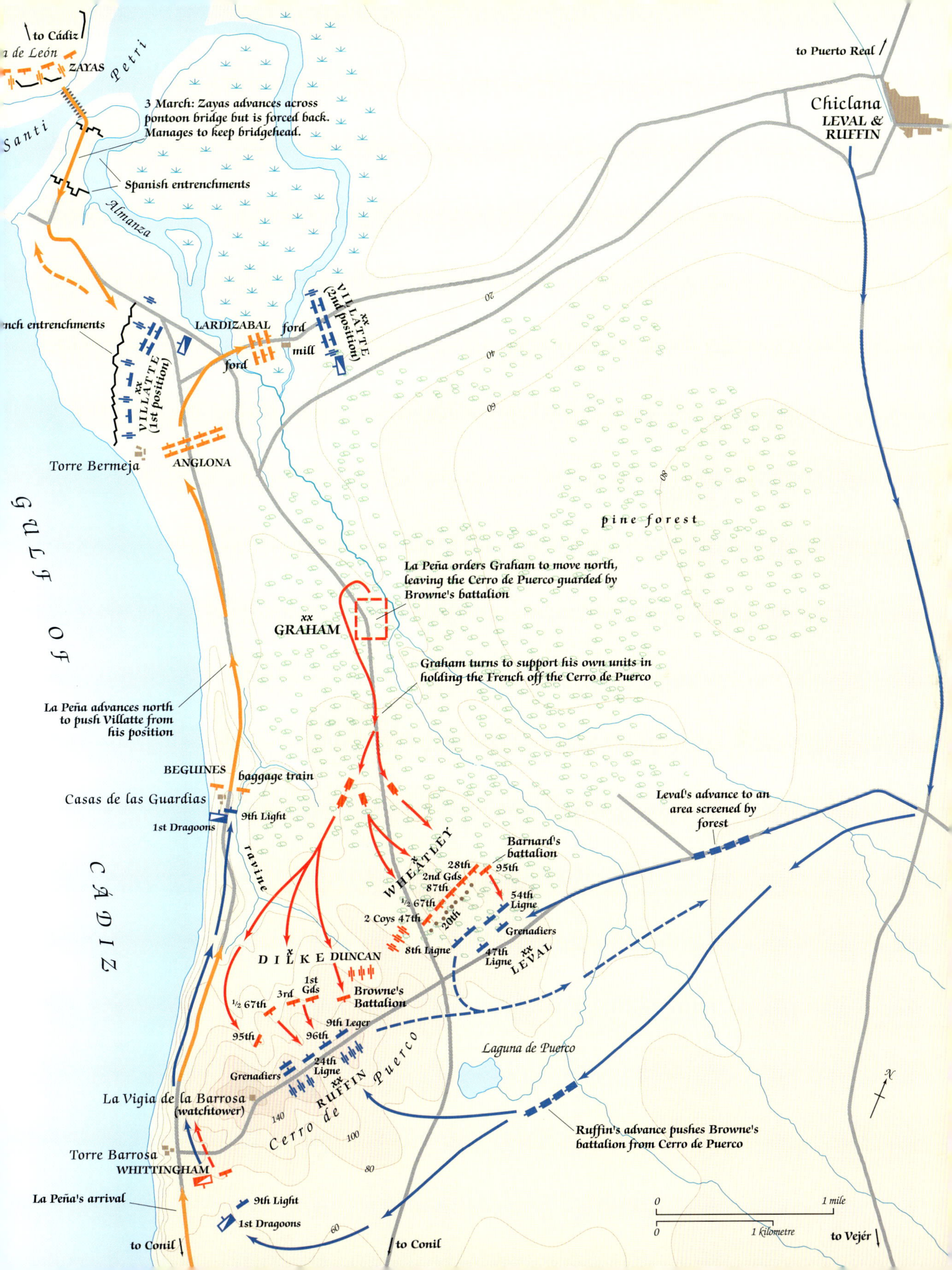

to Cádiz
a de León
ZAYAS
Santi Petri
3 March: Zayas advances across pontoon bridge but is forced back. Manages to keep bridgehead.
Spanish entrenchments
Almanza
to Puerto Real
Chiclana
LEVAL & RUFFIN
ench entrenchments
LARDIZABAL
ford
mill
ford
VILLATTE (2nd position)
VILLATTE (1st position)
Torre Bermeja
ANGLONA
GULF OF CÁDIZ
pine forest
La Peña orders Graham to move north, leaving the Cerro de Puerco guarded by Browne's battalion
GRAHAM
Graham turns to support his own units in holding the French off the Cerro de Puerco
La Peña advances north to push Villatte from his position
BEGUINES
baggage train
Casas de las Guardias
9th Light
1st Dragoons
ravine
WHEATLEY
Leval's advance to an area screened by forest
Barnard's battalion
28th
2nd Gds
87th
95th
½ 67th
54th Ligne
2 Coys 47th
20th
Grenadiers
8th Ligne
47th Ligne
LEVAL
DILKE
DUNCAN
1st Gds
3rd
Browne's Battalion
½ 67th
9th Leger
95th
96th
24th Ligne
Grenadiers
RUFFIN
Laguna de Puerco
Cerro de Puerco
La Vigia de la Barrosa (watchtower)
140
100
80
60
Torre Barrosa
WHITTINGHAM
Ruffin's advance pushes Browne's battalion from Cerro de Puerco
La Peña's arrival
9th Light
1st Dragoons
to Conil
to Conil
0
1 mile
0
1 kilometre
to Vejér
N
20
40
60
80

20 The Battle of Fuentes de Oñoro I

3–5 May 1811

Intent on redeeming his lost reputation if not re-gilding his tarnished laurels, Masséna returned to the fray in early May,[1] aiming to relieve Almeida, when a stubbornly fought encounter with the Allies took place at Fuentes de Oñoro, west of Ciudad Rodrigo. The granite-walled village formed the southern bastion of Wellington's position,[2] aligned east of the gorge of the Turones (or Tourões), and extending south from Fort Conception,[3] on the main road between Ciudad Rodrigo and Almeida, along which Masséna was expected to advance. In this northern sector, the 5th and 6th Divisions faced those of Reynier's Corps near Alameda, just south of which stood Solignac's.[4]

Picton's 3rd Division, supported by Craufurd's,[5] and Spencer's 1st, supported by Houston's 7th (new to the Peninsula), were deployed immediately west of Fuentes itself. Facing them stood Loison's Corps, with D'Erlon's in support.

In the event, on the afternoon of 3 May, it was Fuentes itself that Loison attacked, and frontally, with Gen. Ferey in the van, but although briefly gaining a foothold, several waves of impetuous thrusts across the shallow Dos Casas rivulet were fiercely resisted, and enemy units were withdrawn that evening, having suffered some 650 casualties: those of the Allies were about 260.

There was a lull next day, during which some the contending troops discreetly fraternised while collecting their wounded and burying their dead. Meanwhile, Masséna moved several of Loison's units and Montbrun's cavalry further south, towards a position east of Nave de Haver. But Wellington sensed that Masénna might attempt to turn his flank and, to counter this threat to his communications, ordered Houston's Division south towards Poço Velho, and his cavalry to Nave de Haver, already held by Julian Sanchez's Spanish guerrillas. With foresight, Craufurd, with the Light Division, was directed to proceed to a position from which he could provide adequate support to Houston, should the latter be hard pressed. The alternative would have been to shift his whole line south, which would uncover Almeida, threatened by the columns first seen.

---

1 With 42,200 infantry, 4,660 cavalry, and 38 guns.
2 Wellington had 23,000 British troops, 11,500 Portuguese, 1,870 cavalry, and 48 guns with him.
3 Although partly blown up the previous July, it was still a formidable obstacle.
4 Solignac's units were to move south during the night of the 4th.
5 Craufurd, who had been on leave, only reached Fuentes on the evening of the 4th.

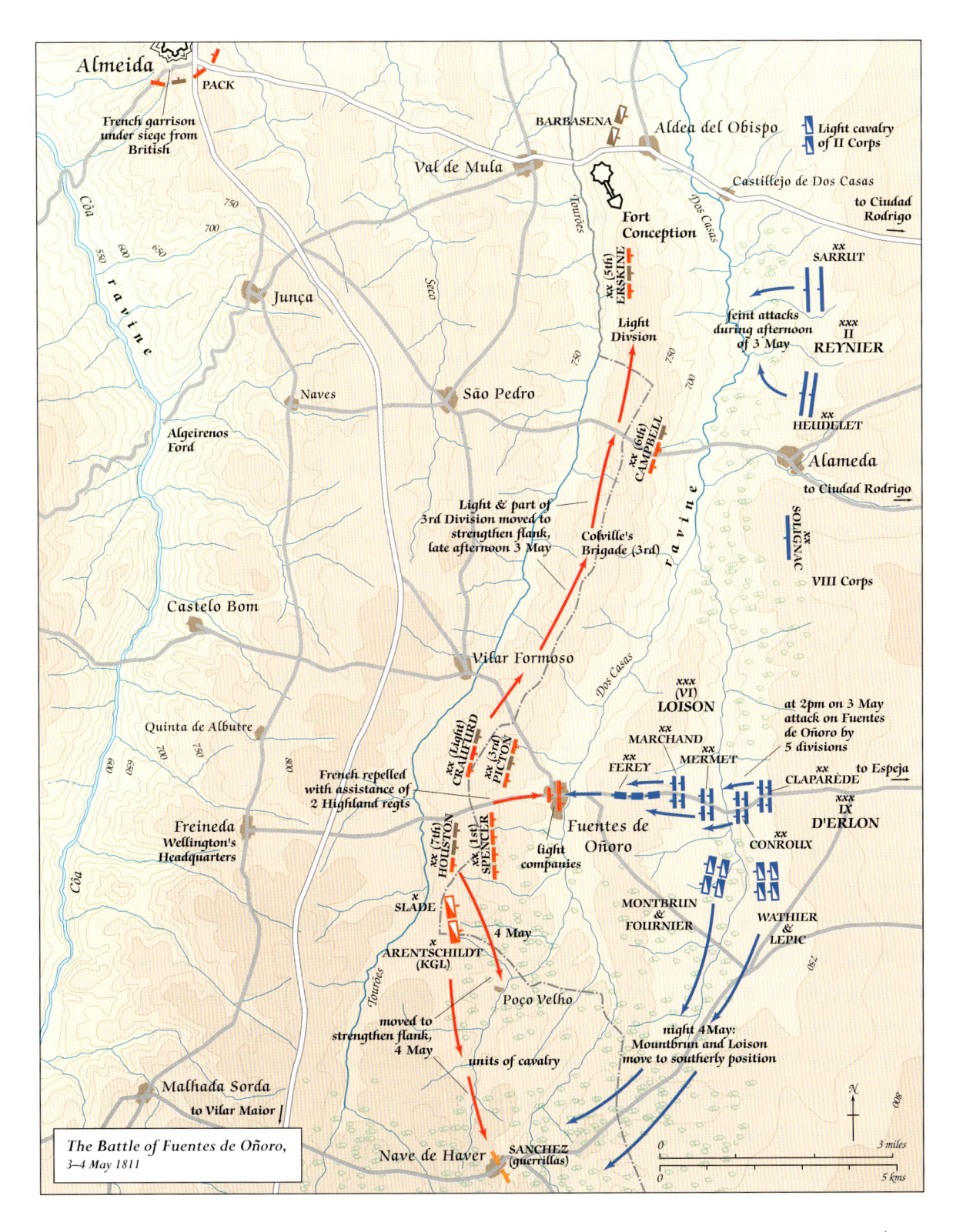

THE BATTLE OF FUENTES DE OÑORO I | 59

21 The Battle of Fuentes de Oñoro II

3–5 May 1811

Sanchez's guerrillas were surprised on the misty dawn of the 5th by the impetuous advance of French cavalry and, heavily outnumbered,[1] Wellington's cavalry was forced back on Poço Velho. It was only with difficulty that this attempt to outflank Fuentes, seriously threatening the Allied line of communications and retreat, was halted. In essence, Craufurd's brilliant 'shepherding' operation may be explained as follows. The over-extended 7th Division was protected from the convergence of artillery fire by the expedient of keeping his line battalions in mobile squares and his riflemen in groups of skirmishers which, whenever they found cover, would keep up a galling fire on the enemy and, whenever they were charged, would sprint into a square. Meanwhile, British cavalry would charge their guns, and horse-artillery would fire from positions taken between each square.[2] 'Leap-frogging' back in this disciplined fashion and in almost perfect order, over 2 miles were covered with negligible casualties on the part of Craufurd's men. Somewhat shaken, the 7th reached the western extremity of Wellington's new defensive alignment and faced about, while Sánchez's men went to protect the village of Freineda. By then, the 1st and 3rd Divisions had been redeployed facing south immediately west of Fuentes. Unusually, Wellington then ordered his troops to 'dig in' behind breastworks along this front, where a sporadic artillery duel ensued until the French guns were eventually silenced.

Units within the virtually impregnable village, now forming the hinge of the Allied position, had been repelling repeated infantry attacks throughout the day,[3] the blood-soaked lanes being the focus of horrid hand-to-hand fighting, with bayonets driven home and volleys exchanged at point blank range. The struggle was over by the early afternoon. French cavalry attempted, unsuccessfully, to find a gap in the Allied defences next day, and Masséna lingered on the battlefield for another two, but realising that it would be fruitless to continue offensive operations without suffering additional heavy losses which he could ill afford,[4] after feeding his men with the supplies intended for Almeida,[5] the army commenced their withdrawal to the east of the Agueda.

Wellingon admitted privately to Lord Liverpool shortly after the battle that, until then, it had been the most difficult one he was ever concerned in, and against the greatest odds.

---

1 See footnotes 1 and 2 to Plan 20.
2 At one point, Norman Ramsay's two guns were surrounded, but he coolly limbered up and both guns and caissons were escorted back at a gallop, his mounted gunners, with drawn swords, slashing their way as they ran the gauntlet of the encircling mass.
3 One member of the 71st recorded that he had fired 107 rounds during the day: the recoils had so bruised his shoulder that he could hardly touch his head with his right hand! Allied casualties here were c. 800; the French c.1,300.
4 French casualties had been c. 2,850; those of the Allies, 1,800. It was to be Masséna's last battle: Napoleon's decision to supersede him by Marmont had already been taken.
5 Much to Wellington's mortification, and largely due to the negligence, among others, of the egregious Gen. Erskine, 900 of the garrison were able to elude capture during the night of 10 May by crossing the unguarded bridge at Barba del Puerco, causing Wellington to comment privately: 'I begin to be of the opinion that there is nothing more stupid as "a gallant officer". They [the blockading force] had … allowed the garrison to slip through their fingers and escape … There they were, sleeping in their spurs even, but the French got off.'

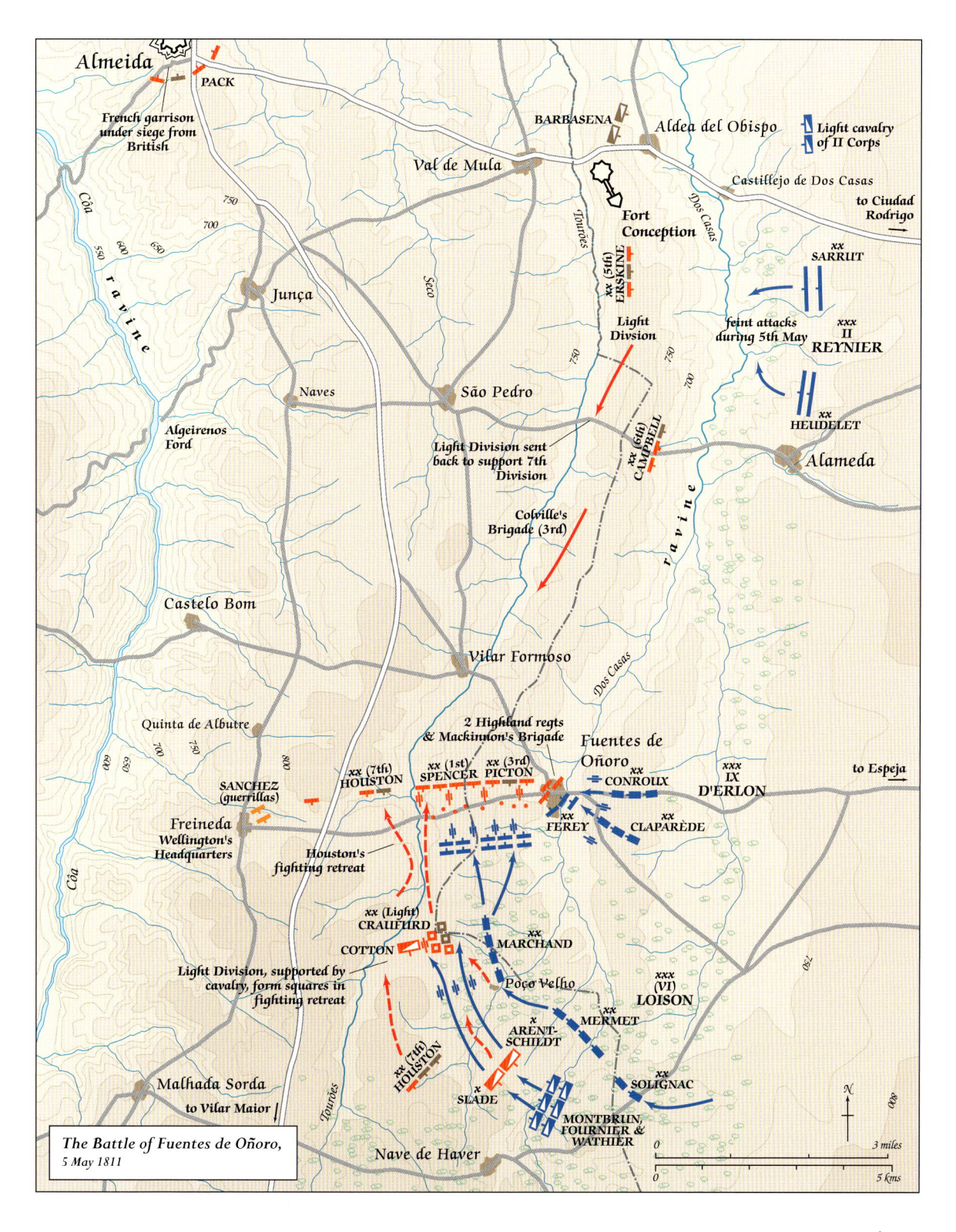

The Battle of Fuentes de Oñoro II | 61

22 South-west Spain

Mid March to Mid May 1811

During the second week in January, Wellington received intelligence that Soult had detached troops from opposite Cadiz and was advancing north-west into Estremadura, probably with the intention of relieving Masséna. Soult had taken Olivenza by the end of the month, after a brief siege, and partly invested Badajoz, held by a Spanish garrison under Gen. Menacho, who continued to put up a strong resistance. Troops under Mendizabal held the north bank of the Guadiana, but they were surprised by the French crossing further upstream, and thoroughly defeated at the battle of the Gebora (19 February).

Soult now blockaded Badajoz. Menacho was killed by a chance shot on 3 March, and Imaz, his successor, although well provisioned, cravenly capitulated on the 10th, albeit aware that relief was on the way.[1] Soult returned south, leaving Gen. Mortier in command, with Badajoz itself being garrisoned by Gen. Phillipon. Alburquerque surrendered to Mortier on the 15th, as did Campo Maior on the 21st.

While the bulk of the Allied army was in pursuit of Masséna (see Map 18), Wellington had already ordered the 2nd Division to march from opposite Santarém towards Abrantes, reached on 10 March, and there await the 4th Division (returning south from Espinhal, and crossing the Tagus at Tancos by a bridge of boats floated down from Abrantes) before proceeding south-east towards Portalegre.[2] Together, they would form a Corps of some 18,000 men commanded by Beresford, who, riding from Tomar, arrived at Portalegre on 20 March. By the 24th, most of this force was at Arronches, next day surprising Latour-Maubourg's units at Campo Maior.[3] The outcome of the ensuing combat would have been far more advantageous had not Gen. Long's cavalry run out of control in their pursuit, as far as Badajoz itself, and suffered unnecessary casualties.[4] The Allied vanguard entered Elvas on the 26th.

To invest Badajoz, Beresford, leaving the fort of San Cristóbal and the bridgehead on the north bank on the Guadiana in enemy hands, constucted a pontoon and trestle bridge further west at Juromenha, which was crossed by 8 April together with his available artillery, and preparations made to besiege the fortress. Meanwhile, Spanish forces had recaptured Valencia de Alcántara and Alburquerque and offered to take part in the ensuing campaign; other Spanish troops were promised.[5] Leaving the 4th Divison surrounding Badajoz, on 10 April the 2nd Division, with Long's cavalry and other units, advanced south-east towards Latour-Maubourg's forces at Fuente del Maestre,[6] beyond which, at Los Santos, Long's cavalry dispersed those of the French, who retired on Llerena on the 19th.

Meanwhile, riding south from Vilar Formoso on the 15th, Wellington reached Badajoz on the 20th to reconnoitre and discuss siege operations, and authorised Beresford to fight a general action if certain of his strength, should Soult advance to its relief. Wellington had agreed that La Albuera, some 15 miles south-east, would be the best of several indifferent sites in the area in which to confront Soult; but if threatened, Beresford's siege train and stores should be returned to Elvas, its resources having been depleted. On the 25th, Wellington started back north to face the predictable advance of Masséna's army: see Plan 20.

Beresford was preoccupied by the rising of the Guadiana, which swept away his frail bridge, making communications hazardous, but this was restored by the 29th.[7] On that day Gen. Colborne advanced on Llerena, together with Spanish cavalry. Several French foraging parties were dispersed, together with a force at Azuaga, which retreated to Guadacanal. Colborne extended operations as far east as Belalcázar before returning to Almendralejo on 11 May. Beresford had received a report the previous day that Soult was on the march from Seville.

Although Badajoz had been fully invested by then, and parallels dug near the three outworks, the ground near the transpontine fort of San Cristóbal was so rocky that little progress was made, and several engineers were wounded by fire from the fort, from which sorties were also taking place: see Plan 27.

62 | An Atlas of the Peninsular War

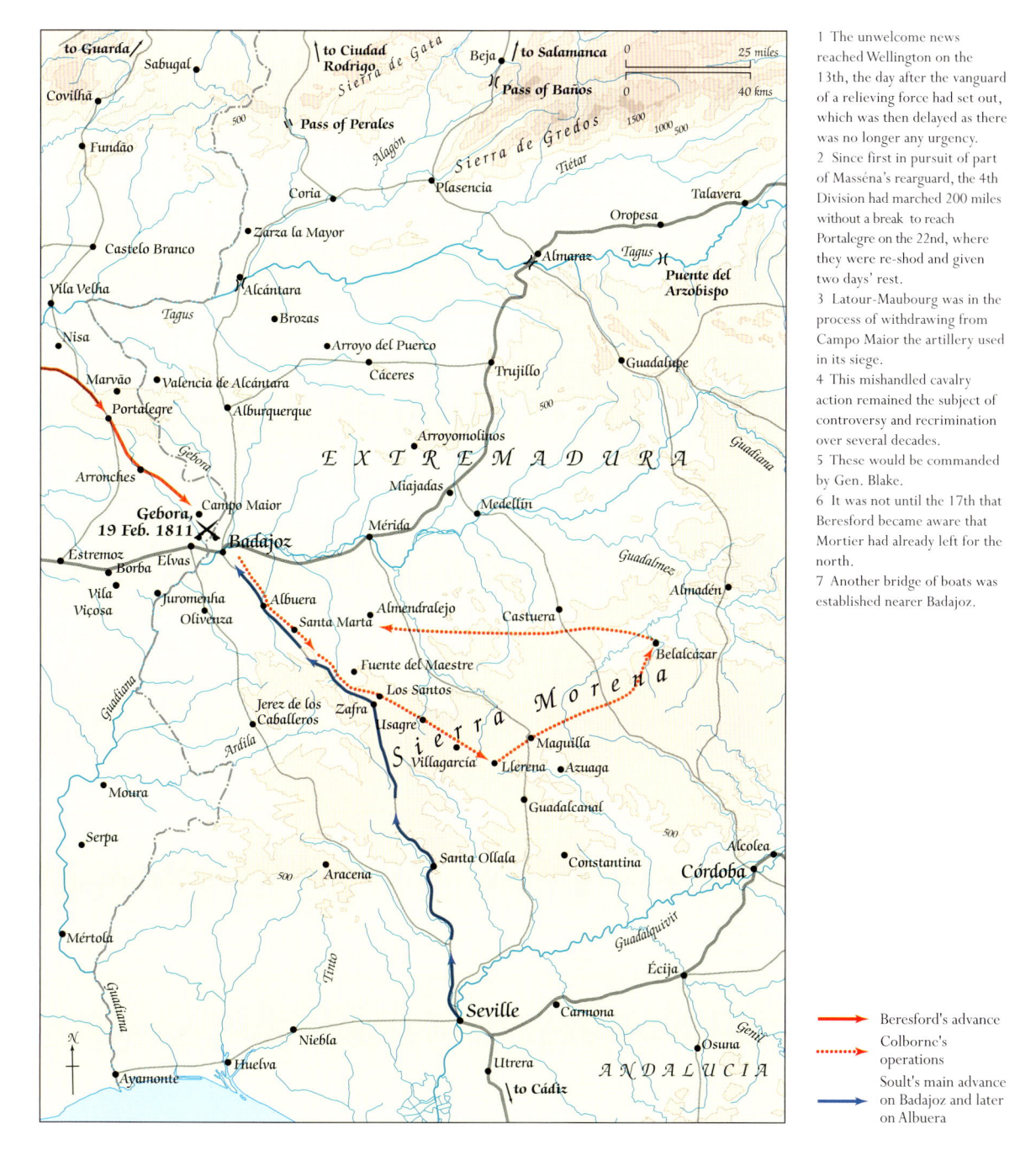

1 The unwelcome news reached Wellington on the 13th, the day after the vanguard of a relieving force had set out, which was then delayed as there was no longer any urgency.
2 Since first in pursuit of part of Masséna's rearguard, the 4th Division had marched 200 miles without a break to reach Portalegre on the 22nd, where they were re-shod and given two days' rest.
3 Latour-Maubourg was in the process of withdrawing from Campo Maior the artillery used in its siege.
4 This mishandled cavalry action remained the subject of controversy and recrimination over several decades.
5 These would be commanded by Gen. Blake.
6 It was not until the 17th that Beresford became aware that Mortier had already left for the north.
7 Another bridge of boats was established nearer Badajoz.

→ Beresford's advance
⋯▶ Colborne's operations
→ Soult's main advance on Badajoz and later on Albuera

Hearing on the evening of 12 May that Soult's vanguard had already reached Santa Ollala, Beresford ceased operations, having already withdrawn his artillery. His advance guard, under Long, retired rapidly from Los Santos to Santa Marta and, by late on the 15th, Beresford's Corps, with the exception of some units of the 4th Division (stranded north of the Guadiana, again in flood), together with substantial Spanish reinforcements, was being deployed at Albuera to await Soult's attack: see Plan 23.

SOUTH-WEST SPAIN | 63

23 The Battle of Albuera I

16 May 1811

Some ten days after the battle at Fuentes de Oñoro, but some 120 miles as the crow flies further south over rugged country, a confused and the most sanguinary encounter of the war (in proportion to the numbers engaged) took place at the village of La Albuera between Soult and Beresford, reinforced by Spanish units commanded by Gen. Blake.

The village lay 15 miles south-east of Badajoz on the Albuera, a tributary of the Guadiana, just south of which was the confluence of two minor streams, the Nogales and Chicapierna (Little-leg). The river was spanned by two bridges, one immediately east of the village; the other, and then a ford, lay further south.[1] Trees on and beyond the tongue of land between the two rivulets obscured a clear view of Soult's approach along the road from Santa Marta from Beresford's initial position (Stewart's 2nd Division in the centre) on higher ground west and north-west of La Albuera, with Blake's contingent further south. Otway's Portuguese cavalry protected the left flank; Spanish cavalry, the right, being placed on the hill-side west of the Arroyo de Valdesevilla.[2] Cole, with the 4th Division, had not yet reached the front.

As expected, the French vanguard (Godinot's brigade) directly attacked the village (defended by Alten's KGL units), with their cavalry facing Otway's, supported by artillery, to which Allied guns replied; but this was largely a feint.[3] Although skirmishing took place near the southern bridge, it was not until 9 a.m. that any change in front was suspected, and then only when a part of Latour-Maubourg's cavalry, on traversing fords between the bridge and the juncture of the streams, had wheeled left, presumably with the intention of attacking the Spanish infantry.

Meanwhile, indistinct movements had been noticed further south beyond the trees. In fact, Girard's and Gazan's infantry brigades, together with Werlé's (which had been in Godinot's wake),[4] were crossing the Nogales much further south to circle west and swing round towards a ford of the Chicapierna. Not only did they then advance due north towards the Spanish, but the main body of Latour-Maubourg's cavalry had also thrust further west, beyond the Allied flank, now seriously threatened.

Advised of this threat, Beresford ordered Blake to redeploy his troops in two parallel lines facing right and further south, where Zayas's units were to take the brunt of the first attack. The entire 2nd Division (brigades of Colborne, Hoghton, and Abercromby) was moved to the right to support the Spanish line, while Cole's 4th Division, now arriving, was also to change its front, advancing south. With them were España's units, which deployed at both extremities of the Spanish line. Gen. Lumley (who had replaced Long) ordered the bulk of the cavalry to the right rear to support the Spanish cavalry.

---

1 The latter crossed by the present main road.
2 This has been dammed recently to form an inundation west of the present bypass.
3 Some of Godinot's units were able to enter the village, only to be ejected.
4 It is uncertain where, precisely, Werlé's brigade had crossed the streams.

The Battle of Albuera, movements prior to 10 am

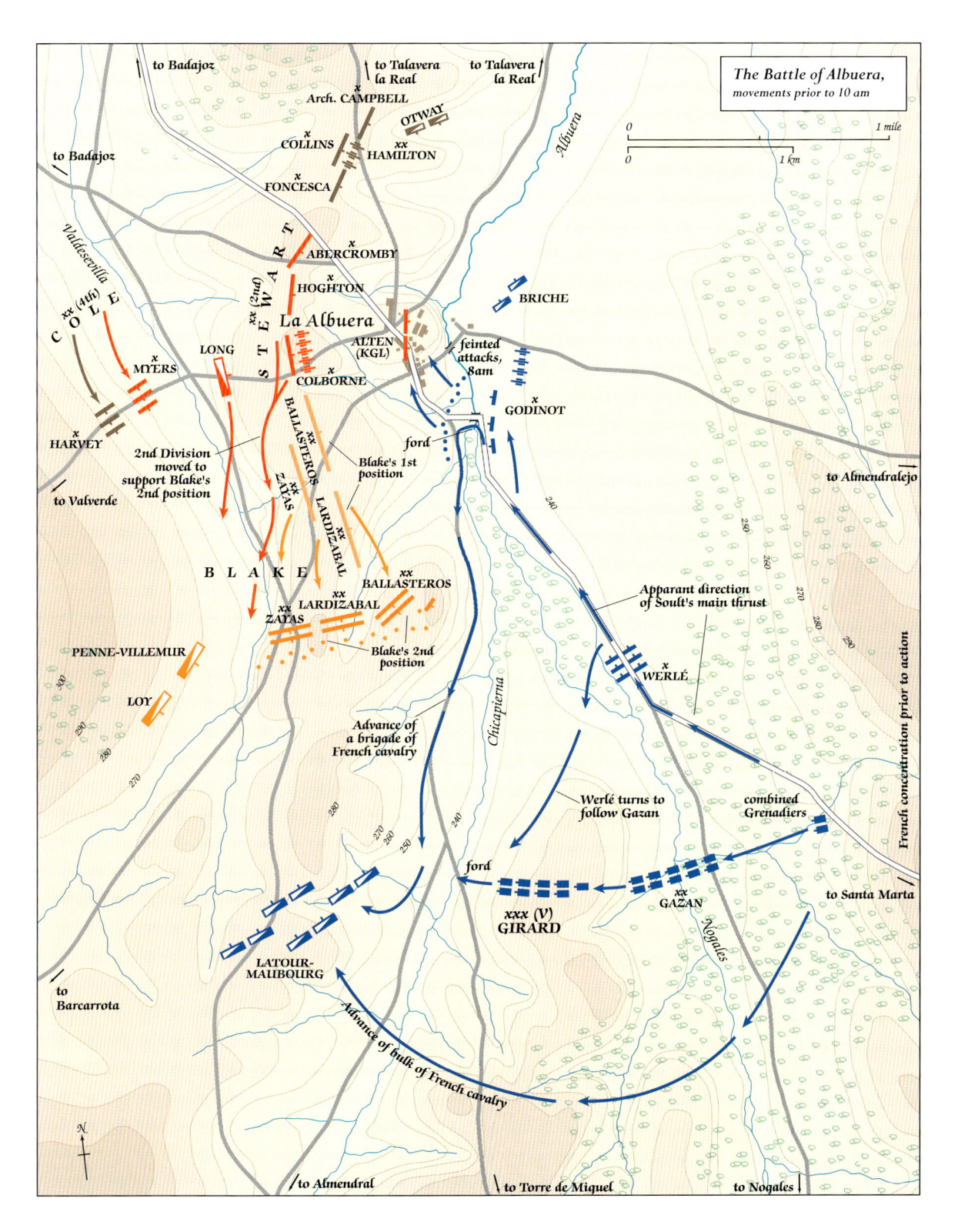

THE BATTLE OF ALBUERA I | 65

24 The Battle of Albuera II

16 May 1811

Girard's column, with Gazan's behind them, now engaged in an extended musketry duel with Zayas's line, which held firm, although gradually thinning, while Colborne's Brigade moved ahead to protect and extend beyond it's right flank, their superior firepower causing heavy losses among the massed ranks of the enemy. The 3rd ('the Buffs'), in the van, then charged. Too late, they found that 800 Polish lancers from Latour-Maubourg's cavalry had swept forward behind the over-extended formation, a movement veiled by a sudden rain and hailstorm, which also caused their muskets to misfire, and wrought havoc among their ranks. The mayem decreased slightly as the undefended flanks of Colborne's other three regiments were charged, only the last being able to form square and repulse the lancers.[1] In the confusion, Beresford and his staff were overrun, but the leading regiment of Hoghton's Brigade now arriving was able to disperse the rampaging lancers (an arm they were unused to face), after which there was a lull in the battle as the downpour receded. Lumley was now able to reinforce the cavalry opposing the numerically overwhelming enemy squadrons, and the lines of Spanish infantry were replaced by Hoghton and Abercromby. By now, Gazan had brought forward his infantry, which mingling with those of Girard's exhausted units, presented a compact target of 8,000 men, of which only 1,200 could return the fire of 2,000, but Hoghton himself was killed in the ensuing firefight.[2]

Cole's 4th Division was brought forward, if belatedly, and bore down obliquely on the massed French, now reinforced by Werlé's Brigade, who found themselves in a destructive cross-fire, and were then charged by Myers's Brigade.[3] The downpour recommenced. The contending forces had been locked in the stubborn struggle for no less than four hours before the French started to give way. They had been suffering heavy casualties from the Allied artillery, belatedly deployed on the hill west of the Chicapierna. Meanwhile, the French guns had been withdrawn to the tongue of land between the two streams, south of which their cavalry still hovered menacingly; but by then the battle had ground to a halt: no further action was possible.

That afternoon and the following day were spent recovering the wounded from the blood-soaked field. Casualties on both sides had been appalling.[4] Allied losses totalled 5,915: those of the enemy have been estimated at between 7,000 and 8,000, of which some 4,000 less badly injured were carried off in all available carriages.

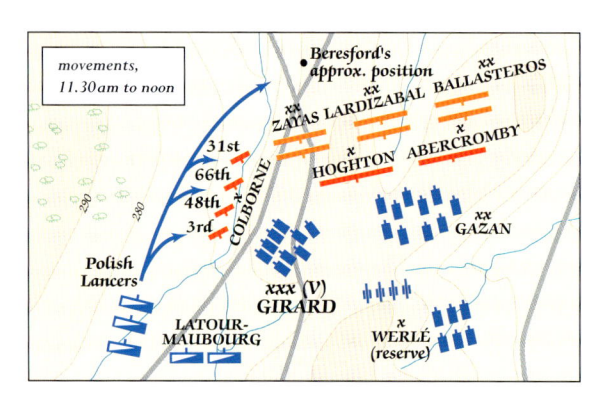

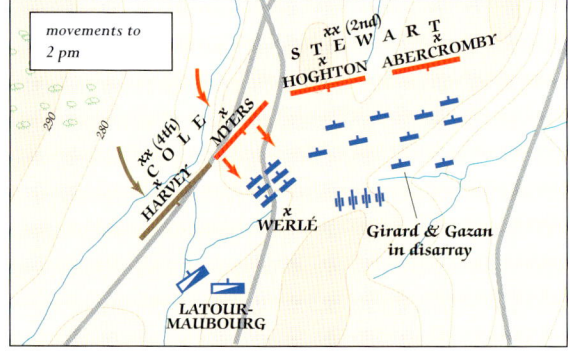

Soult retreated east early on the 18th, his cavalry acting as a rearguard, and from Almendralejo veered south-east via Usagre, reaching Llerena by the 24th. Lumley's cavalry followed cautiously in their wake. Soult then sent Latour-Maubourg's cavalry back up the road to check the strength of any units which might be following him, but they were surprised in a skilful action at Usagre, one brigade being decimated, while Lumley returned to Badajoz with almost 100 prisoners. Beresford's reputation suffered from reiterated criticism, notably from Napier, of his generalship and the muddled handling of his troops, which have remained the subject of controversy and recrimination.

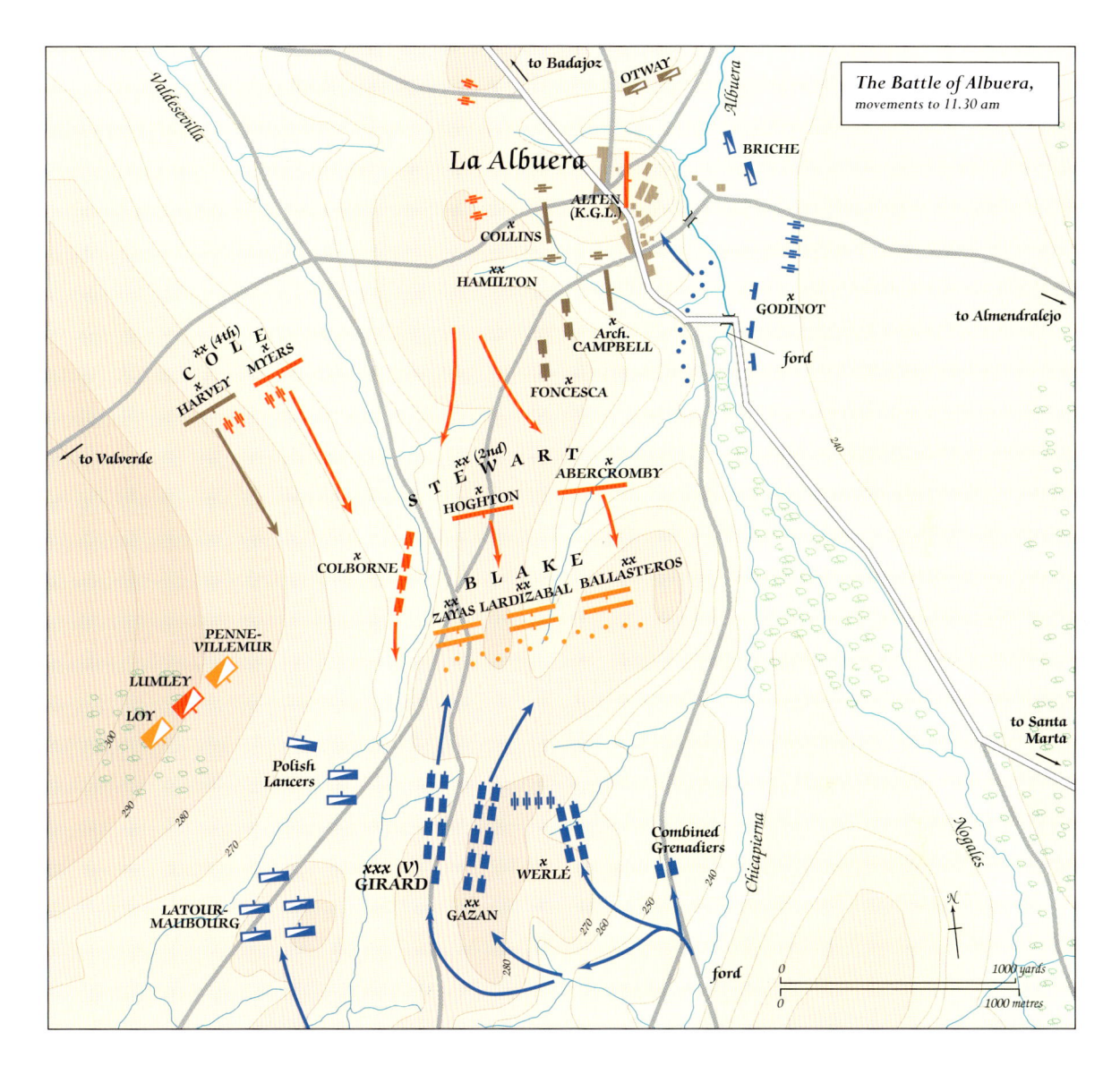

1 Casualties in the 3rd were 643 of the initial 755, and 343 of 452 in the 48th.
2 In which 56 of the 95 officers and 971 of the brigade's 1,556 rank and file present were casualties.
3 Myers himself was killed, while 1,045 of 2,015 of Cole's officers and men were casualties in this action.
4 A disproportionate number were among the British infantry: 4,039 of the 8,738 taking part in the battle.

25 Combats of El Bodón, and Arroyomolinos de Montánchez

25 September, and 28 October 1811

Wellington reached the battlefield of Albuera on 21 May, by which time Beresford had already re-invested Badajoz,[1] for there was a slight chance that the fortress might be taken before the Allies found themselves outnumbered by the probable convergence of Marmont's forces with D'Erlon's 5th Corps and Soult's surviving units, which together would amount to some 60,000.

This attempt to seize the fortress went badly; despite progress made, two assaults on the breaches failed, and on 10 June Wellington reluctantly abandoned the siege. He then withdrew across the Guadiana to a defensive position facing east between the Caia and the Gebora and abutted to the north by Ouguela (but with temporary headquarters at Portalegre[2]) to await any combined movement against him once the enemy had relieved Badajoz, which they did on 20 June.[3] But the French had serious logistical problems to resolve, and they could not remain concentrated for long. Soult retired south again on 27 June, and Marmont decamped on 15 July to re-cross the Tagus, after leaving Badajoz well supplied and garrisoned, while D'Erlon remained in the vicinity of Merida.

On taking stock of the situation, Wellington decided that it would be better to focus on capturing Ciudad Rodrigo before besieging Badajoz again, and established Headquarters at Fuenteguinaldo. But on 3 September, an intercepted dispatch indicated that Marmont and Gen. Dorsenne would be combining to advance against him in force, in the face of which he had little alternative but to abandon his blockade and place his troops – c. 46,000 – in cantonments along his lateral communications, where they remained during the ensuing winter (see inset), with the 2nd Division stationed further south, around Portalegre.

A sudden thrust by 2,500 cavalry against 1,000 Allied infantry and 500 cavalry precipitated a hard-fought minor action at El Bodón (south-west of Ciudad Rodrigo) on 25 September, after which Wellington concentrated his troops in a stronger position further west, nearer the Côa. Marmont cautiously pulled back his army, allowing the fortress to be again isolated.

Little movement took place on this front during the next month, apart from Headquarters being transferred to Freineda (west of Fuentes de Oñoro) until 26 October, when Hill advanced from Alburquerque towards Caceres,

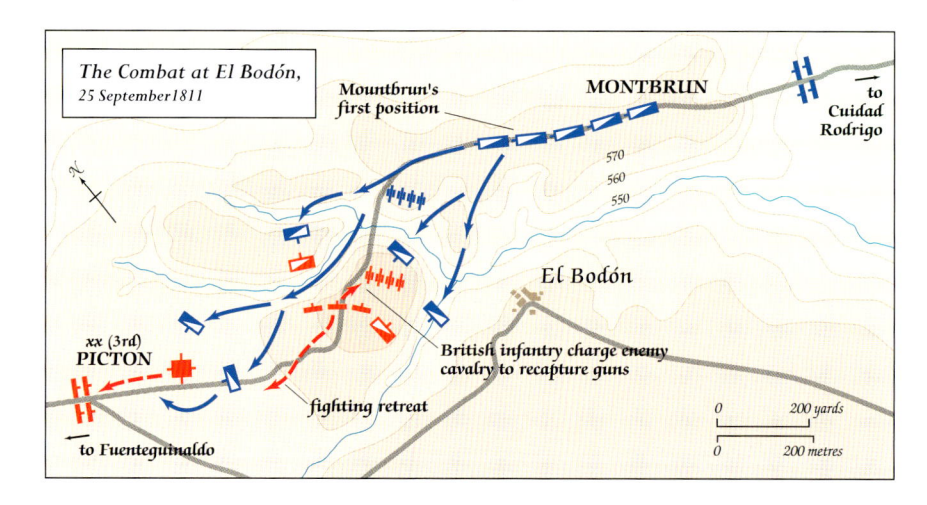

The Combat at El Bodón, 25 September 1811

which Gen. Girard abandoned, moving south-east to Arroyomolinos, below the Sierra de Montánchez.

By making a forced overnight march from Alcuéscar in appalling weather, Hill surprised Girard at dawn on the 28th, dispersing his troops, inflicting several hundred casualties, taking 1,300 prisoners, and all their artillery and baggage, with minimal casualties (7 killed; 64 wounded). This brilliant operation caused more than a flurry among the French dovecotes, and several redeployments which took some pressure off Wellington, facing Ciudad Rodrigo.

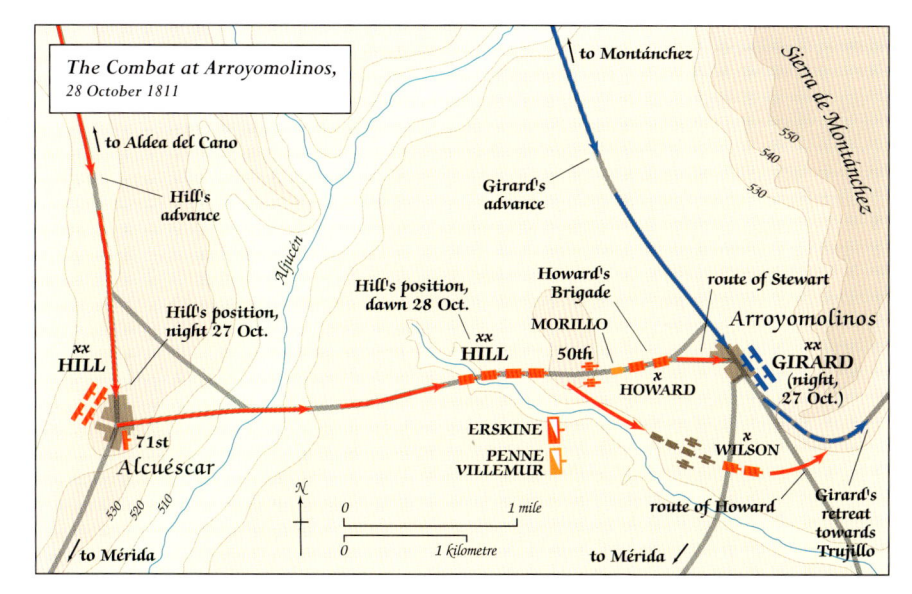

1 Beresford was to relinquished command here shortly afterwards, and the right-wing Corps of Wellington's extended front passed to Gen. Hill.
2 Well-positioned on the corridor between the two fronts, should his presence be required urgently in the northern sector, where Graham replaced Gen. Spencer.
3 There was skirmishing between opposing cavalry when Latour-Maubourg made a reconnaissance in force across the Guadiana and surprised picquets of Long's Brigade.

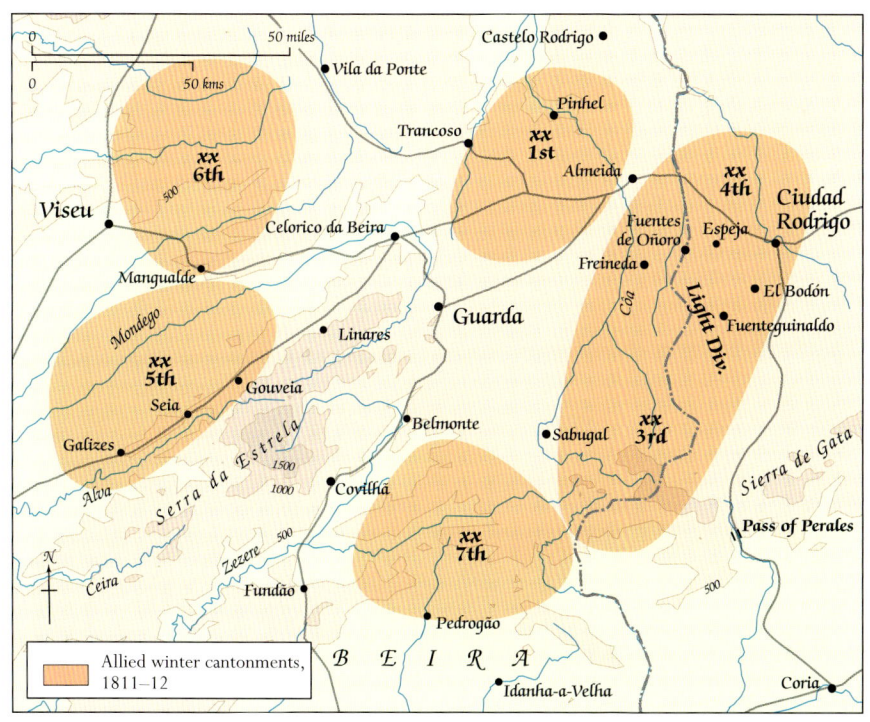

26 The Siege of Ciudad Rodrigo
8–19 January 1812

On 8 January, with the ruse of widely publicising that 'field sports' would be taking place that day at Fuenteguinaldo, the 2,000 strong garrison of Ciudad Rodrigo were surprised to find themselves tightly invested. The fortress stood on the summit of a rocky bluff commanding a bridge over the Agueda, with a suburb to the north-east. Its main weakness was the proximity of two connected hills to the north-west – the Lesser and Greater Tesons (the latter rising 14 feet higher than the town walls) – which it would be necessary to occupy first.[1] This was done forthwith, the garrison of 60 in the redoubt erected there being overwhelmed at the cost of 26 casualties; parallels (partly following the line of those dug by the French, and since filled) were excavated in the frozen soil and batteries, including siege-guns, were bombarding the walls by the afternoon of the 13th. Two convents in the suburbs were occupied during the next few hours with little resistance.

By the 19th, two breaches had been made, the larger where the walls had been previously weakened, the smaller being some 250 yards further east, and both appeared practicable. The assault took place that same night, with the main breach being attacked by the 3rd Division; other units advanced over the bridge to escalade outworks, and from behind the Santa Cruz convent, to scale the outer wall and sweep round to the breach, while from behind the San Francisco convent the lesser breach would be approached and stormed by Vandeleur's brigade of the Light Division, among other units, with a diversion being made at the south-east of the enceinte. At one time, the Allied position was extremely precarious, having met several unexpected hazards, paticularly when a mine placed below the main breach exploded, causing substantial casualties among the 3rd Division, including Gen. Mackinnon, while Craufurd was mortally wounded when assaulting the lesser breach.[2]

The French surrendered without much further fighting,[3] but many of those who had stormed the place then ran amok; several buildings were set alight, and it took some time before discipline was restored. The breaches were then repaired, the trenches filled, the fortress re-provisioned and an adequate Spanish garrison installed, and the main Allied army proceeded south towards Badajoz. To confuse the enemy, Wellington himself did not follow it until 6 March.

---

1 The French had placed their batteries here when breaching the walls, since repaired, in 1810.
2 Craufurd was later buried in the breach where he fell.
3 Their casualties were some 530, but the garrison of 1,937 was marched off as prisoners, leaving behind their siege train, including 250 heavy guns. Allied casualties amounted to 1,100, 568 of them in the storming, of which 125 were killed.

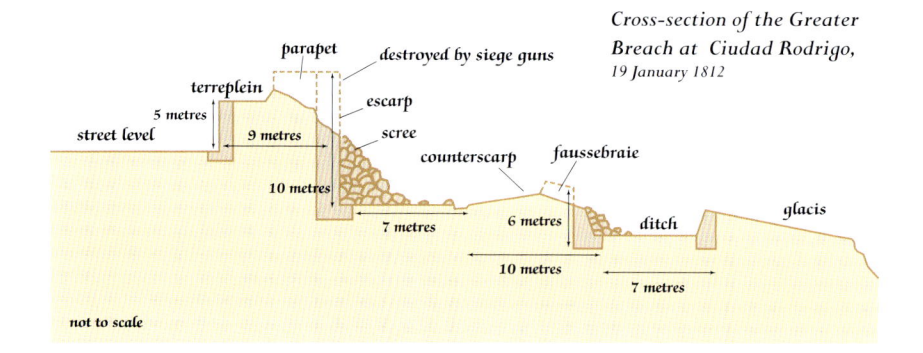

Cross-section of the Greater Breach at Ciudad Rodrigo, 19 January 1812

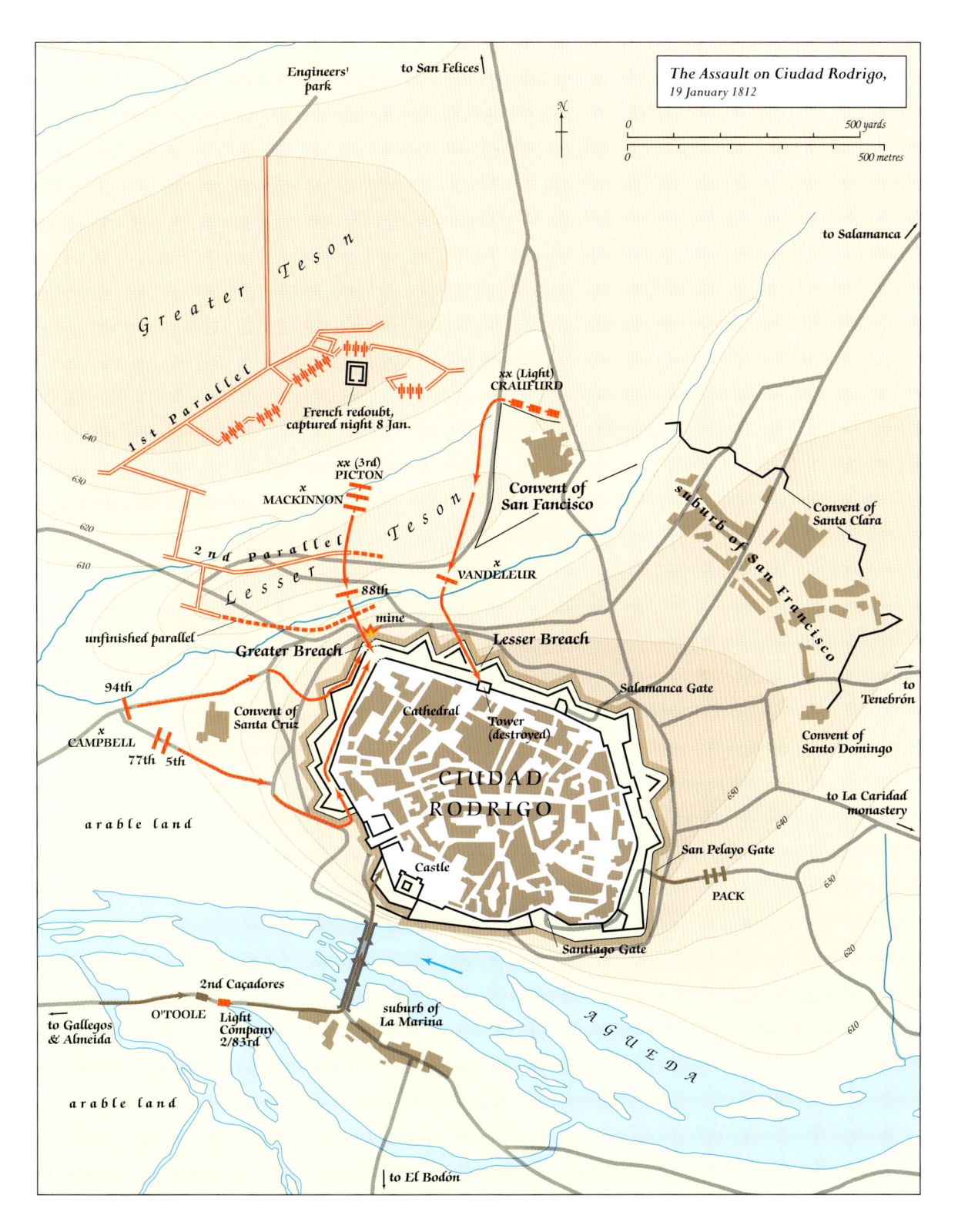

THE SIEGE OF CIUDAD RODRIGO | 71

27 The Final Siege of Badajoz

17 March to 6 April 1812

Wellington was well aware that Badajoz would be a harder nut to crack, for its defences were more formidable than those of Ciudad Rodrigo, and its garrison – 4,500 effectives – was commanded by Phillipon, a resourceful general. Of the total of 60,000 Allied troops in the southern sector, 19,000 under Graham advanced south-east towards D'Erlon's forces and to keep a weather eye on Soult, while Hill, with 14,000, pushed east beyond Merida, lest Marmont re-cross the Tagus and approach from that direction.

The fortress was closely invested by 17 March,[1] but since the previous June the French had connected the Pardeleras outwork to the town walls, while the Rivillas stream had been dammed to form an inundation, beyond which Fort Picurina had been strengthened. The position of recently placed mines was revealed to Wellington by a deserter, which decided him to attack from the south-east, between the Santa María and Trinidad bastions, to approach which parallels were dug,[2] and, on the 25th, 28 heavy guns opened fire, and the Picurina was stormed. Additional guns battering the walls had made three breaches which would be practicable by 6 April. These were stormed at 10 p.m. that evening by the Light and 4th Divisions; the 3rd escalading the dominating castle (NE), the 5th assaulting the San Vicente bastion (NW), and a feint attack being made on the San Roque lunette, protecting the dam, while Portuguese units threatened the bridgehead. The breaches had been strengthened by an elaborate *chevaux de frise*, among other obstructions and hazards which had also to be negotiated, and this was only done after the divisions storming them had suffered very heavy casualties.[3] It was only after the secondary assaults had been successful, and those belatedly, that those defending the breaches, now threatened from the rear, surrendered.[4]

Regrettably, the frenzied rank and file commenced to rampage through the town, which their officers were powerless to control, and several were shot in attempting to restrain them from the worst excesses in the ensuing scene of bedlam; it was a full three days before 'the tumult rather subsided than was quelled' (in Napier's words).

Meanwhile, Soult and D'Erlon were converging to relieve the fortress, which movement Hill and Graham had

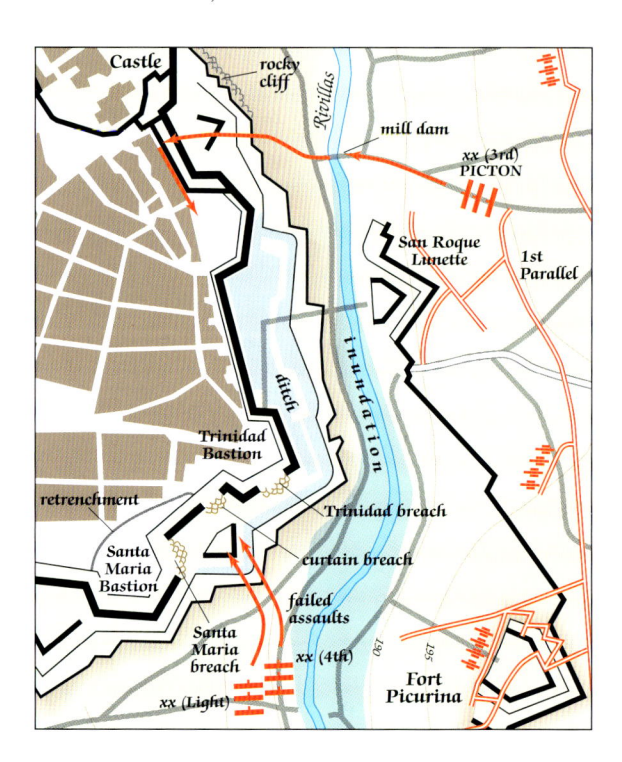

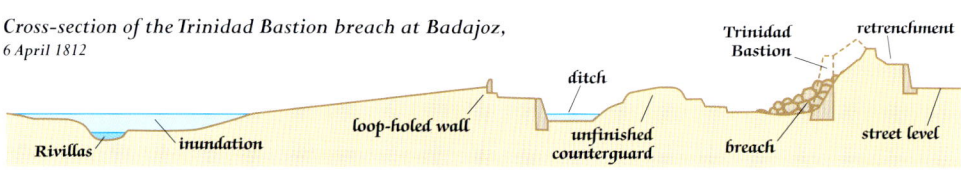

Cross-section of the Trinidad Bastion breach at Badajoz, 6 April 1812

section approx. 200yds (218.7m) wide

72 | AN ATLAS OF THE PENINSULAR WAR

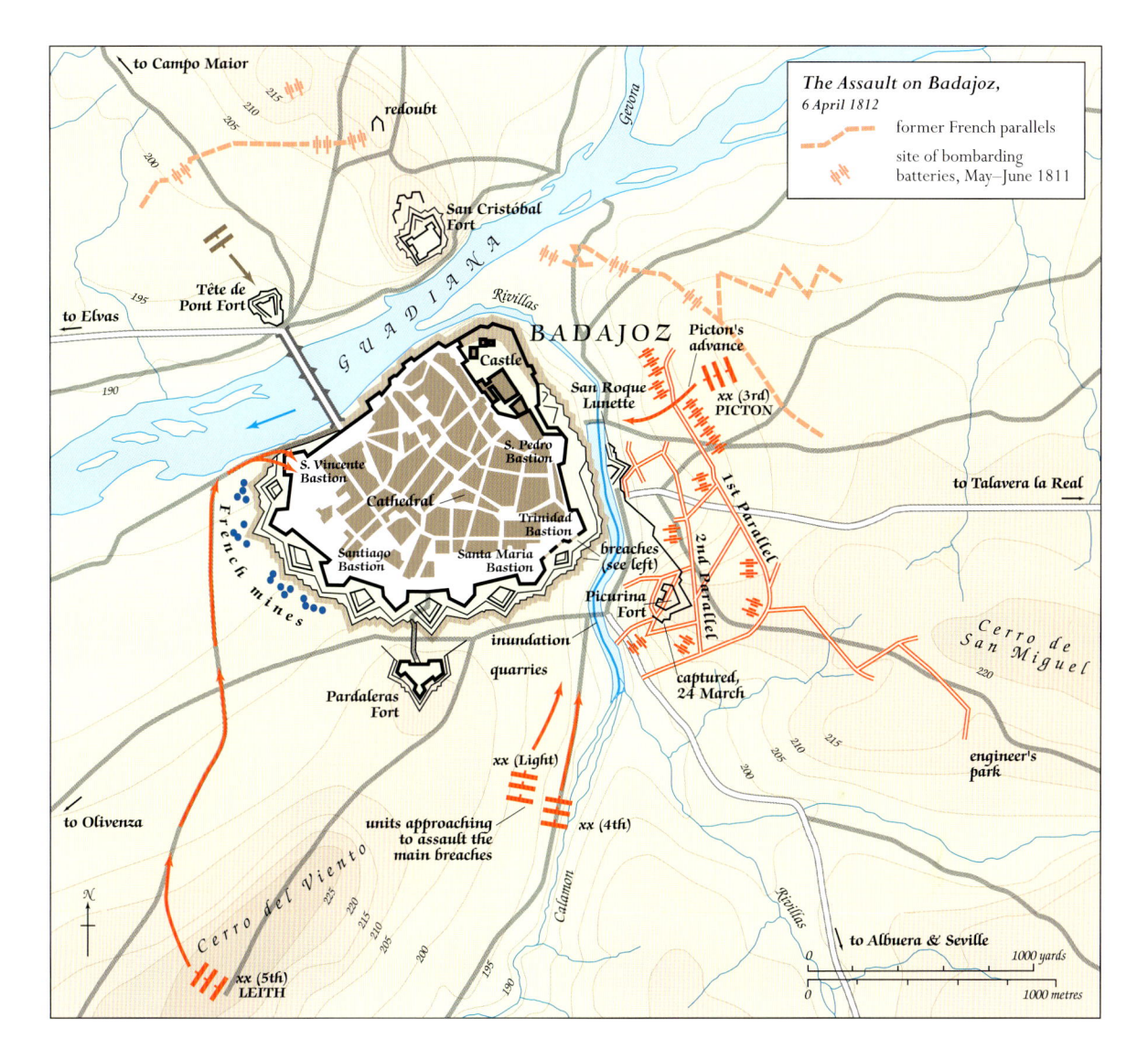

been ordered to counter; but the French reached Villafranca and Fuente de Maestre only on the afternoon of the 7th, the day after Badajoz had fallen, and so then hastily turned back, retreating south-east.

Although Gen. Clausel had pushed south-west as far as Castelo Branco by 12 April, on hearing of the fall of Badajoz on the 15th, and that Wellington's vanguard was already crossing the Tagus at Vila Velha, Marmont evacuated Guarda, which he had briefly occupied, and converged with Clausel, who had retired on Sabugal. It was not until the 22nd that Marmont had re-crossed the Agueda and marched for Salamanca, still unaware that Allied forces were close behind him.

1 Transpontine Fort Cristóbal was invested on the 22nd.
2 On the 25th, a storm flooded these, and swept away the pontoon bridge, temporarily dividing Allied units.
3 Allied casualties during the siege were some 4,650, of which 3,713 (with 744 killed) were suffered in the storming alone, 929 and 935 in the Light and 4th Divisions respectively; a high proportion was among officers.
4 Fort Cristóbal, to which some of the garrison escaped, capitulated next morning.

THE FINAL SIEGE OF BADAJOZ | 73

28 The Almaraz Expedition

19 May 1812

To consolidate his position of advantage along the Spanish frontier by improving his own communications and impairing those of the enemy, Col. Sturgeon was sent from Elvas to Alcántara on 2 May to form a removable suspension bridge across the destroyed arch of the Roman bridge there, which had been blown up almost three years earlier. Completed within a few days,[1] it enabled Wellington to transfer troops across the Tagus some distance east of the usual crossing at Vila Velha.

Hill, still keeping an eye on D'Erlon's units, set out from Merida with three brigades, a regiment of cavalry, and artillery, to make what might be referred to as a preemptive strike, by destroying the pontoon bridge further east at Almaraz, which would very considerable delay the transit of enemy reinforcement from either bank of the Tagus to the other. The only enemy troops stationed anywhere near, that might interrupt the operation were some distance further east, at Talavera.

From Trujillo, entered on 15 May, Hill proceeded discreetly past Jaraicejo to approach the Puerto de Miravete. On finding this defended by two small forts and outlying works dependent on the strengthened old castle of Miravete, which both effectively commanded the pass and were too inaccessibly sited to be taken without a proper siege, Hill changed his initial plan. As any attempt to cross the pass with his guns would be hazardous, he divided his force, leaving half under Gen. Tilson-Chowne to demonstrate against the castle, a ploy which might distract the garrison of the forts defending the Almaraz bridge – the destruction of which was the main objective of the expedition – when these were attacked.

The other half, commanded by Gen. Howard, was detached to undertake the difficult operation of descending to the Tagus by night, and by a roundabout route. Guided by a peasant over the minor Puerto de la Cueva (3 miles east of the main pass), this force, carrying cumbersome scaling-ladders and following what was little more than a goat-track in single file, climbed steeply down through intricate terrain and, after skirting the hamlet of Romangordo,[2] reached the valley floor. The drop from the Puerto de la Cueva (now locally referred to as the Collado de los Ingleses) to the Tagus was slightly over 400 metres. At dawn, the vanguard of 900 was able to assemble within a short run of their first objective, Fort Napoleon, guarding the south bank of the Tagus. Although its garrison was not taken entirely by surprise, it was soon overwhelmed, as was that of Fort Ragusa, on the opposite bank. Both fortifications were then entirely destroyed, together with 20 pontoons, 18 guns, and a great deal of *matériel* and provisions. Losses among the 700-strong garrison were about 400, including some 280 prisoners; Hill's casualties were 189, including 35 killed; but in the words of Gen. D'Urban at the time: the raid was 'of infinite importance both real and moral, and is indeed the most advantageous Coup of the Second Class during the War'.

A contemporary plan of the Tagus at Almaraz.

1 By which time the new span could take the weight of heavy artillery.
2 The Puerto de la Cueva is now crossed by a motorway, which then swings north-west, leaving Romangordo on the far side of a valley.

AN ATLAS OF THE PENINSULAR WAR

THE ALMARAZ EXPEDITION | 75

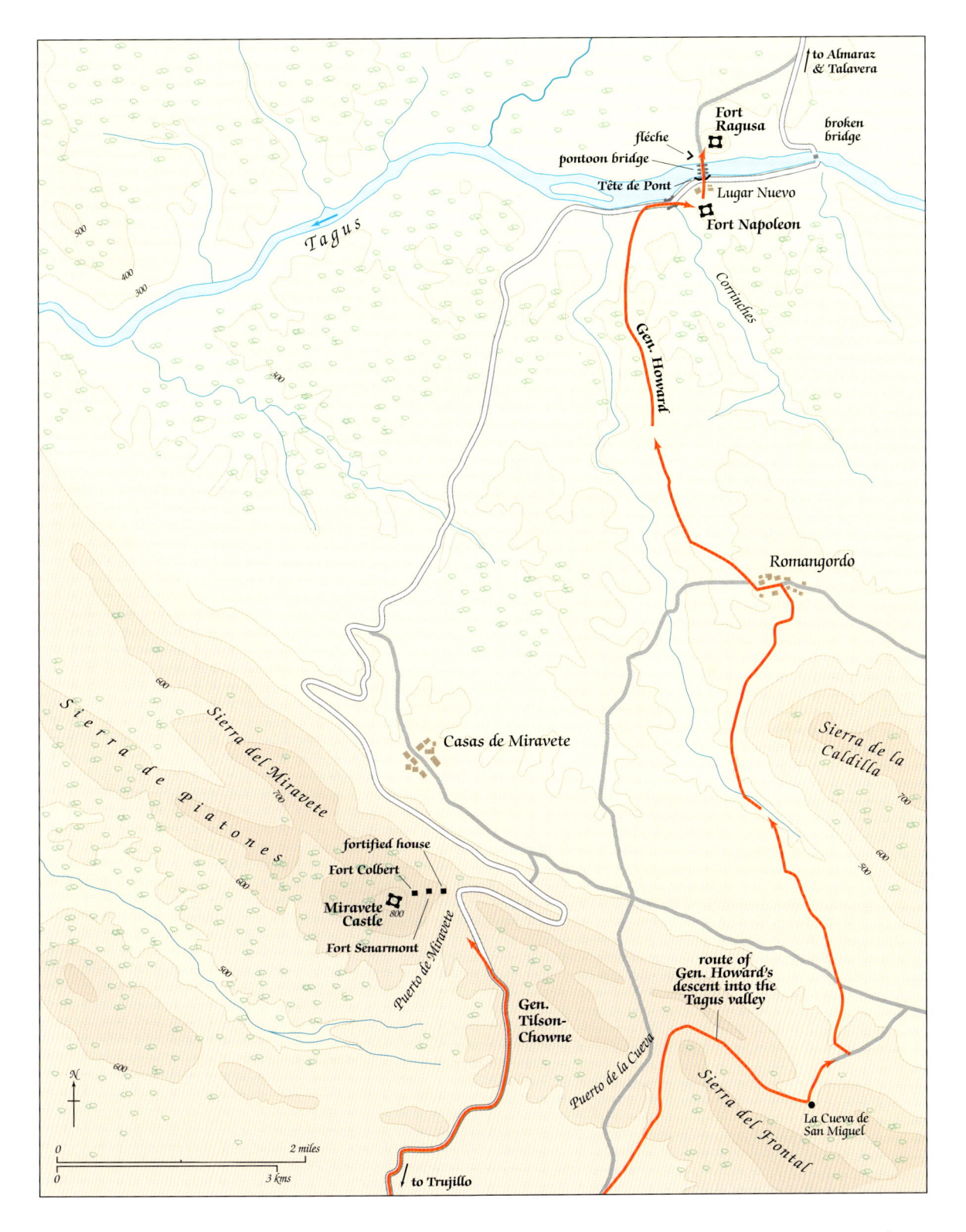

29 Manoeuvring prior to Salamanca, and the Fall of the Forts

13 June – 21 July 1812

At about this time, there were five French armies in Spain: Suchet had 60,000 on the Levante coast; in the centre were two forces: Gen. Caffarelli to the north with 48,000, and Marmont with 52,000; Soult controlled 54,000 in Andalusia; while in the vicinity of Madrid were another 18,000, nominally under Joseph Bonaparte and Jourdan: altogether some 230,000 effectives – but not including many thousand sick and wounded. Many units were dispersed, pinned down by guerrilla bands or in defending threatened communications. Wellington was encouraging Spanish commanders to make any offensive moves they could which might divert the enemy from concentrating against his 60,000 regulars, while avoiding direct confrontations.[1]

On 13 June, Wellington, with a force of 48,500 assembled on the Agueda, proceeded east towards Salamanca (entered on the 17th), in the face of which Marmont withdrew, having left 800 men to garrison the fortified dependences of three convents in the western suburbs. Wellington was aware of their existence and had brought forward siege guns, but the forts resisted stubbornly, and progress in taking them was slow, the last not capitulating until the 27th, after being set alight by red-hot shot.[2]

Meanwhile, Marmont had warily approached the city, but did not attack on the 21st as expected. A deal of jockeying for position took place during the ensuing days, with each manoeuvre made by Marmont being appropriately countered. As Wellington succinctly summarised his position at about this time: 'Marmont will not risk an action unless he should have an advantage; and I shall certainly not risk one unless I should have an advantage; and matters therefore do not appear likely to be brought to that criterion very soon.'

Once the forts had fallen, Marmont retired towards the Duero, hoping that he might receive substantial support from Caffarelli, but he was reinforced only by a division under Gen. Bonnet on 7 July.[3] This made the numbers of the contending forces nearly equal, although the Allies were stronger in cavalry. Wellington advanced in Marmont's wake and, before long, troops from both banks of the Duero were seen bathing together.[4]

The brief lull lasted until 17 July, when Marmont went on the offensive again, the bulk of his troops crossing the

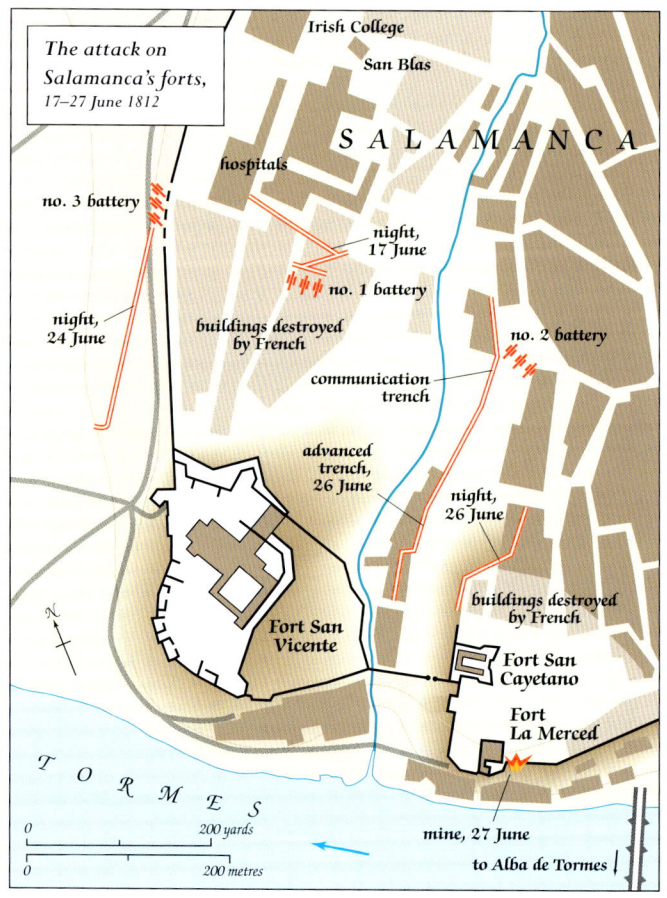

The attack on Salamanca's forts, 17–27 June 1812

Duero at Tordesillas, while those who had made a feint crossing at Toro passed the river at Pollos, and concentrated between Rueda and Nava del Rey. Confused actions took place next day at Castrejón and at Castrillo, as Wellington retired south-west towards Salamanca.

On 18 July, the contending armies were marching parallel to each other, with 'sharp cannonading from both sides', but not closely engaged; nor were they on the 21st, when both made a gruelling march of over 20 miles under a blistering sun. The French infantry, travelling lighter, could march faster, and were able to ford the Tormes at Huerta, east of Salamanca, which threatened Allied communications, but Wellington had already sent west his baggage and inessential supplies. By nightfall, both armies were across the river and had taken up parallel positions within its wide bend, the French vanguard occupying Calvarrasa de Arriba, on a road to Alba de Tormes.

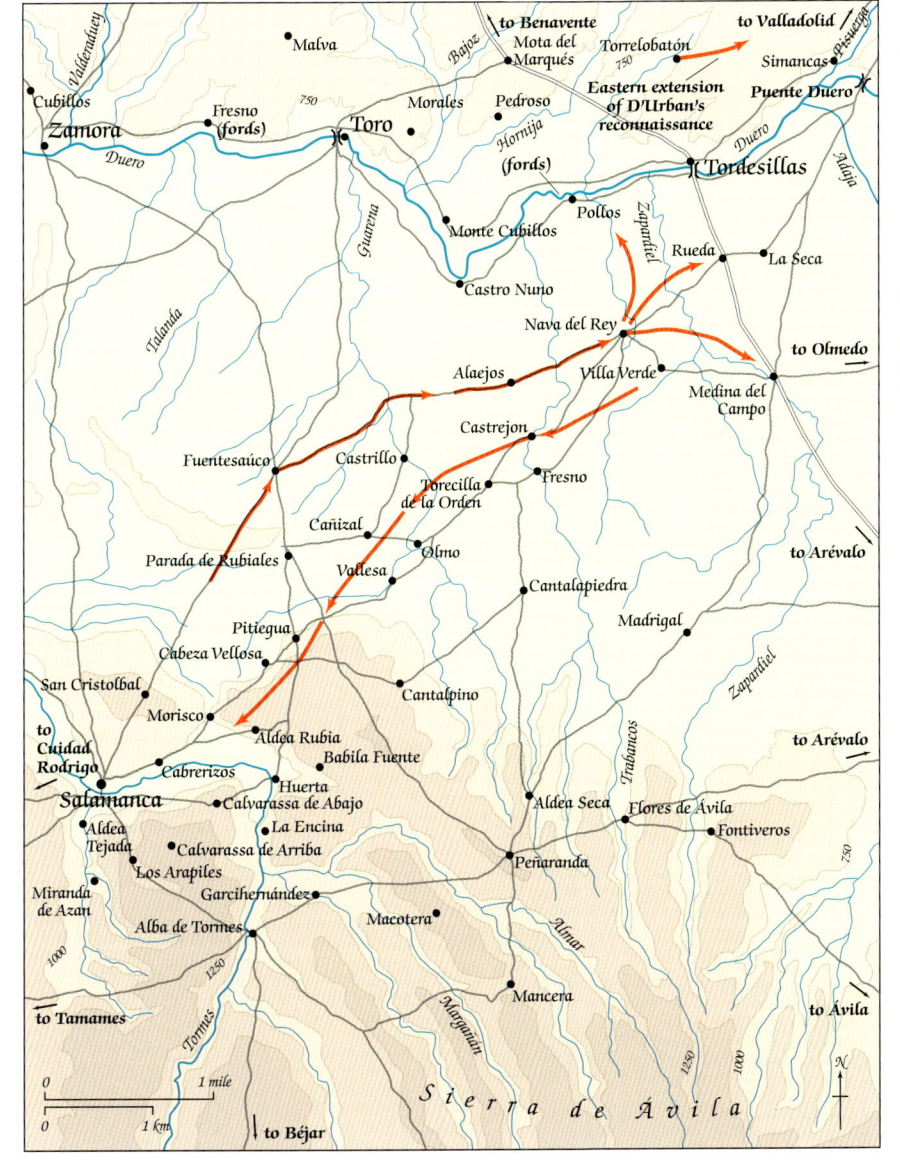

1 An expeditionary force under Lord William Bentinck, intended to threaten Suchet on the east coast, unfortunately set out belatedly.
2 Allied casualties were 430; those of the French, 200 plus 600 prisoners.
3 Since 30 June, cavalry units under Gen. D'Urban, on crossing the Esla, had been reconnoitring both banks of the Duero as far as Valladolid, reporting on its fords and on any reinforcement reaching Marmont from that quarter. On 15 July, D'Urban received orders to rejoin the main army and by the 19th he had re-crossed the Duero to take up a position at Parada de Rubiales, south of Fuentesaúco, closer to the Allied divisions retiring rapidly towards the Tormes.
4 By 9 July the Allies were concentrated near Pollos, with the Light Division at Rueda, the 1st and 7th at Medina del Campo, the 5th at Nava del Rey, and the 6th at Alaejos.

THE MANOEVRING PRIOR TO SALAMANCA, AND THE FALL OF THE FORTS

30 The Battle of Salamanca I

22 July 1812

The terrain in the vicinity of Salamanca is largely an open, rolling, plain, with slight elevations and troughs, while cork-oak woods (more plentiful at the time) extend further south-east towards Alba de Tormes. The Tormes, flowing north there, made a sharp turn west at Huerta (where there were fords) before reaching Salamanca, south-east of which rose the only hills of consequence, the characteristically steep-sided but flat-topped Lesser Arapile and, some 800 yards further south, the Greater Arapile. Beyond them, a slight ridge (the Monte de Azan[1]) merged with more undulating country further west.

By dawn on 22 July, the contending armies were marching parallel to each other towards the bald Arapiles, with the Allies occupying the nearer and lower. Most of Wellington's troops were concentrated, half-hidden, behind a low hill (the Teso de San Miguel), just north of the village of Los Arapiles,[2] with the exception of the Light and 1st Divisions (facing south-east across the Pelagarcia stream and towards the hill-top chapel of Calvarrasa de Arriba, near which Foy was stationed) and the 3rd (then commanded by Gen. Pakenham), which had only just crossed the Tormes at Salamanca and was marching towards the hamlet of Aldea Tejada to protect the right flank.

By late morning, with the torrid July sun beating down as at Talavera almost exactly three years earlier, most Allied divisions had been deployed in line from west to east just north of the village of Arapiles, facing south, for the foremost of Marmont's divisions (Thomières's), followed by Maucune's, were veering west from behind the Greater Arapile and along the Monte de Azan. By then, the 3rd Division, together with the majority of Wellington's cavalry, including Le Marchant's brigade, were stationed between Aldea Tejada and the hamlet of Las Torres (behind and west of his right flank), leaving Bock's cavalry brigade defending his far left.[3]

The main action commenced with Maucune attacking the village of Arapiles, from which they were expelled; but Thomières's troops had by then passed behind them and were extending west along the exposed ridge of the Monte de Azan, with Clausel's division some distance in the rear, followed by Bonnet's. Indeed, their van was imprudently advanced, presumably intent on cutting the road to Tamames and threatening Allied communications. It was about 2.45pm when Wellington ordered a general attack, with D'Urban's and Arentschildt's cavalry wheeling round to charge the foremost enemy column from the south-west,[4] while the 3rd Division would halt their further advance. Given no time to form square, Thomières's troops were rapidly scattered. Marmont himself was severely wounded before he could rectify the hazardous position in which he had noticed that this foremost division had been placed, and as several subordinates were wounded soon after, the French were briefly without a commander-in-

---

1 At its western extremity rose the Pico de Miranda, with the hamlet of Miranda de Azan to the south.
2 In Spain, the battle is known as that of Los Arapiles, rather than of Salamanca.
3 This remained in the area throughout the ensuing battle, in which the brigade suffered not a single casualty.
4 Arentschildt took over command when V. Alten was wounded early in the action.

George Hennell, *Sketch of Fort San Vicente made the day after its surrender.*

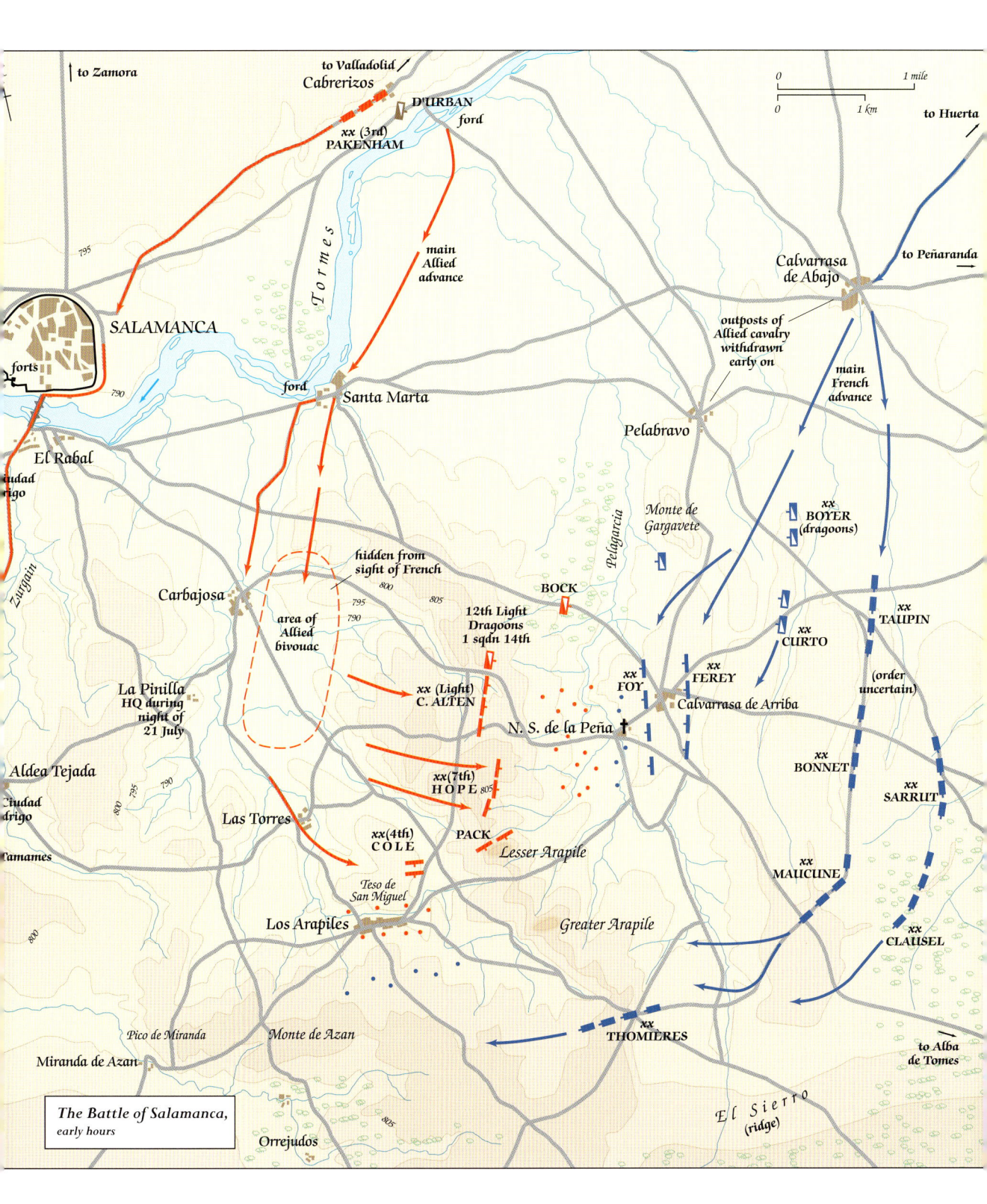

The Battle of Salamanca, early hours

31 The Battle of Salamanca II

22 July 1812

chief.

The 5th Division (with the 7th in its rear), and Cole's 4th (supported by Clinton's 6th) abutting it to the east, had now moved forward, while Le Marchant's dragoons swept down obliquely on Maucune's flank, which virtually disintegrated, as did the leading regiment of Taupin's 6th Division.[1] Clausel, now in command, counter-attacked, and the firefight in the intervening valley became increasingly confused and ferocious, but Bonnet's 8th Division was unable to withstand the advance of Clinton's line (which had relieved Cole's) and, although Clausel ordered up Ferey's 3rd

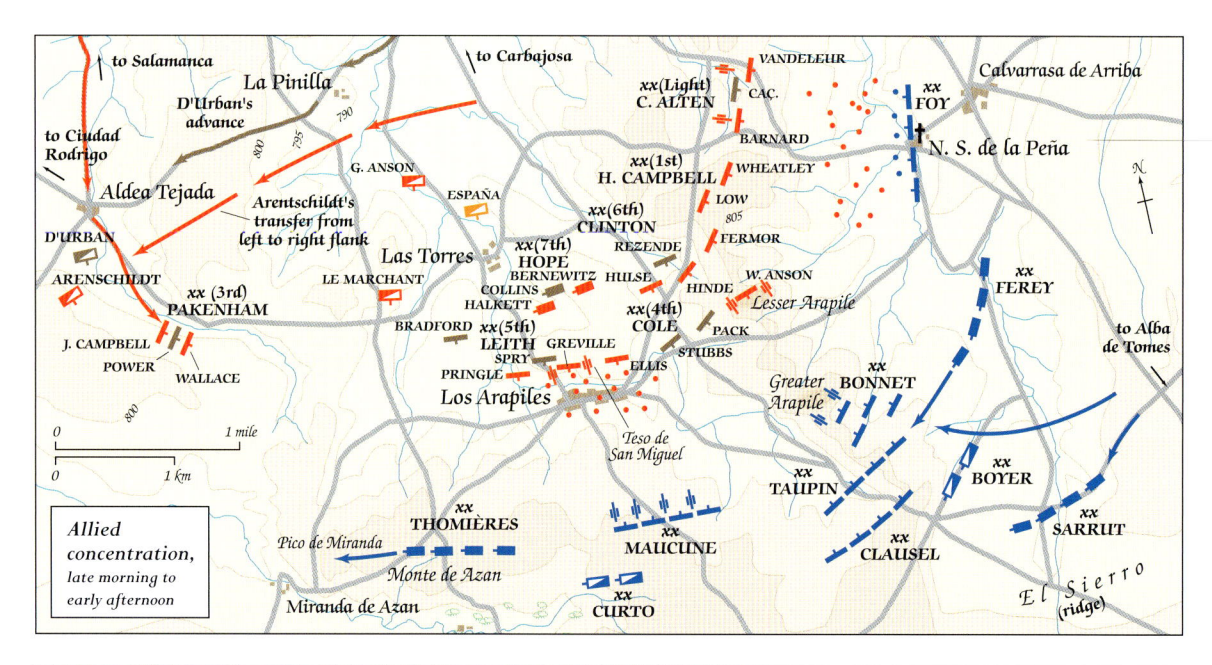

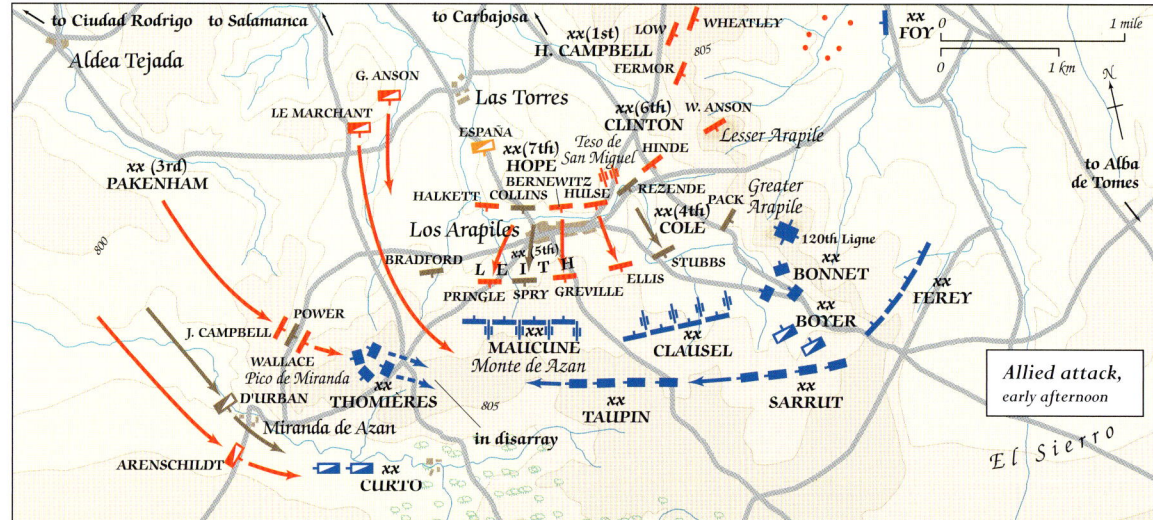

Allied concentration, late morning to early afternoon

Allied attack, early afternoon

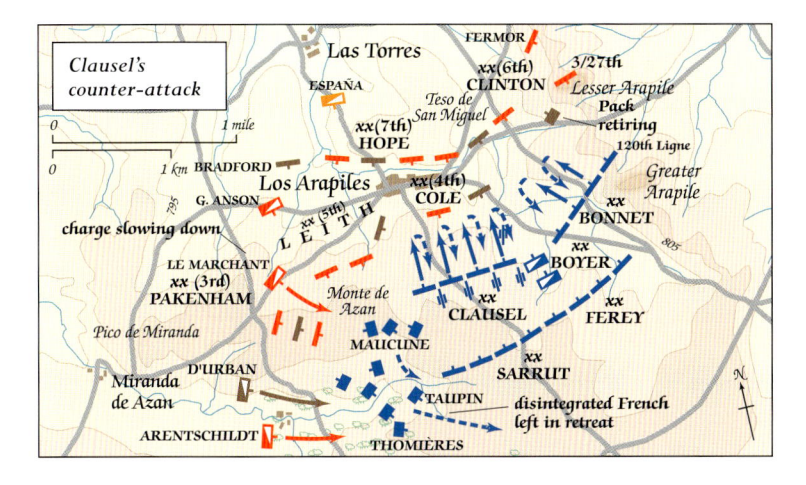

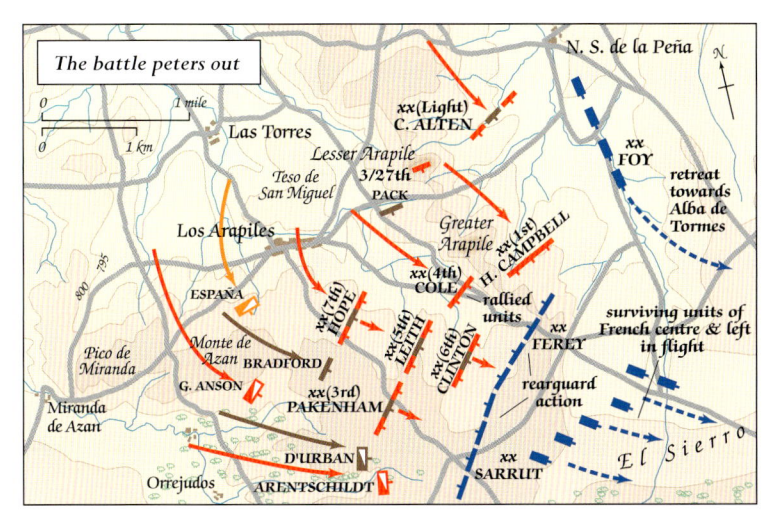

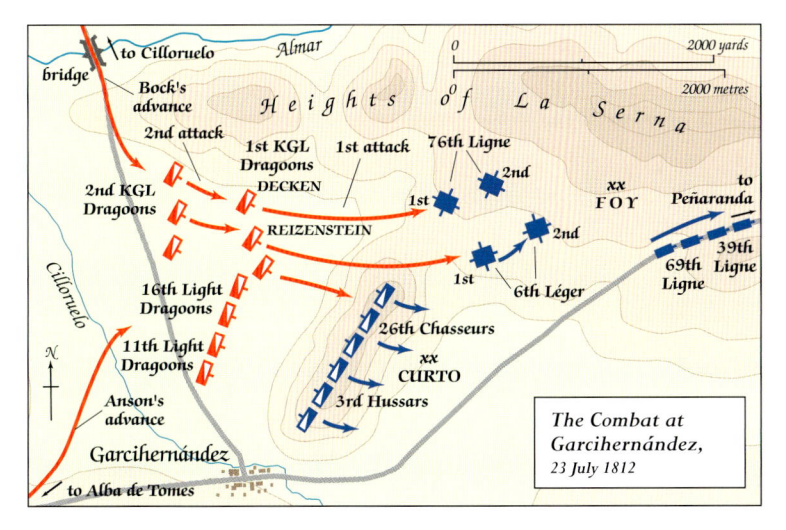

Division to hold Clinton at bay and defend the line of retreat, it was likewise dispersed by fire from batteries from the 1st and Light Divisions. Foy himself was powerless to make any stand against the Allied onslaught and, as darkness fell, the French retreat developed into a stampede as they fled south-east through the woods, despite the fact that the Allies were by then too exhausted to pursue vigorously.

Wellington had every reason to believe they would find themselves trapped, as Spanish units had been instructed to hold the bridge at Alba de Tormes at all costs. Until some cavalry, sent forward to investigate, reported back that the fugitives had escaped, he was unaware that Carlos de España had withdrawn his troops, contrary to specific orders.

The Allies suffered some 5,000 casualties in the battle, almost 700 being mortal; French losses were at least 12,500, half of them prisoners, and they left 20 guns on the field.

On the following afternoon, Bock's and Anson's cavalry brigades attacked the French rearguard near the village of Garcihernández (north-east of Alba), where a spirited action took place, in which the Allies had 127 casualties, those of the enemy amounting to about 1,100 including prisoners.

Essential reading for a proper understanding of this battle is Rory Muir's *Salamanca 1812*. Without doubt – and as Foy himself candidly admitted – it had been Wellington's most brilliant offensive battle to date. It greatly enhanced his reputation and encouraged the Spaniards to maintain their resistance.

1 French sources confirm that Taupin, not Brennier, commanded this division throughout the campaign.

32 The advance on Madrid and Burgos, and retirement to Portugal

23 July to late November 1812

Napoleon had already set in motion his invasion of Russia, when news reached him of the disaster sustained by Marmont's army at Salamanca and of the subsequent Allied occupation of Madrid, which was to cause Soult to evacuate Sevilla and then Andalusia.

Wellington followed the defeated army north-east to beyond Valladolid, which he entered on 30 July. Having knocked Clausel out of the ring for the time being, leaving a Galician division to watch the line of the Duero, and the 6th Division at Cuellar, he decided it would be more advantageous politically to capture Madrid, which served as the main military depot and hub of communications in French-occupied Spain. He could then join forces with Hill, advancing up the Tagus valley, and together they could face the probable convergence of Soult's and Joseph's forces. Marching via Segovia, the capital was entered on 12 August. The garrison of 2,500 surrendered after token resistance, while a vast accumulation of *matériel* was seized, much of the captured equipment then being distributed among the Spanish. Several thousand *afrancesados*, collaborators, and hangers-on fled. Wellington did his best to revitalise resistance among the local politicians and military, but privately expressed the view that the only way 'to get them to do anything on any subject' was 'to *frighten* them'. He remained preoccupied by the possibility of being outnumbered by the combination of French armies – for Clausel had re-occupied Valladolid.

Leaving Hill's Corps (some 28,000, plus 8,000 Spaniards) near Aranjuez, to defend the capital, and having sent ahead 23,000 men, Wellington left Madrid on 31 August, re-crossed the Duero on 6 September – Clausel retiring before him – and proceeded north-east towards Burgos, entered on 18 September.

Several changes in enemy dispositions took place during the ensuing siege – see Map 33 – for Gen. Southam, superseding Clausel, now commanded an army of 42,000, and could be reinforced by another 11,000 under Caffarelli (occupied quelling guerrilla bands further north).[1]

***

After dark on 21 October Wellington pulled back his field army from Burgos, joined unobtrusively by the besieging units, to gain a head start along the road to Valladolid. His rearguard of 1,300 cavalry soon found themselves hard-pressed by 6,000 enemy cavalry, and several sharp rearguard actions took place during ensuing days (as at Venta del Pozo and Villamuriel). The Duero was crossed at Boecilla in torrential rain, and the retreat continued through Rueda.[2] The rain continued to fall unceasingly; rations were short; and discipline deteriorated as the disconsolate troops, harassed ceaselessly by Soult's cavalry, waded south-west, chagrined by the indignity of having to retreat in the face of the enemy they had trounced only three months earlier.

Soult's and Joseph's forces, having belatedly converged between Hellín and Almansa,[3] were now advancing on Madrid, which was re-occupied on 2 November; but Wellington had already instructed Hill to evacuate his position south of the capital and cross the Guadarrama to meet him in the vicinity of Arévalo.[4]

By 8 November the entire Allied force (52,000 Anglo-Portuguese plus 18,000 Spaniards) was concentrated east of Salamanca, deployed in positions very close to those occupied previously.[5] On the 15th, Soult's army forded the Tormes at Galisancho (south-west of Alba) in an attempt to sever Wellington's communications, but this thrust coincided with a further deterioration in the weather. Although Soult's cavalry continued to pick up and take prisoner hundreds of stragglers, his artillery did little harm, shot falling into the sodden earth. A minor action took place near the Huebra bridge at San Muñoz as Wellington's army tramped on towards the comparative security of Portugal. The French now gave up the pursuit, dispersing to find food, forage, and shelter wherever they could, for the winter nights were bitterly cold.

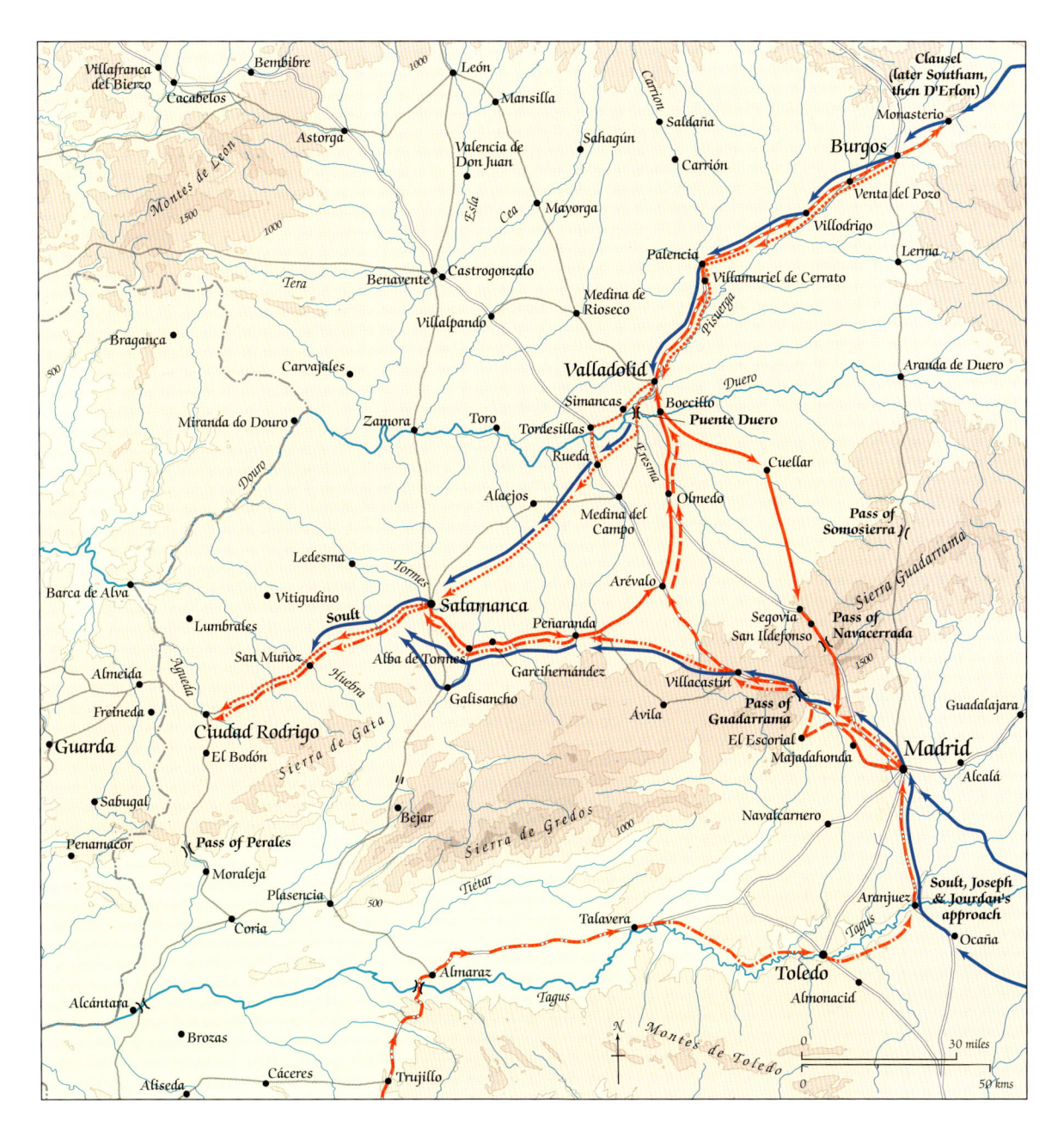

1 Southam himself was replaced by D'Erlon in mid-November.
2 In a dispatch from Rueda on 31 October, Wellington admitted: 'I have got clear in a handsome manner of the worst scrape I ever was in'.
3 *c.* 200 miles south-east of Madrid.
4 On 2 November, on reaching Villacastín, Hill received orders to veer west directly towards Alba de Tormes and Salamanca.
5 By then, Soult's forces greatly outnumbered the Allies, on whom as many as 90,000 men could have converged.

- → Allied pursuit of the French to Valladolid and their advance on Madrid
- → Wellington's advance on Burgos
- → Hill's advance on Aranjuez
- → Wellington's retreat
- → Hill's retreat
- → French in the wake of Allied retreats

THE ADVANCE ON MADRID AND BURGOS, AND RETIREMENT TO PORTUGAL | 83

33 THE SIEGE OF BURGOS

19 September to 21 October 1812

The reduction of the formidable citadel of Burgos, which crowned a height immediately north of the town, and with a well-provisioned garrison of 2,200 commanded by Gen. Dubreton, was vital before Wellington could advance further north-east; but the outlying redoubt of San Miguel, known as the Hornwork, would have to be stormed and taken first.[1] This took place on the evening of 19 September, when a few field-guns were captured; but casualties were heavy. Wellington, not expecting a strong resistance, had no proper siege train to hand, or the means of transporting adequate ordnance,[2] nor had he yet been provided with a body of trained sappers and miners.[3]

Although the outer walls of the castle eventually fell, it was not until 18 October that the main assault took place, and that failed.

In the face of growing enemy concentrations – two of Souham's divisions had advanced to test the strength of the Allies on 20 October, only to retreat, smarting – Wellington reluctantly decided to withdraw next day: see Map 32. The whole undertaking had gone badly. Several officers concurred with the opinion of Capt. Bowles (Coldstream Guards) that Wellington had 'shown rather more of a quality nearly allied to obstinacy than is to be wished', having been 'repeatedly told by those whom he consulted previous to commencing operations, his means … were totally insufficient'. Total casualties during the siege were over 2,000, a quarter of which were mortal;[4] casualties among the garrison amounted to 623.

François-Joseph Heim, *The French besieged at Burgos.*

1 This stood c. 500 yards north-east of the citadel. To what extent it was wooded at the time, as it is now, is uncertain.
2 On 26 September a Dispatch sent to Commodore Popham, off the Cantabrian coast near Santander, to unload powder-barrels, only reached Burgos on 5 October. Two 24-pounders, leaving the coast on 9 October, took nine days to reach Reinosa, still 50 miles away, and were sent back.
3 Some men who had been coal-miners in civil life came forward from the ranks when called to assist.
4 Wellington's most serious single loss was that of Somers Cocks, a brilliant officer killed during Dubreton's sortie on 8 October.

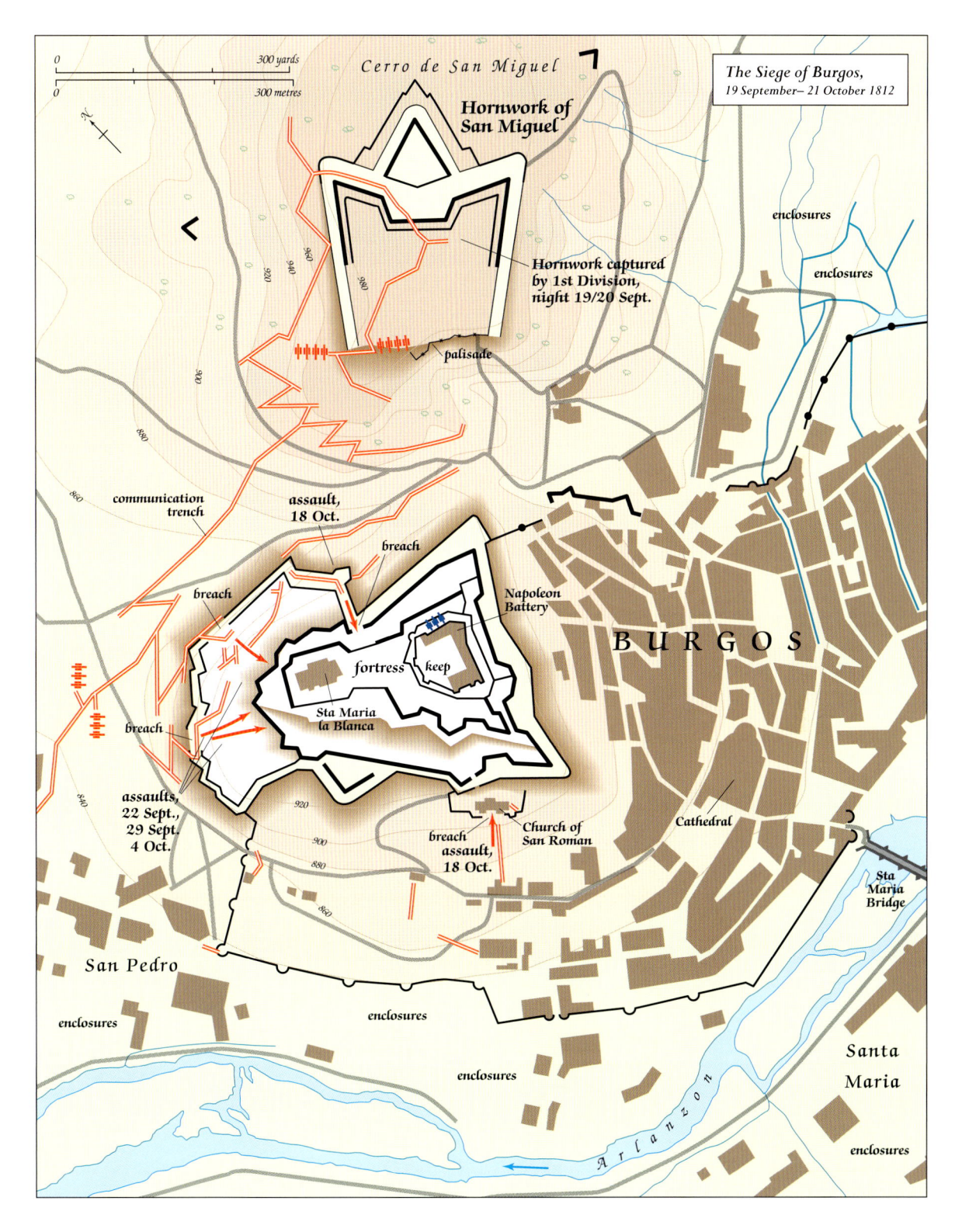

The Siege of Burgos, 19 September – 21 October 1812

34 Winter Cantonments, and Preparing for the Spring

1812–1813

Freineda, just west of Fuentes de Oñoro, was Wellington's headquarters for the second winter in succession. By 19 November most of his regiments were back in their former cantonments within Portugal, with the exception of Hill's Corps (principally brigades of the 2nd Division), which marched south to settle in mountain villages in the vicinity of Coria, with his cavalry further south. The 1st Division was stationed in the upper Mondego valley, between Guarda and Viseu, with the 3rd further north; the 4th was cantoned near the south bank of the Douro near São João da Pesqueira, with the 5th further west, in the vicinity of Lamego. The 6th and 7th lay near Seia, on the northern flank of the Serra da Estrela. The Light Division, together with Alten's Brigade of cavalry, remained east of Guarda and in their familiar billets nearer the frontier. Pack's and Bradford's Portuguese were placed north of the Douro, between Penafiel and Vila Real, while most of the remaining cavalry, apart from D'Urban's units near Braganza, were sent as far west as the coastal plain.

Wellington's hospitals, still with convalescents from Salamanca, were now glutted: the morning states confirmed that as many as 18,000 men were sick.[1] Thirteen regiments had more 'sick' than 'effective'; twelve were less than 300 strong.

It did not take long for Wellington's army to recuperate after the fatigue and exposure experienced in their retreat:[2] being well-fed, re-clothed, re-shod, and sheltered, both their health and morale were restored. They were rigorously drilled throughout the winter, and supplied with blankets and bell-tents, among much other equipment. Their cast-iron camp-kettles were jettisoned and replaced by those of sheet metal. Reinforcements were expected.

Several changes in French dispositions were taking place during the first months of 1813, partly caused by the withdrawal of troops from Spain to make up for staggering losses among Napoleon's armies which had been incurred during the disastrous Russian campaign.[3] The Emperor was also misled into believing that Wellington's casualties had been heavier than they were. Soult was recalled to Paris and replaced by Gazan; Joseph and Jourdan were instructed to withdraw any units remaining south of the Guadarrama range. Madrid was evacuated, and by 23 March headquarters had been established at Valladolid.

There had been a very considerable increase in guerrilla activity, notably in the Basque provinces,[4] which was seriously threatening the extended French lines of communication. The redeployment of forces should place them in a better position to frustrate these depredations. Clausel superseded Caffarelli, but he was no more successful in combating guerrilla incursions.

Meanwhile, to prevent the possible concentration against him of units from Marshal Suchet's army – with between 60,000 and 70,000 men, the largest enemy force in Spain – Wellington had instigated a diversionary measure. Some 15,000 Anglo-Sicilians, commanded by Gen. Sir John Murray, after a creditable action at Castalla (23 miles north-west of Alicante) on 13 April, were transported up the Levante coast to land at Tarragona in mid May. But Murray's operations, when attempting to take the fortress, were a fiasco, and his troops were re-embarked.[5] However, these diversions – see Map 2 – did have the effect of engaging Suchet's attention to the extent that he sent not a single man to support Joseph and Jourdan.

---

1 The site of the main General Hospitals, as opposed to Regimental hospitals, had been established earlier at Lisbon, Abrantes, Coimbra, Elvas, Oporto, Celerico, and Ciudad Rodrigo. Later in the war, others were sited at Vitoria, Bilbao, Fuenterrabia, Santander, Pasajes, and Toulouse. Smaller hospitals were often located in the vicinity of the larger (as at Vila Viçosa, near Elvas). Naturally, temporary and/or field hospitals had been set up in the towns or villages nearest to recent battlefields, among them Salamanca, Albuera, Fuentes de Oñoro, and later at Orthez and Aire, for example, as described in Martin Howard's *Wellington's Doctors*.

2 Private Wheeler had estimated in early December that since their advance from Ciudad Rodrigo eleven months earlier, he had marched 2,328 miles, and that was besides 'counter-marching, when near the enemy. If I had averaged ten miles per diem I think I should not have over rated it.'

3 This would still leave 200,000 French troops in Spain.

4 Supplies were reaching them from ports along the north coast, while Longa's partisans were collaborating with Commodore Popham in the autumn. Among many other partisan leaders then harassing the French were Mina, Porlier, El Empecinado, Jauregui, Duran, and Mendizabal.

[5] Murray was later court-martialled.

WINTER CANTONMENTS | 87

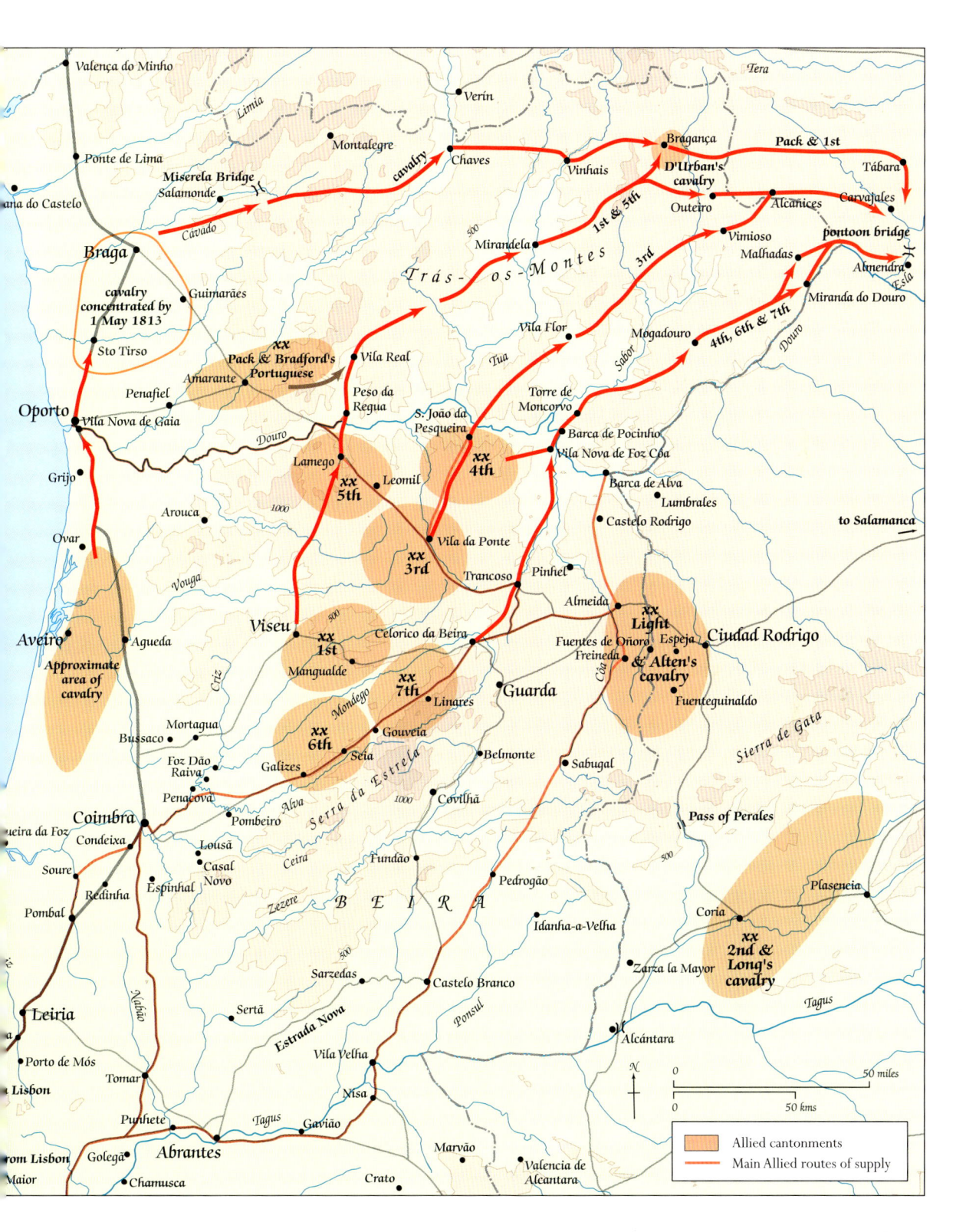

35 The Advance on Vitoria

Late May – 21 June, 1813

Despite the setback of the autumn, Wellington had every intention of thrusting the French back to the Pyrenees in his next campaign. As Spanish authorities had recently invested him *Generalissimo* of their armies, the numbers under his command were considerably augmented. Apart from their 4th Army (Giron's 18,000 infantry; 3,000 cavalry), he could expect to have Longa's 'army' and Silveira's Portuguese (formerly Hamilton's) at hand among other reasonably well-equipped and disciplined troops. The Anglo-Portuguese contingent included 67,000 infantry, 8,000 cavalry, and 102 guns in 17 batteries.

George Murray's staff had been accumulating first-hand topographical information, reporting on the passages of the Douro and mapping extensive areas through which the planned advance, scheduled for early May, would take

The position of the Headquarters of each column during the advance on Vitoria

	Column I *Giron's Galicians*	Column II *Graham*	Column III *Wellington*	Column IV *Hill*
May 26/28				Salamanca
29	approaching from		Miranda do Douro	
30/31	the direction of		Carvajales	
June 1	Benavente		Zamora	approaching Toro
2–3			Toro	
4	Villalpando	Villar de Frades	Mota del Marqués	Morales/La Mota
5	Villafrechos	Medina de Rioseco	Castromonte	Torrelobatón
6	Villarramiél	Villerías/Torremormojón	Ampudia	Mucientes
7	Becceril de Campos	Grijota	Palencia	Dueñas
8	Villodo	San Cebrian de Campos	Amusco/Tamara	Torquemada
9	Villasarracino	Santillana de Campos/Osorno	Amusco/Tamara	Villalco
10	Herrera de Pisuerga	Zarzosa	Melgar de Fernamental	Pedrosa del Principe
11	Herrera de Pisuerga	Sotresgudo	Castrojeriz	Barrio de Sta Maria
12	Pradanos de Ojeda	Sotresgudo	Castrojeriz	Bilviestre
13	Aguilar del Campóo*	La Piedra	Villadiego	Villarejo
14	Polientos	San Martin de Elines	Masa	Montorio
15	Soncillo	Villarcayo	Quintana/Puente Arenas	Villaescusa del Butrón
16	Quintanilla de Pienza	La Cerca	Medina de Pomar**	Villalain
17	Villasana de Mena	San Martin de Lastres	Quincoces del Yuso	La Cerca
18	Valmaseda	near Berberana	Berberana	Membliga
19	Arseniega	Osma	Subijana Morilles	Añana (Salinas de)
20	Orduña	Murguia	Subijana Morilles	Pobes
21	Battle of Vitoria			

*Where the column was joined by Porlier's Galicians
**Where the column was joined by Longa's Cantabrians

place. This enabled him to issue routes to assembling units, even if, due to a lack of rain, on which fresh forage depended, their start was delayed.

However, on 12 May, Larpent noted that there were indications of an impending move at Headquarters in Freineda, 'such as the packing of Lord Wellington's claret, etc.' By the end of the month, reinforced by Hill's Corps marching from Béjar,[1] Wellington had pushed forward to re-enter Salamanca, where he deliberately flaunted his presence, hoping that the enemy would assume that the entire Allied field army faced them: in fact it was a mere 30 per cent of the total, which by then amounted to some 81,000 effectives.

In previous weeks, with remarkable circumspection and secretiveness, the major part of the Allied army had been transferred north, crossing the Douro well within Portugal, and then tributaries of the Esla in the neighbourhood of Carbajales. The cavalry, according to William Bragge (3rd Dragoons), reached Braganza on 22 May, 'in as good order as could be expected after having crossed the Province of Tras os Montes by a Route never before attempted by British Cavalry and which never ought to have been marched. We were two Hours getting up one Hill, and for three Days never got the Regiment out of single Files, scrambling over Rocks, Mountains, and Precipices for 8 Hours every Day.' According to Private Wheeler, the infantry, during its progress, was 'continually starting hares …being provided with some good greyhounds, the fatigue of marching was much enlivened. So great was the quantity of game … that it was no uncommon thing to have half a

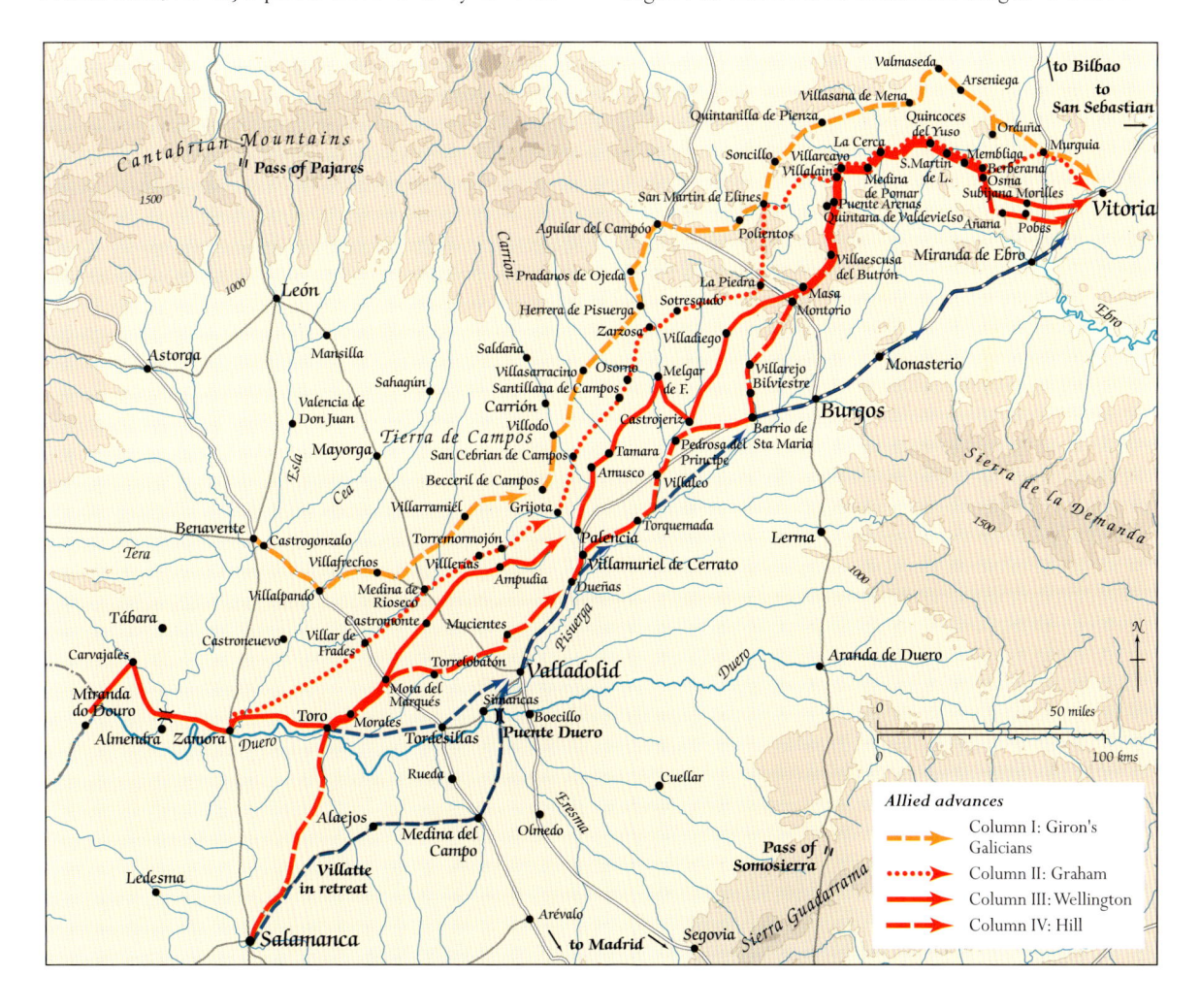

THE ADVANCE ON VITORIA | 89

dozen up at once, some of which would be running through the intervals of our column.' On 24 May, they reached the position assigned for their encampment. Wheeler recalled the amazement of some Spaniards in the vicinity to whom he was talking: 'We were in full view of our division but the tents were not pitched.[2] I heard the bugle sound to stand by the tents. I managed to draw the people's attention into the opposite direction … till the bugle sounded again … I then pointed to the camp [where a] minute before nothing was to be seen but the soldiers, now … studded with several hundred bell tents as white as snow and as regularly placed as if it had been the work of much labour and time. To a people so naturally superstitious … it must appear like magic … for they expressed their astonishment in a volley of "Caravos [*carajos*, a common oath]," then devoutly crossed themselves exclaiming "Jesu Maria – these English are the Devil".'

On 29 May, barely accompanied, and having ridden some 50 miles from Salamanca the previous day, Wellington traversed the gorge of the Douro at Miranda to join the army at Carbajales. Now occurred one of the more spectacular movements of the war. By the following evening, three divisions of infantry, together with cavalry and artillery, had crossed the Esla on a pontoon bridge[3] and, swarming east, outflanked and completely surprised the French defending the right bank of the Duero (so-spelt in Spain). A few minor rearguard actions took place, as at Morales, during their retreat to converge with the main bulk of the army, commanded by Joseph and Jourdan. This, out-manoeuvred by Wellington's advance,[4] was meanwhile retiring precipitately along the highway from Valladolid, their temporary headquarters, to Burgos, hampered by a vast train of baggage and plunder.

The Allies pressed rapidly north-east in four columns across the Tierra de Campos: the left flank consisting of Spanish units under Gen. Giron, parallel to which marched Graham's brigades; next came Wellington's column, flanked by Hill's Corps. Their progress was graphically described by Surtees, as they traversed 'one continuous plain of waving corn, mostly wheat … There are no hedges or dikes … so that its appearance is like an immense sea … the long corn undulating in the wind as the waves in the ocean'; while Broughton remarked on the 'concourse of mules, carrying the baggage of the army, and the various camp followers, [that] occupied more than treble the space of the army itself, and presented a moving scene so far as the eye could reach on all sides.'

On 13 June, the French blew up the fortifications of Burgos in the wake of their headlong retreat through the Pancorbo pass to approach Vitoria. Meanwhile, the Allies had swung north into the Montes de Oca and across the upper reaches of the Ebro, the descent to its thickly wooded valley being described by one major as 'down two miles of road cut through solid rock & steeper than any I had ever attempted to lead a horse down before…' This was the 5 mile (8km) descent from the Puerto de la Mazorra (just over 1,000m) to the river 600m below. By the 15th, headquarters were at Villarcayo, near Medina de Pomar. Several minor actions took place during ensuing days, during which Graham's troops worked their way round to approach a line of hills north-west of Vitoria, with Giron's Spaniards circling east nearer the coast.[5] Demoralised by the rapidity of their retreat, induced by the relentless pressure exerted by the outflanking Allied columns, on approaching Vitoria the French army was brought to a halt in the Zadorra valley, into which Wellington allowed them to debouch: they would find themselves in a cul-de-sac, for its exits were obstructed by an immense accumulation of carts and carriages which would take days to clear. Unless prepared to abandon the lot, they would be forced to fight.

1 Hill's Corps later converged on and crossed the Duero at Toro by a makeshift structure (the bridge having been broken) and fords to form the Allied right-hand column. By 4 June, the entire army was established north of the river, leaving Spanish units at Salamanca and to mop up along the south bank.
2 Belatedly, a large consignment of Trotter's bell tents had been shipped out from England.
3 With immense trouble, these had been transported overland on wagons during previous weeks.
4 The abnormal speed of the advance caused a severe strain on the Commissariat. As S.G.P. Ward has emphasised, once a bullock-cart was loaded from a depot, it rarely travelled faster than 12 miles a day. This was normally no problem, but the velocity of the infantry and cavalry thrust now stretched the system beyond its limits, notably on 16 June, five days before the battle of Vitoria. By then, three weeks had passed since the start of the advance, and the troops, outrunning their supplies, had to subsist as well as they could off the country, which accounted to some extent for their fatigued state, and the slowness of the ensuing pursuit.
5 Auxiliary units under several other Spanish commanders, among them Longa, Espoz y Mina, Morillo, and Porlier, were more in evidence at this period.

36 The Battle of Vitoria

21 June 1813

Shaken by the precipitancy of their retreat, and by the inexorable pressure of the outflanking Allied columns, the French debouched into the wide valley of the Zadorra, where, massed facing west, Joseph, Jourdan, and Gazan awaited the approach of Wellington's vanguard.[1] To the south, the valley was commanded by the Heights of Puebla, extended to the west by the Sierra de Morillas, to the north of which rose the hills of the Sierra de Arrato. The Zadorra coiled diagonally south-west across the French front, forming an abrupt turn round a hillock before curving east below the knoll of Ariñez, which rises in a central position of the valley floor, and flows south-west through a defile.[2]

Allied columns advanced into the valley early on the 21st, with Hill's Corps ascending the Heights of Puebla to attack Gazan's left flank. Wellington himself had a point of vantage on a low hill just west of the Villodas bridge, from which he could observe most of the future battlefield; but further advance was delayed until he *heard* firing from the north-east, which area was masked by the Ariñez hill. It was from this direction that Graham, with 20,000 men, having meanwhile worked his way behind the Sierra de Arrato to outflank the French and threaten their main line of retreat,[3] would be making his attack.

Once firing from that quarter was heard, Wellington unleashed his central columns in a vigorous attack, with Kempt's brigade swarming over the bridge of Tres Puentes, their approach to it being masked from the French by the hillock within the sharp bend of the river. Meanwhile, Picton's 3rd Division had stormed across the Mendoza bridge and rolled back the flank of Gazan's units defending the knoll of Ariñez. The French were unable to consolidate their line and, with Hill's Corps pressing their left, the 3rd and Light, now reinforced by the 7th, forcing back D'Erlon, the 4th was launched into the gap between D'Erlon and Gazan and broke the French centre. On learning this, Reille's two divisions, having long attempted to hold Graham at bay, gave way.

The bridge of Tres Puentes, looking east from Barnard's Hill.

[1] Joseph commanded 66,000 men, including 11,300 cavalry and 138 guns; the Allies had almost 79,000, including 8,300 cavalry and 90 guns.
[2] Although fordable at this time of year, the Zadorra was crossed by several bridges, some barricaded but not destroyed. The road from the Bayas valley crossed it by the Nanclares bridge; further north, it was spanned by those of Villodas, Tres Puentes, Mendoza, Arriaga (due north of Vitoria), Gamarra Mayor, and Durana, the last bearing the highway leading north-east towards the frontier.
[3] Longa's troops had cut the main road north-east by noon.
[4] Although some 55,000 men escaped, their total losses must have far exceeded 8,000, while Allied casualties have been estimated at 5,150, of which 840 were killed.

By late afternoon Joseph, who narrowly evaded capture, ordered a general retreat. Now entirely demoralised, what had been his army decomposed into milling groups. Once aware that their main escape route had been cut, panic ensued and, virtually disintegrating, they fled east, flinging away packs and even muskets in an endeavour to hasten their flight, in which all but two of their guns were abandoned, plus an immense amount of booty, which effectively delayed any rapid pursuit, in which only 2,000 prisoners were taken.[4]

The Battle of Vitoria, 21 June 1813

92 | An Atlas of the Peninsular War

THE BATTLE OF VITORIA | 93

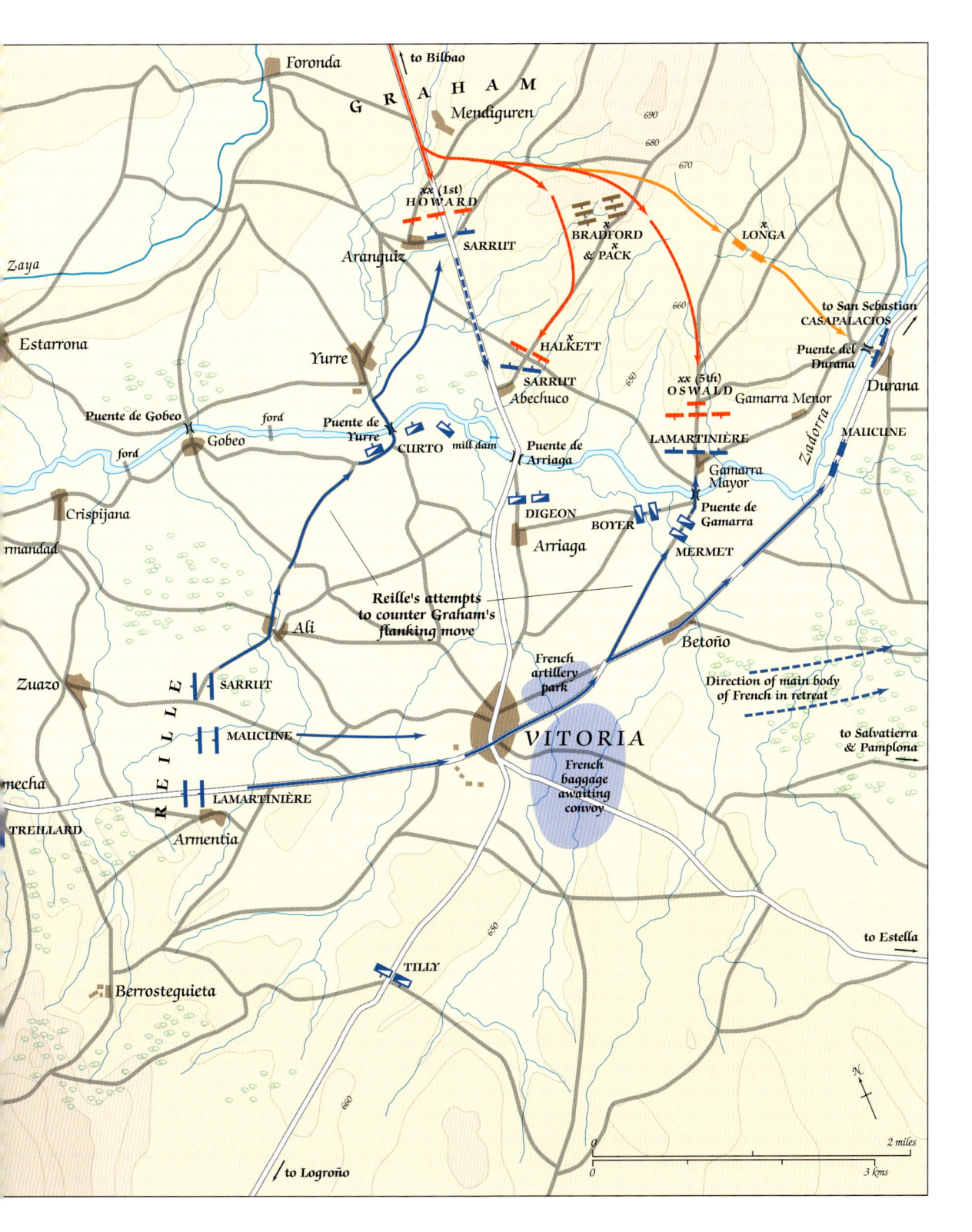

37 The Pyrenean Quadrilateral

Late June and first half of July, 1813

Not surprisingly, a General Hospital had to be set up at Vitoria. The bulk of the Allied army, flanked by Graham's and Hills' units to the north and south, proceeded east towards Irurtzun and Pamplona,[1] but belatedly, for they had briefly out-marched their provisions and, as new bases on the coast had not yet been established,[2] they were also running short of ammunition.

Meanwhile, Longa's troops, and then those of Giron, followed the French under Maucune retreating down the highway to San Sebastian, where at Vergara they were reinforced by Foy's units. In an unsuccessful attempt to intercept them at Villafranca (now named Ordizia), part of Graham's force peeled off at Salvatierra to traverse the Sierra de Urquilla by the Puerto de San Adrián. After dislodging rearguard resistance at Tolosa, Graham pressed north-east to invest San Sebastian, into which Foy had thrown a garrison, and reached the Bidasoa, marking the frontier, on 30 June.

On hearing of the disaster at Vitoria, Clausel's army had rapidly retreated east via Logroño and Tudela towards Zaragoza, eventually escaping across the Pyrenees via Jaca and the Somport Pass. Hill, sent from Pamplona towards Tafalla on a wild-goose chase to cut them off, was obliged to give it up at Cáseda, near Sangüesa. On 4 July, after returning towards Pamplona, Hill veered north through foothills of the Pyrenees, beyond the Puerto de Velate entering the Baztan valley, from which any lingering French were expelled. By 10 July, Headquarters were at Zubieta, not far west of Santesteban.

Hills's route had also been the main one followed by the retreating French for, from Irurtzun, after bypassing Pamplona (already garrisoned), Joseph and D'Erlon had swung due north via the Baztan and Maya pass. Reille's units had been sent north-east across country from Irurtzun to Santestéban, to descend the narrow valley of the Bidasoa; Gazan's units, making for St Jean-Pied-de-Port, had crossed the range at Roncesvalles.[3]

The whole frontier area was remarkably mountainous terrain, in which few passes were clearly defined, and it was easy to lose one's way. The foothills on the Spanish side were a confusing jumble of rounded peaks separated by rugged wooded valleys and tumbling watercourses, but cross-tracks between valleys were few and tortuous: communications were extremely difficult.[4] On the French side, although the valleys were steeper, the ascents between the wooded spurs to the summit of transverse ridges and passes were shorter. Apart from the coastal highway from Bayonne, the main French base in south-western France, the Pyrenees were crossed by a steep road up the narrow Val Carlos from St Jean-Pied-de-Port, from which (further east) a Roman road, still passable by wheeled traffic, also wound up via the Puerto de Ibañeta to Roncesvalles, there bearing south-west to Pamplona. The barrier range was traversed as well by a track up the Bidasoa valley and, between the two, another climbed from Ainhoa and Urdax to the Col de Maya (Puerto de Otsondo), from there descending past Maya to Elizondo in the Baztan valley.[5]

As it would be impossible to defend a front of over 40 miles in extent with the 60,000 troops at his disposal, Wellington placed limited numbers in depth along the principal avenues of approach by which the enemy were likely to penetrate in force, and kept the rest in reserve to reinforce any sector being threatened: but no counter-attack in the immediate future was expected.

---

1 The fortress was blockaded, eventually surrendering on 31 October when on the verge of starvation.
2 The most important of which would be the land-locked harbour of Pasajes, just east of San Sebastian.
3 No attempt has been made to indicate on the accompanying map the often cross-country tracks taken by the French in retreat. While the progress of the Allies towards the frontier and the posts taken up are shown, they are approximate only, for several units were in constant movement or being repositioned.
4 How very different would be the cross-country ride between any two points compared to a canter over the rolling plains of Salamanca!
5 Naturally, there were numerous other tracks traversed over the centuries by hardy Basque smugglers, who knew every nook and cranny of their mountains.

THE PYRENEAN QUADRILATERAL | 95

38 Soult's Counter-offensive, and Retreat

23 July to 1 August 1813

Soult entered Bayonne on 11 July with orders from Napoleon to re-group and re-vitalise Joseph's recently defeated and still disorientated army in the frontier area, take the offensive, and relieve both San Sebastian and Pamplona as soon as possible.[1] His forces were divided into three Corps in all but name, comprising three Divisions each, commanded by Reille, D'Erlon, and Clausel, with Villatte retaining a large Reserve at Bayonne. Within twelve days, Soult's columns were already on the march, but with only four days' rations in hand.[2] The advance he had planned was risky unless results were rapid and decisive, for it would be impossible to live off the land in such inhospitable country; both food and ammunition would run short if there were any delay. But Soult was confident that his superior force (55,400 men) could ascend and cross the watershed far faster than Wellington could muster and move sufficient troops across country to offer substantial resistance.

The ensuing campaign, the 'Battles of the Pyrenees' (see Plans 39 and 40) took place within the mountainous triangle between San Sebastian, St Jean Pied-de-Port, and Pamplona. The foothills of the main range, entered with comparative ease from the north, gave the French an advantage.

Until the latter stages of his advance on Vitoria, Wellington had not found himself in anything like such rugged country since defending the 'damn long hill' at Busaco: his 'lines' covering Lisbon lay along comparatively low hills. There would be several different problems of communication to resolve in such labyrinthine terrain, with which he was entirely unfamiliar, and in which it was easy to go astray, the more so as mist and low clouds frequently blew in from the sea to obscure the heights.

***

Soult's retreat from the battlefield of Sorauren (see pp.100-1) was undertaken with great difficulty. He was in a dangerous situation, having run out of rations, and there was virtually no food at hand: morale had plummeted.

Any attempt to break through past Lizaso towards Tolosa and separate the Allied armies from each other was given up after Hill, at first obliged to give ground, received reinforcements (among them the 7th Division) on the 30th, which left Soult and D'Erlon (with 35,000 men) little alternative but to continue their retreat due north over the Doñamaria passes to reach the elbow of the Bidasoa at Santestéban.

Cole's troops had already blocked any French attempt to approach the Baztan valley and the Maya pass and were threatening their right flank,[3] while Picton's had cut all practicable routes north-east towards Roncesvalles. Nevertheless, joined by isolated and straggling units, Foy had managed to escape by setting off north across trackless mountains, through which some 10,000 men, in a state of utter destitution, percolated back into France via the Aldudes valley.

At Yanci, when running the gauntlet of the narrow rock-bound valley of the Bidasoa, Soult's troops were assailed by the Light Division, approaching through mountainous country to the south-west, but they were just too late to cut them off.[4]

A sharp rear-guard action took place at Echalar, where remnants of Conroux's division, caught unawares by the rapid advance of the 7th Division, were routed. Other units ordered to reinforce Conroux, on seeing his predicament, turned away and likewise retreated across the frontier, under pressure from the 4th Division and in danger of being outflanked by the Light. Soult's fruitless nine-day offensive petered out at Vera, after which his surviving units dispersed to take up what defensive positions they could. By 2 August, Wellington was back at his HQ at Lesaca. See p.98.

Casualties had been high in the 'Battles of the Pyrenees': those of the Allies were some 7,000 of the 40,000 engaged; Soult's were some 13,500 of the 53,000 men in action.

1 Joseph himself had been recalled in disgrace.
2 The rapidity with which Soult restructured and mobilised his troops certainly took Wellington by surprise, even if he was loath to admit it except in faint praise, as when later remarking to Stanhope that, in his opinion, Soult was not equal to Masséna: 'He did not quite understand a field of battle: he knew very well how to bring his troops on to the field, but not so well how to use them when he had brought them up.'
3 They surprised and captured a large convoy. The escorting troops were expecting an uninterrupted march on Pamplona, being entirely ignorant of the disaster that had overtaken Soult.
4 The Light Division had made a laborious roundabout march from Lecumberri via Leiza and Zubieta, and from Elgorriaga had followed a mountainous track north above and parallel to the Bidasoa valley.

SOULT'S COUNTER-OFFENSIVE, AND RETREAT | 97

39 The Combats at Roncesvalles, and Maya

25 July 1813

Although intelligence had been reaching Wellington that enemy units were moving east, he assumed this was a feint on Soult's part, and that the main thrust would be at the mouth of the Bidasoa. Early on 25 July, worried that the scheduled assault had failed, Wellington had ridden over to San Sebastian from his HQ at Lesaca, unaware until his return late that evening that a major offensive to relieve Pamplona was under way against his right wing.[1] Not only was D'Erlon's Corps of 21,000 ascending from Urdax towards the Puerto de Otxondo or Col de Maya (after the village of Maya in the upper Baztan valley) but, simultaneously, almost 34,500 infantry, and two cavalry divisions, under Clausel and Reille, together with Soult in person, having concentrated near St Jean Pied-de-Port, were climbing laboriously towards the Puerto de Ibañeta and Roncesvalles in two immense columns. Defending these passes were Cameron's and Pringle's brigades of Stewart's 2nd Division and Barnes's brigade of the 7th at Maya, and Cole's 4th Division together with Byng's brigade of the 2nd (13,000 men) at Roncesvalles.

Reille's units made their way up the Val Carlos and along a spur flanking it to the west to approach Roncesvalles from the north-west, near the Linduz peak; Clausel's followed the Roman road towards the Col de Bentarte and height of Altobiscar, to converge on Roncesvalles from the north-east.

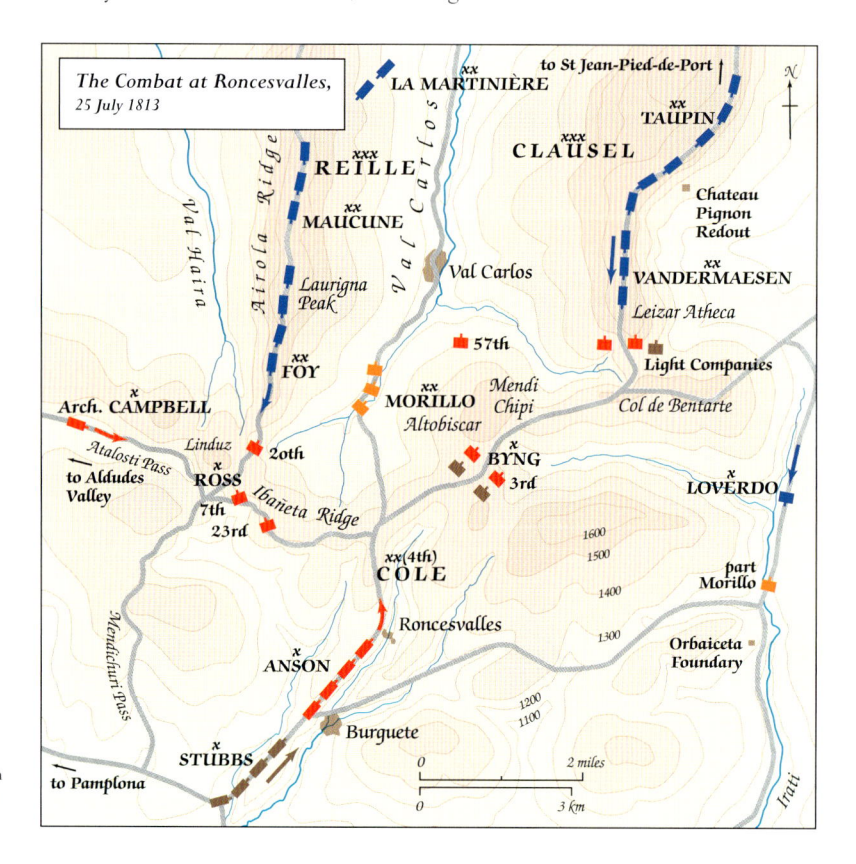

[1] On the assumption that both passes could be forced with ease, the French planned to march on and relieve Pamplona, attack the Allied flank and threaten their rear.

98 | An Atlas of the Peninsular War

Cole's picquets had been alarmed and retired to warn Byng, whose men were able to delay the advance of three divisions for four hours before being driven back by overwhelming numbers to a stronger position on the slope of the Altobiscar, where they continued to hold the pass, although their right flank was in danger of being turned further east near Orbaiceta.[2]

Meanwhile, further west, Ross's brigade among other units had kept at bay the van of Reille's column on a narrow front below the Linduz when suddenly the whole Roncesvalles area was enveloped by dense low cloud, restricting visibility to 20 yards and bringing fighting to a standstill. The opposing forces could only bivouac within sound of each other. In the circumstances, although initially ordered to hold on at all costs, Cole judged it wiser to retire downhill south-west to avoid being entirely cut off, although his dispatch confirming this retrograde movement did not reach Wellington until the evening of the 26th.[3]

***

Having ridden south-east with Hill to investigate the firing near Roncesvalles. Stewart was not present at the Col de Maya when the head of D'Erlon's column was first seen approaching from the Gorospil knoll, east of the main pass. Although the advance was tenaciously resisted for 40 minutes, Pringle's and Cameron's men were eventually forced back, despite reinforcements reaching them from the west. An attempt to stem the tide was made by Grant's brigade of the 7th Division, taking up a position near the Alcorrunz peak, but it was not until part of Barnes's brigade, advancing rapidly from the west along the 'Chemin des Anglais' and taking them in flank, that the balance swung against the enemy. Although, as night fell, they retained the actual pass, their attempt to cross it had been delayed for ten hours.[4] Discreetly, the Allies retired down the Baztan valley in the night, during which Wellington had received Hill's dispatch and ridden up the Bidasoa valley towards the upper Baztan.

The Combat at Maya, 25 July 1813

2 Defended by Morillo's Spaniards.
3 Wellington had received this when at Almandoz, on the north flank of the Puerto de Velate.
4 Allied casualties had been about 1,500 (including half of the 1,900 present in Cameron's brigade); the French lost some 2,100.

40 The Battles of Sorauren

28 and 30 July 1813

Having warned Graham to prepare against a French thrust towards San Sebastian, Wellington, still in ignorance of Cole's situation, instructed the Light Division and Dalhousie's 7th to support Hill; Pack's 6th was sent south. On reaching Almandoz and receiving Cole's belated dispatch, he ordered both Cole and Picton (then near Pamplona) to hold the French advance from Roncesvalles at Zubiri, in the Arga valley.

By 10 am on 27 July Wellington had entered Olagüe, in the Ulzama valley south of the Puerto de Velate, only to learn that Cole and Picton were already much further south in the parallel valley. Wellington and Fitzroy Somerset pressed on, to reach the bridge at Sorauren, where the later was sent back with an instruction to QMG Murray to re-route Pack to enter the valley much further south. By then, Cole's Division had taken up a position on a ridge between the two valleys (later known as 'Cole's'), to which Wellington ascended,[1] first skirting the base of a 1½-mile-long parallel ridge along which Clausel's troops were deploying. The two ridges were connected by a wide saddle of land further east before reaching the Arga valley and a separate hill (defended by Spanish troops) commanding the village of Zabaldica, towards which Reille's vanguard was advancing. Further south, the road to Pamplona was blocked near Huarte by Picton (facing Foy), with additional Spanish units defending ridges extending west.

Soult was cautious, and it was not until next morning, after a stormy night,[2] that the action commenced. Five French divisions – heavily outnumbering the Allies facing them – descended into the intervening valley to attack Cole's ridge, the column crossing the saddle being the first to come into collision with the defensive line, which had the musketry advantage. The Allied left flank was pushed back until Wellington ordered a counter-attack, reinforced by units from Byng and Stubbs, an onslaught which sent the enemy sprawling back into the valley and to the safety of their own ridge, although stiff fighting took place to retain the Spanish-held hill.

The 6th Division had now entered the Ulzama Valley from the west, but Conroux's Division, when making a preemptive attack on it was savaged.[3] Meanwhile, additional artillery and ammunition arrived and was hauled to the summit of Cole's Ridge; but although four hours of daylight remained, Soult did not return to the attack. To frustrate the possibility of D'Erlon's juncture with Clausel, Wellington had sent orders to Hill to take up a position near Lizaso, where he might receive support from the Light Division, which by then was approaching Irurtzun.

***

The 29th was largely spent by the contending armies in attending to their wounded. Already, the French had suffered as many as 4,000 casualties, but those of the Allies were also heavy: some 2,650. Soult was in a hazardous situation: he could only retreat, but to do so without putting himself at great risk would require careful planning.

Ominous sounds of movement were heard before dawn on the 30th. As day broke, the bulk of Soult's army was seen hurrying up both the Arga and Ulzama valleys, although some units were also moving towards the village of Sorauren itself, which, together with 'Clausel's Ridge', was now subjected to a vigorous bombardment prior to a coordinated attack from Cole's Ridge.

Maucune's Division was effectively wiped out; but Foy's units, in and near Zabaldica, were able to extract themselves from a perilous situation between Cole and Picton, and flee north. The only troops retreating comparatively unscathed from Sorauren were those retiring up the Ulzama valley, although losing many prisoners en route. For the ensuing engagement near Beunza and Lizaso, and Soult's subsequent retreat, see Map 38.

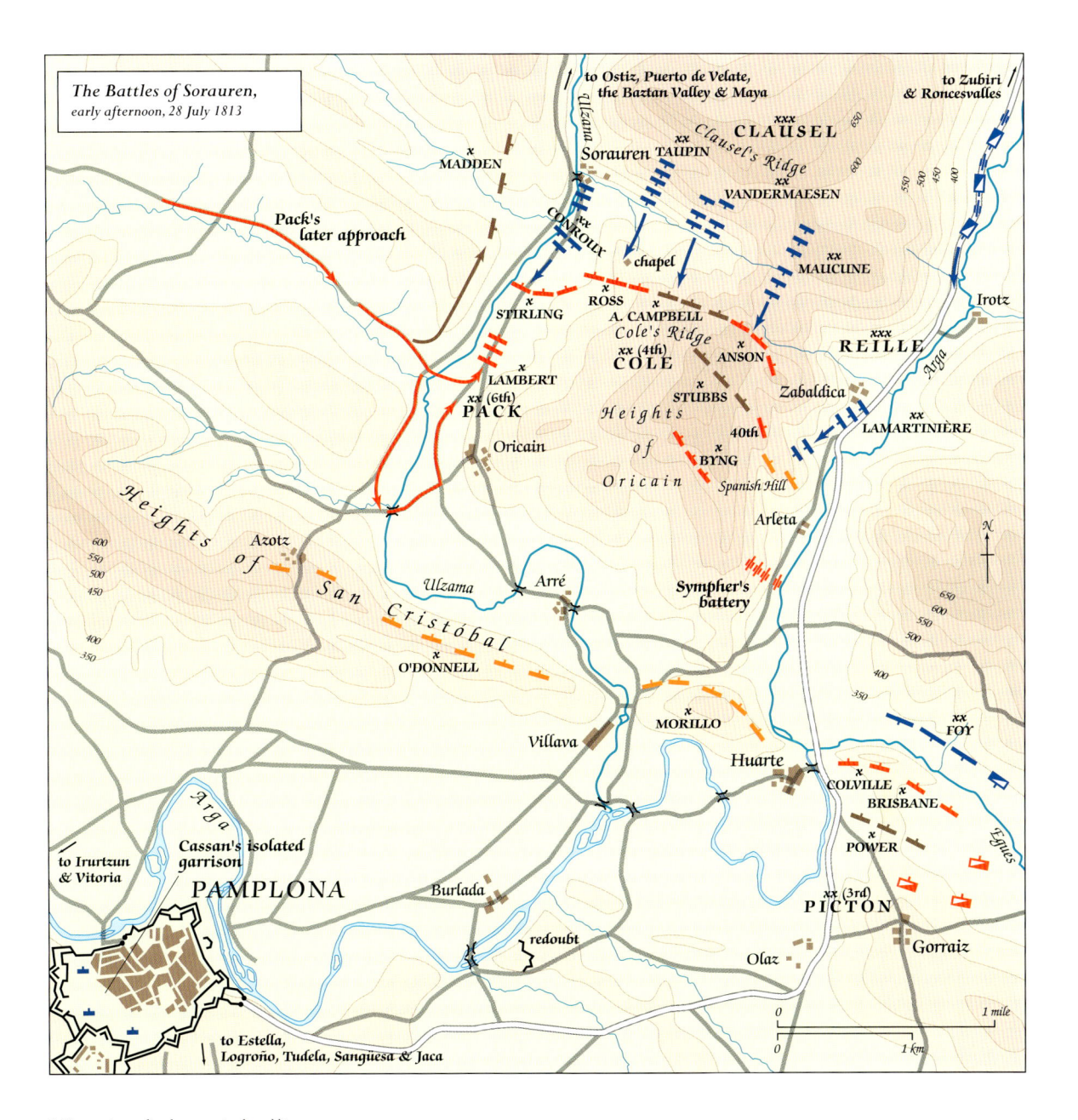

1 He was immediately recognised, and his presence acknowledged by welcoming shouts of 'Douro' from Campbell's Portuguese.
2 The 28th was coincidentally the fourth anniversary of Talavera.
3 Pack was wounded in this action, and replaced by Pakenham.

THE BATTLES OF SORAUREN | 101

41 THE SIEGE OF SAN SEBASTIAN

7 July – 8 September 1813

Advancing from Tolosa, by 28 June Gen. Graham had invested San Sebastian, where Gen. Rey commanded, and reached the estuary of the Bidasoa at Irún two days later. Siege ordnance soon began to land at adjacent Pasajes – a far handier port of supply than Santander – before being hauled into position facing San Sebastian. The compact walled town straddled a narrow isthmus between a sandy crescent bay (*La Concha*) and the mouth of the tidal Urumea, spanned by a destroyed bridge. Monte Urgull dominated it to the north, surmounted by the citadel (*La Mota*). To the west, beyond the rocky island of Santa Clara, rose Monte Igueldo; to the east, beyond a stretch of dunes (*Los Chofres*) covered by water at high tide,[1] the fortress was dominated by Monte Ulia, part of the long coastal ridge (later that of Jaizkibel) extending towards Fuenterrabía. To the south-west of the fortifications rose the Heights of San Bartolomé, with its convent; other hills rose steeply to the south-east.

On 12 July, Wellington visited the front to supervise preparations for the siege being conducted by Sir Richard Fletcher,[2] whose plan of placing guns on both the isthmus and the sandhills he approved. On a second attempt, San Bartolomé was successfully stormed on the 17th, from which parallels approaching the walls were completed by the 23rd. Batteries were positioned; breaches were soon made, and a mine was exploded in the already severed water main entering the town, blowing down the counterscarp of the western flank of the hornwork. The assault made at dawn on the 25th failed, due partly to too hurried preparations, and the discovery that an additional wall and ditch had been run up behind the first line of defences.

Additional consignments of siege guns were being landed after the 19 August and new batteries established, some guns being dragged up to the summit of Monte Ulia, from which – even at such a distance – high-trajectory fire caused severe damage to the interior defences and made life uncomfortable in the citadel. Some 100 sappers and miners disembarked also, the first time such specialist troops were used in the Peninsula. The artillery re-opened fire on the 26th, and a false assault was delivered three days later, but Gen. Rey did not take the bait. Nevertheless, their guns defending the eastern wall overlooking the Urumea were soon silenced, a stretch of wall crumbled, a smaller breach was made further north, and the demi-bastion at the south-east angle was destroyed.

The main attack was scheduled for noon on 31 August, after a heavy preliminary bombardment was lifted, with the same positions as before being stormed. Columns of Portuguese troops, with 900 yards to cover, started 30 minutes later to cross the sand-hills and exposed banks of the Urumea to assault the lesser breach, near which an additional ford had been discovered the previous night. On wading through 3 feet of water at the double, a lodgement was gained, which enabled them to enfilade the French, who meanwhile were keeping up a furious fire on troops attempting to break in further south. On seeing the impetus of the attack slacken here, Graham sent the unusual order to forward batteries and, by semaphore to others, to resume fire on the enemy defending the curtain wall, even if this target was immediately over the heads of storming units (a margin of less than 40 feet vertically). One shell touched off a mine below the main breach, which blew up 300 of the defenders, clearing the way for the storming parties, who carried the ramparts and jumped down past burning houses to enter the close-packed town, where tenacious street fighting continued until the survivors of the garrison, a little over 1,000, retired to the citadel. Any attempt to extinguish the spreading flames, fanned by the wind, was given up as the inevitable ransack of the place commenced.

Naturally, the holocaust was blamed on the British, whom the Spanish claimed were jealous of San Sebastian's economic prosperity, a calumny firmly denied by Wellington in his dispatch: 'Several people urged me …

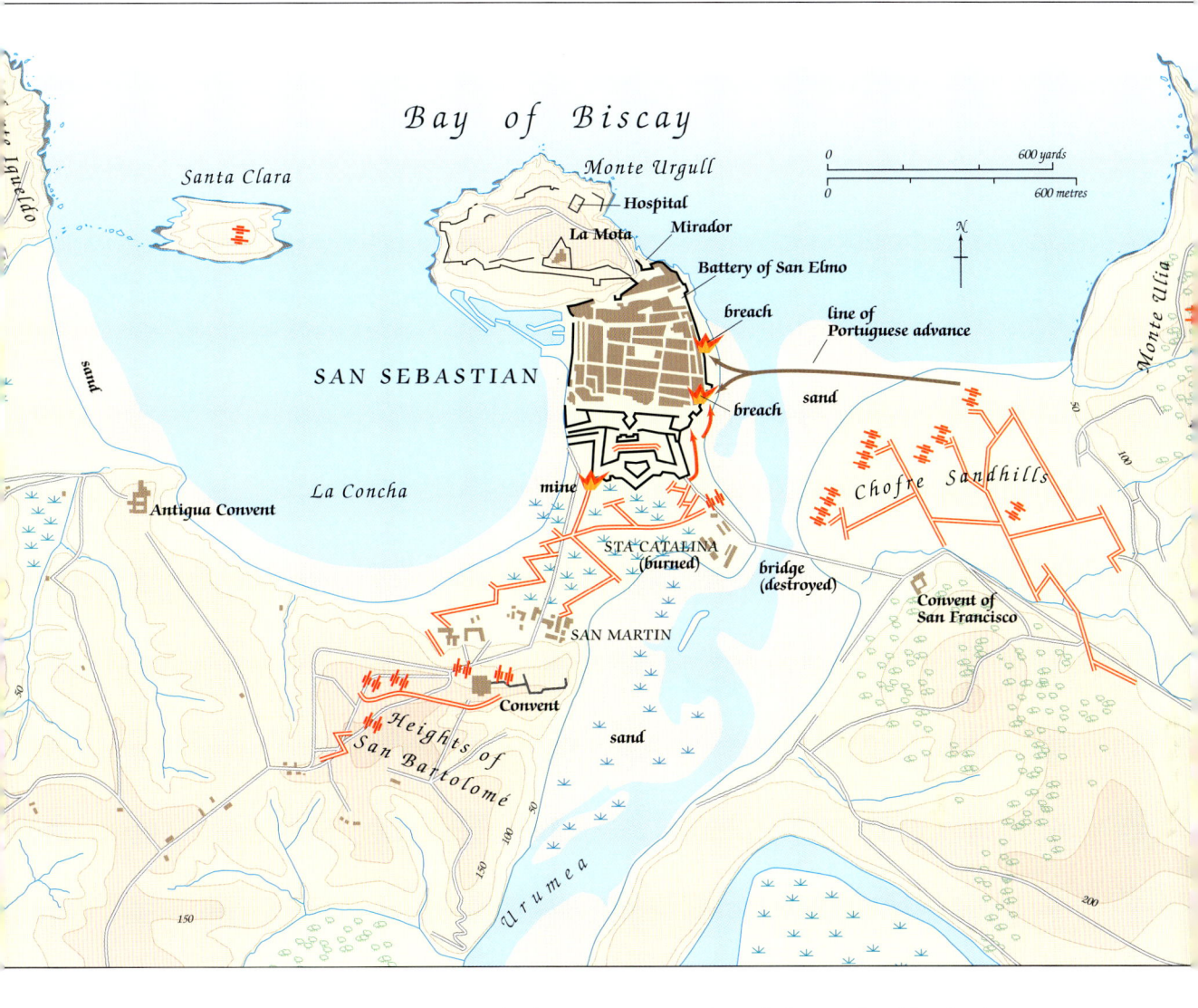

to allow it to be bombarded, as the most certain mode of forcing the enemy to give it up. This I positively would not allow for the same reason as I did not allow Ciudad Rodrigo or Badajoz to be bombarded; and yet if I had harboured as infamous a wish as to destroy the town from motives of commercial revenge, or any other, I could not have adopted a more certain method than to allow it to be bombarded.'

Rey and his garrison, encumbered by wounded and prisoners, although refusing the demand to surrender on 3 September, could not long resist the guns and mortars which continued to pound them, and with any remaining defences being levelled to the ground, and fearing the main magazine might explode, capitulated five days later, descending into the charred ruins to lay down their arms before bring be shipped off to England as prisoners.

Allied losses in the first assault were some 570; in the second they amounted to over 2,300, of which 870 were mortal, a high proportion of killed to wounded, largely caused by canister firing into a compact mass at close range.

1 There was mean difference of some 16 feet between tides.

2 Regrettably, he was killed by a musket ball only minutes before the assault commenced.

THE SIEGE OF SAN SEBASTIAN | 103

42 The Frontier Triangle

September 1813 to mid February 1814

During the ensuing winter months, almost all the fighting took place within the area confined to the south by the Bidasoa, there marking the frontier as far as Vera; and to the east by the river Nive (flowing north-east from St Jean-Pied-de-Port), which entered the Adour at Bayonne, at the apex of this triangle. There were political reasons also for the long lull,[1] but heavy rains in this region at that season made any extensive movement of troops and equipment a formidable operation.

Before Wellington placed any of his brigades in secure winter quarters, he had to occupy the line of commanding foothills between the coast and the peak of Artzamendi (926m) rising not far south of Itxassou (on the Nive upstream from Cambo), behind which, from such conveniently sited small ports as those of Pasajes and (later) St Jean-de-Luz, regular supplies of every kind could be distributed to them.[2]

Meanwhile, after mustering his dispersed forces, Soult deployed them along a discontinuous front extending inland for some 30 miles. Elaborate field fortifications and gun emplacements were constructed at every defensible site, the whole being supplied from his strongly fortified base at Bayonne, and the hinterland. Reille's divisions were placed near the coast, abutted by Clausel's, and extended to the east by those of D'Erlon.

Leading south from Bayonne, the main lines of communication were the highway running parallel to the coast to St Jean-de-Luz; a road bearing south-east up the Nive valley via Ustaritz towards Espelette and Ainhoa; and, between the two, a cross-country road via Arcangues and St Pée, which, not far south of the bridge of Amotz, divided to approach both Sare and Ainhoa.[3]

Behind Wellington's front, other than a track skirting the bank of the Bidasoa to Vera, there was no practicable direct route for wheeled vehicles between his left wing and the right, now facing Ainhoa.

---

1 It was not until 3 September that Wellington learned that Austria had re-entered the war against France, and another twelve days before he heard of Vandamme's defeat at Kulm.
2 Wellington was also provoked by contemptible behaviour on the part of the Spanish government, which expected the British not only to clothe and arm, but also to feed and pay, Spanish forces. Conflicting orders were also being sent to them behind his back after it had been agreed that he would be in overall command, while Spanish bureaucratic interference and inefficiency were also delaying the landing of essential supplies. Although he could rely on the troops of Longa, Giron, Mina, and Morillo, Wellington was justifiably reluctant to lead them into France, where their proclivity to plunder and take revenge would set the whole country against him.
3 Off the latter road, another veered towards Urdax, eventually ascending to the Col de Maya.

THE FRONTIER TRIANGLE

43 | The Combats at San Marcial and Vera

31 August 1813

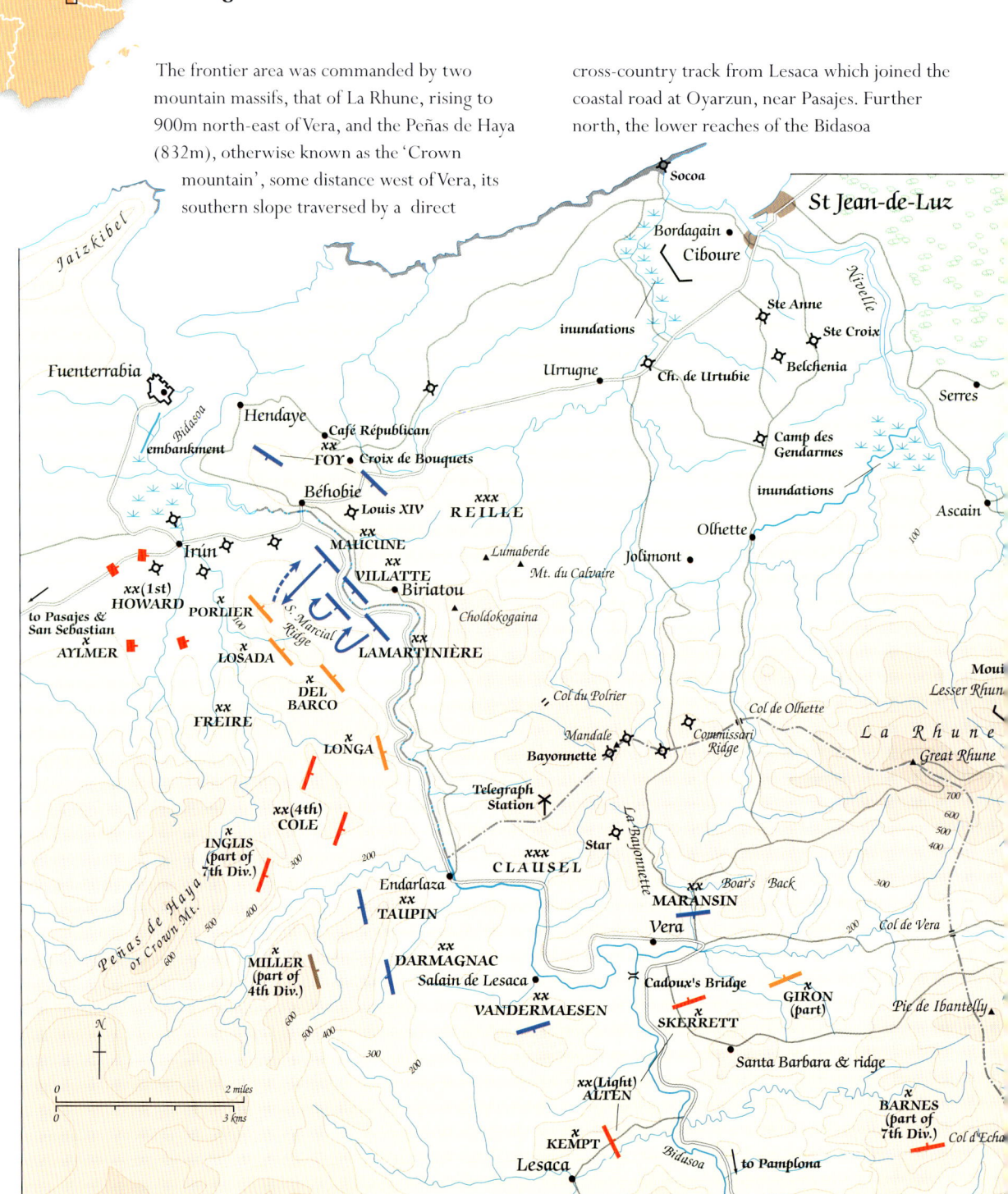

The frontier area was commanded by two mountain massifs, that of La Rhune, rising to 900m north-east of Vera, and the Peñas de Haya (832m), otherwise known as the 'Crown mountain', some distance west of Vera, its southern slope traversed by a direct cross-country track from Lesaca which joined the coastal road at Oyarzun, near Pasajes. Further north, the lower reaches of the Bidasoa immediately east of Irún were dominated by the ridge of San Marcial, along which three Spanish divisions commanded by Gen. Manuel Freire were deployed. Further inland, and as far as the gorge of the river, stood Longa's troops. These rocky narrows extended south for some 5 miles before the valley briefly opened out towards Vera.

On 31 August, the sound of the preliminary bombardment of San Sebastian (prior to the storming of the main breach) was drowned by the thunder of gunfire on the Bidasoa as Reille's four divisions waded across several fords below the village of Biriatou. They formed the northern of two diversionary thrusts – the second being made upstream near Vera by Clausel – in Soult's 11th-hour attempt to relieve the fortress.

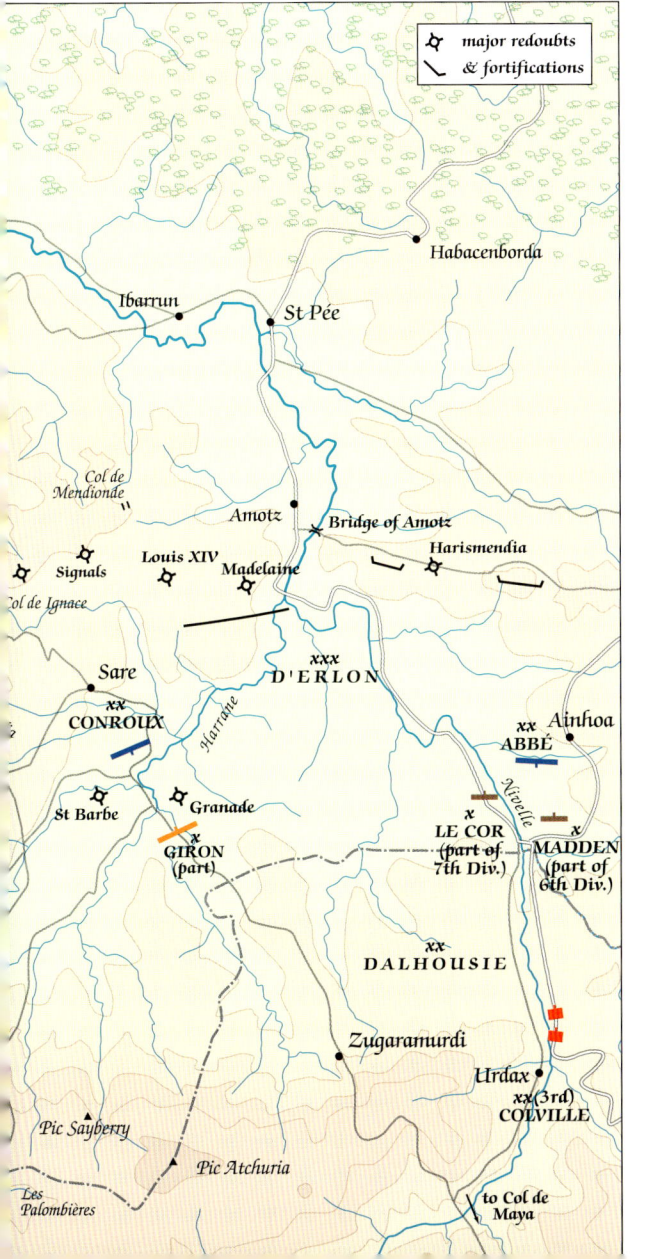

Two French columns, as they ascended the ridge of San Marcial through dense morning mist, were not expecting to be met by volleys at short range followed by a vigorous charge from Freire's Spaniards; and, after fierce hand-to-hand fighting, they were forced back towards the river bank. At noon, a third column had pressed forward and gained a foothold on the western end of the ridge. Freire sent an urgent request for help, but Wellington, who had been watching the proceedings from the Peñas de Haya, declined to send any, replying that the Spaniards had already shown their capacity to defeat the enemy, and could do so again, for the French, being unsupported, could not possibly hold the 300 yards of the crest.[1] Thus encouraged, the Spaniards counter-attacked, and indeed pushed the enemy back down to the Bidasoa.[2]

Wellington had already given orders to Dalhousie, on his right wing, to demonstrate against any probable attack by Clausel's divisions on his right flank while San Sebastian was being stormed. Although only desultory fighting took place in this sector, Soult felt his left wing sufficiently threatened to order Foy's Division back from its temporary position near the mouth of the Bidasoa to support D'Erlon's, guarding Soult's left flank.

Torrential rain flooded the fords by which Clausel's troops had advanced west from Vera that morning, and their eventual retreat across a narrow bridge under cover of darkness was delayed for two hours by Capt. Cadoux and 80 riflemen, who inflicted 200 casualties. Cadoux and many of his men were killed in this gallant action, in which Gen. Vandermaesen was mortally wounded.[3]

[1] Wellington had also noticed that the French, aware of his presence with additional troops, were already about to withdraw.
[2] Wellington later referred to having made the Spaniards win the action unaided, which in their account of the war 'is represented as one of their greatest battles – as a feat that does them the highest honour'. In fact, British officers who witnessed the engagement reported that as at one time so many ran away, a brigade of guards close to their position actually received orders to form a guard in order to 'stop all Spanish soldiers who were not wounded', one of them adding: 'had you seen the ground they were formed upon you would have said that it was impossible for the enemy ever to have come near them, nor could they have done so, had the Spaniards stood their ground like men'. Spanish casualties approached 1,700; those of the French were about 2,500.
[3] French casualties in this sector that day were at least 1,300; those of the Allies were some 850.

44 The Passage of the Bidasoa and the Ascent of La Rhune

7 October 1813

The position of certain stretches in the tidal estuary of the Bidasoa which might be fordable at low tide had been pointed out to Wellington as early as 15 September,[1] and as the next low tide would not occur until 7 October, he had time to prepare such a crossing. Although defended by earthworks, the French right flank (Reille's) was less heavily manned than their centre or left; and the latter, raided on 30 September, had put Soult on the alert.[2] At the centre of their line rose the massif of La Rhune, descending south from the bald 900m summit of which were two spurs, the more westerly (the Bayonette) pointing almost directly towards Vera, nearer which, at the intersection of a lateral ridge, stood the 'Star redoubt'. From a point further east, by the 'Boars' back' hill, a track climbed towards the Commissari ridge, forming the long western slope of the La Rhune. To attack this height, Wellington deployed the Light Division, supported by Longa's and Giron's Spaniards.

Meanwhile, three brigades of the 5th Division were brought forward and concealed behind fortifications and an embankment between Fuenterrabía and Irún,[3] in readiness to wade across the estuary through 3 feet of water, while the 1st Division waited further upstream nearer the fords traversed by the French a month earlier. They were supported by several other brigades, including Freire's Spaniards, and had pontoons at hand. There were thus 24,000 men ready to be unleashed against the thinnest section of Soult's extended line.

At 7.15 on the misty morning of the 7th, 'holding their firelocks and cartouche-boxes over their heads to keep them dry', the head of their columns being guided by local shrimpers, the 5th Division waded across the estuary, unsuspected and undetected by enemy picquets near the ruined hamlet of Hendaye, outflanked earthworks near the Croix de Bouquets (captured by 9am), and approached Urrugne, while the 1st Division were also half-way across the river before they were observed.

The progress of almost every operation further east went to plan, although stiffer resistance was met at earthworks on the lower southern slope of La Rhune. However, the summit was gained next day at comparatively little loss, for it was not by storming the height but by outflanking it, that it was made untenable. French casualties were heavier, and included several hundred cut off in intervening valleys by the ascending brigades. While the foothold on the north bank of the Bidasoa may not have been deep, the ascent of La Rhune enabled Wellington to dominate – not only visually – a wide sector of the enemy line, now extending inland for some 16 miles (as the crow flies) from St Jean-de-Luz.

1 These were across mud flats between Fuenterrabía and Irún, nearer the river mouth than those crossed by the French on 31 August.
2 On 1 October, Wellington himself had ridden over to Roncesvalles to inspect outposts, already experiencing flurries of snow. On the 5th, both the 2nd and 6th Divisions made a threatening move from the Col de Maya.
3 In part, this survives immediately west of the present airstrip.

The ridge of the Lesser Rhune seen from the summit of La Rhune.

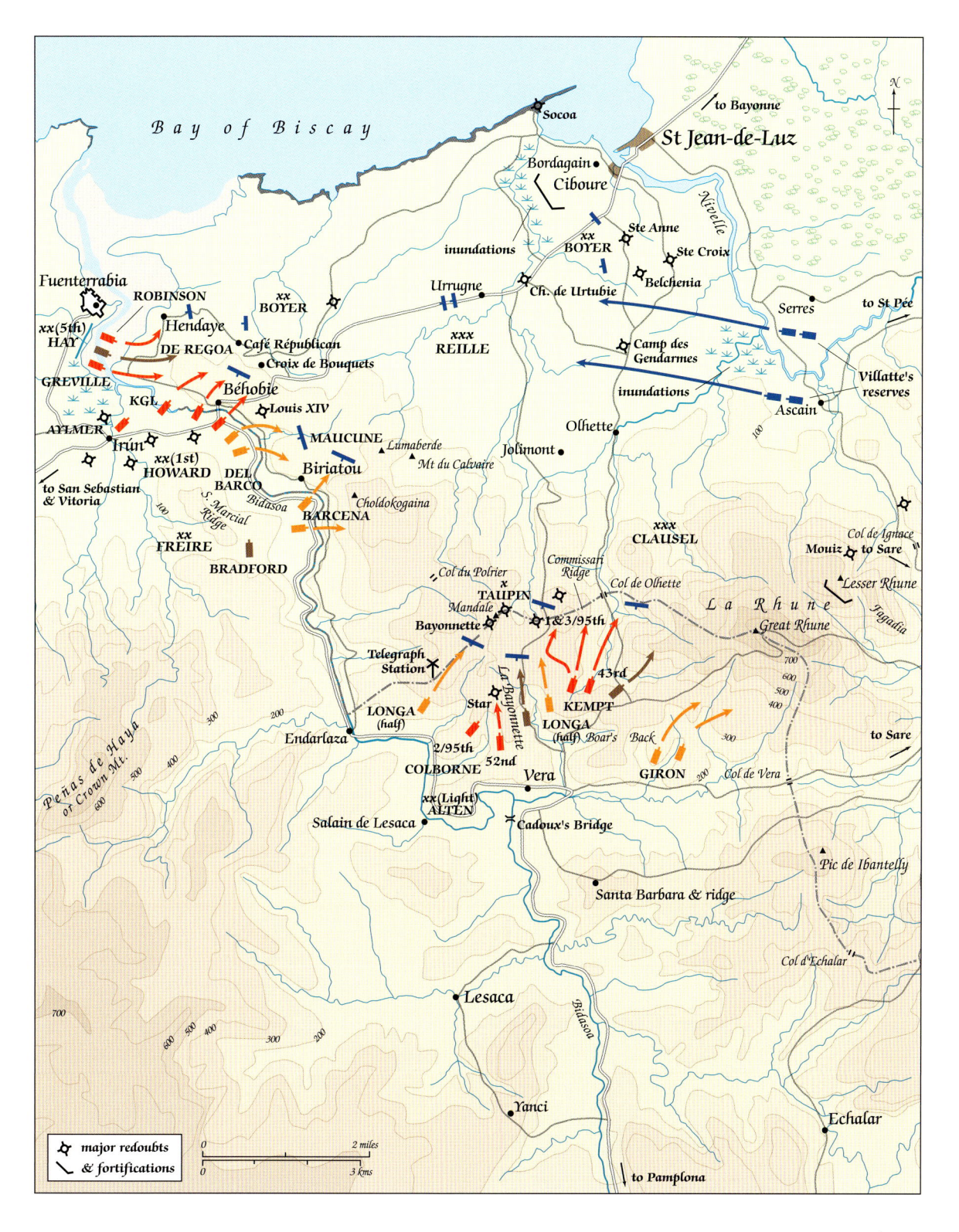

The Passage of the Bidasoa and the Ascent of La Rhune | 109

45 The Battle of the Nivelle

10 November 1813

Soult, who had received reinforcements, still appeared to rely on a static line of earthworks and artillery emplacements, which extended along a series of low ridges rising south of the river Nivelle, of no great consequence in itself. In the seaward sector, from just north of Urrugne to Ascain (one third of his defensive line, and where he had been surprised on 7 October) he had placed Reille's three divisions, with three or four in reserve. Another five (commanded by Clausel and D'Erlon) were deployed along the remaining two-thirds of his front, extending east beyond the bridge of Amotz towards the Pic de Mondarrain; but, as Wellington observed to Colborne, '… the enemy have not enough to man all those works and lines they occupy. I can pour a greater force on certain points than they can concentrate to resist me.'

Below the north-east flank of La Rhune projected the rocky ridge of the Lesser Rhune,[1] which formed a key forward bastion, still in French hands, but one difficult to hold should Wellington decide to break through there. Any such thrust would require careful planning. It was intended initially to take place during the last week of October, although the timing was contingent on the capitulation of Pamplona,[2] and was then delayed by appalling weather until 10 November.

The plan was that the 1st and 5th Divisions among other troops on the coastal sector, now commanded by Gen. Hope (Graham being obliged to take sick leave), would drive in outposts and make strong demonstrations only, but not commit themselves to any serious action.

The bulk of the Allied army was divided into two 'Corps': one commanded by Beresford (with whom Wellington remained throughout), consisting of the 3rd,[3] 4th, 7th,[4] the Light Division, and Longa's and Giron's Spaniards. Hill's usual units were reinforced by the 6th Division (Clinton), and Hamilton's Portuguese brigade. Together, these two Corps numbered some 55,000 men, who would make a concerted attack between Ascain and the Mondarrain, defended by only 40,000.

While Morillo's Spaniards, on his far right wing, threatened the Mondarrain, Wellington's massive thrust commenced at dawn on the 10th, with the Light Division making the difficult approach to and, from its western end, assaulting the several defensive works on the Lesser Rhune, which were in their hands by 8am. By 9am, the village of Sare (below the north-east flank of La Rhune) had been entered by the 4th Division; by 11am the 3rd had taken possession of the bridge of Amotz (by the road to St Pée, which provided a vital lateral communication between the French left and right). Hill's Corps had crossed the Nivelle west of the village of Ainhoa, which was occupied by Hamilton's Portuguese by noon.

However elaborate were the fortifications prepared to hold his line, Soult could not stem the overwhelming tide of those opposing him. By mid afternoon Hill and Beresford had taken all their immediate objectives, and the enemy abandoned their positions (including 59 pieces of artillery) and, with their right flank seriously threatened, retired towards Bayonne.[5]

Hope's troops had demonstrated effectively enough to ensure that the 23,000 facing them remained pinned down, unable to reinforce Soult's centre. Hope occupied Urrugne and approached Ascain without great losses.

In the day's fighting, Anglo-Portuguese casualties were about 2,450; those of the Spaniards, some 800. French losses were 4,350 (2,900 among Clausel's three divisions alone, including 1,200 prisoners); but in the seaward sector they had less than 500 casualties. On both sides, the ratio of officers to other ranks killed was unusually heavy: 1 to 11.

If not the most resounding of Wellington's victories, undeservedly remaining in the shadow of the more spectacular actions at Salamanca and Vitoria, the battle of the Nivelle was one of the most brilliantly conceived operations of the Peninsular War.

1 Altxanga in Basque.
2 This took place on 31 October.
3 Commanded by Colville, replacing Picton, who was on leave.
4 Temporarily under Le Cor, Dalhousie being on leave.
5 Contrary to D'Erlon's order to join him, Foy had advanced south-west and caused some mischief to Hill's rear, before being brought to a halt by Morillo's troops, but then retreated to Cambo to avoid being cut off entirely.

THE BATTLE OF THE NIVELLE

46 THE BATTLE OF THE NIVE
9–10 December 1813

The Allies needed to pause for breath. They were now faced with a hard nut to crack, for Bayonne, straddling both banks of the Nive at its confluence with the Adour,[1] was the most powerful military base in south-west France, surrounded by a complex of Vaubanesque fortifications, and with a substantial garrison which could be reinforced and re-supplied by roads converging on it from the depot of Mont-de-Marsan and from Pau. The Nive was a more serious obstacle than the Nivelle. Although fordable in certain places, its flow was unpredictable, the level rising substantially after heavy rains or melting snow in the Pyrenees.

The French front now extended east from the sea-side hamlet of Biarritz, through the village of Arcangues, to reach the Nive opposite Villefranque. Their bridgehead on the west bank at Cambo had been withdrawn on 16 November.

Wellington, with his headquarters at St Jean-de-Luz from 17 November until late February, planned to continue operations by crossing the Nive between Bayonne and Cambo once the rains ceased and the roads were again practicable, but he was faced with a problem with regard to the Spanish contingents.[2] He still had over 63,000 infantry at hand (36,000 British, 23,000 Portuguese, and Morillo's 4,500 veterans). Three of Soult's divisions faced him on the far bank, supported by cavalry and artillery, while Gen. Paris's division stood further south-east: altogether some 54,500 infantry, plus the sedentary garrison of Bayonne, an additional 8,800.

On 9 December, the day after Wellington had learned of Napoleon's defeat at Leipzig, Hill's Corps waded across fords in the Nive near Cambo and, leaving Morillo to guard their right flank, veered north parallel to the river, later followed by the 6th Division, which had crossed further downstream on pontoons. The three divisions facing them retired on Bayonne. Hope, with the 1st, 5th, and Light Divisions, together with other brigades, also pushed north towards the batteries defending the entrenched camps south of the fortress, there leaving a line of outposts before pulling back.[3] Unwisely, the 1st Division and Aylmer's brigade retired too far, almost to St Jean-de-Luz, which delayed their appearance next day, when Soult counter-attacked.

Early on the 10th, Hope's picquets were attacked in force. The Light Division, opposed by four enemy divisions, put up a stubborn defence at Arcangues, having hastily fortified the church, while the 7th Division, to their east, also brought the French thrust to a halt. Units further west, defending Château Barrouillet, found themselves hard pressed until the 5th Division, with Hope in person, belatedly reached the front, which tilted the precarious balance in their favour.[4] In this 'Battle of the Nive', casualties on both sides were between 1,700 and 2,000, including several hundred prisoners taken when Hope's picquets were overrun. Additional casualties were suffered in indecisive fighting on this front during the following two days. Meanwhile, Hill had moved closer to Bayonne, taking up a semicircular position between the Nive and the Adour.

---

1 The right bank of the Adour was dominated by a strongly bastioned citadel.
2 Longa's troops had plundered and committed atrocities on entering Ascain, causing Wellington to sacrifice his numerical superiority by sending the majority of his Spanish units back across the frontier: he could not rely on them to desist, nor could he afford to provoke the well-disposed civilian population into any form of 'guerrilla war' against his occupying forces.
3 Beyond the strongly-fortified town walls (and moat) lay Soult's entrenched camps of Beyris (south-west), Marracq (south), and Mousseroles (south-east, on the right bank of the Nive). A redoubt defended the highway from St Jean-de-Luz, while the Château de Marrac (burnt out in 1824) formed the main southern bastion of his outer defences south of the Adour. The far bank and the surrounding area were commanded by swivel guns from the citadel.
4 The Château at Barrouillet (or Barroilhet) is a simple mansion often referred to as 'the Mayor House' (being that of the mayor of Biarritz at the time). It survives high above the *péage* or toll on the present motorway, and may be approached from the main road south of the Lac de Mouriscot.

THE BATTLE OF THE NIVE

47 The Battle of St Pierre

13 December 1813

Soult had deliberately withdrawn his troops within the entrenched camps immediately south of Bayonne. From there, he could attack the Allies on either side of the Nive in force while holding them at the other. But Wellington had the foresight to order up a pontoon bridge (defended by the 3rd Division) to span the river at Villefranque, by which he could reinforce Hill's Corps. This was in position by midday on the 11th. The 4th and 7th Divisions remained west of the Nive, while the 6th was nearer Ustaritz.

During the night of the 12th, ominous sounds of Soult's artillery rumbling across the bridges at Bayonne were heard at Hill's camp, which alerted him to expect an attack next day; but this coincided with a sudden rise in the level of the Nive, causing the bridge at Villefranque to give way, thus isolating him.

His hilly 3 mile-long front in the ensuing action (named after the suburban village of St Pierre d'Irube) was divided by mill-ponds into three sectors, the central one traversed by a road; on the ridge nearer the Adour stood the hamlet of Vieux Mouguerre;[1] while a track leading to Villafranque, traversing a lower wooded area, skirted the hill-top Château Larraldea.[2] The latter area was held by Pringle's Brigade of the 2nd Division; Byng's Brigade was positioned on the northern ridge; the rest of the division (Barnes's Brigade and Ashworth's Portuguese) manned the central sector in depth, with Le Cor's troops (Buchan, and Da Costa) held in reserve behind the hill of Horlopo.

Pringle's 1,800 found themselves faced by the approach of 5,000 under Daricau, but were able to hold him at bay: the château was attacked, but never taken.[3] Heavily outnumbered by Foy, Byng's forward units were forced back towards the rest, their position on the Mouguerre ridge being regained after eventually receiving reinforcements. It was Hill's centre, with Stewart in local command, that was most strongly attacked; but with the aid of two batteries of artillery trained on the ascending road, and feeding in units from his reserves, Soult's columns were brought to a halt and held well below the crest for three hours.

Although the struggle was becoming critical, by then Hill was aware that the pontoon bridge had been replaced, enabling the 3rd Division to cross, and that the 6th was also approaching rapidly, having forded the Nive at Ustaritz. Knowing that substantial reinforcements were now close at hand, he ordered a counter-attack which turned the tide of battle, won virtually unaided (although by then Wellington himself had ridden up), and against heavy odds. Hill's casualties (1,775) were light when compared to the 3,300 suffered by Soult, whose troops retired within the perimeter of Bayonne's defences.

---

1 A commemorative obelisk known as the Croix de Mouguerre has embellished a view-point at the western extremity of the ridge since 1917.

2 Its remains were in a forlorn state when last seen by the author.

3 Pringle inflicted 450 casualties, but suffered only 130.

THE BATTLE OF ST PIERRE | 115

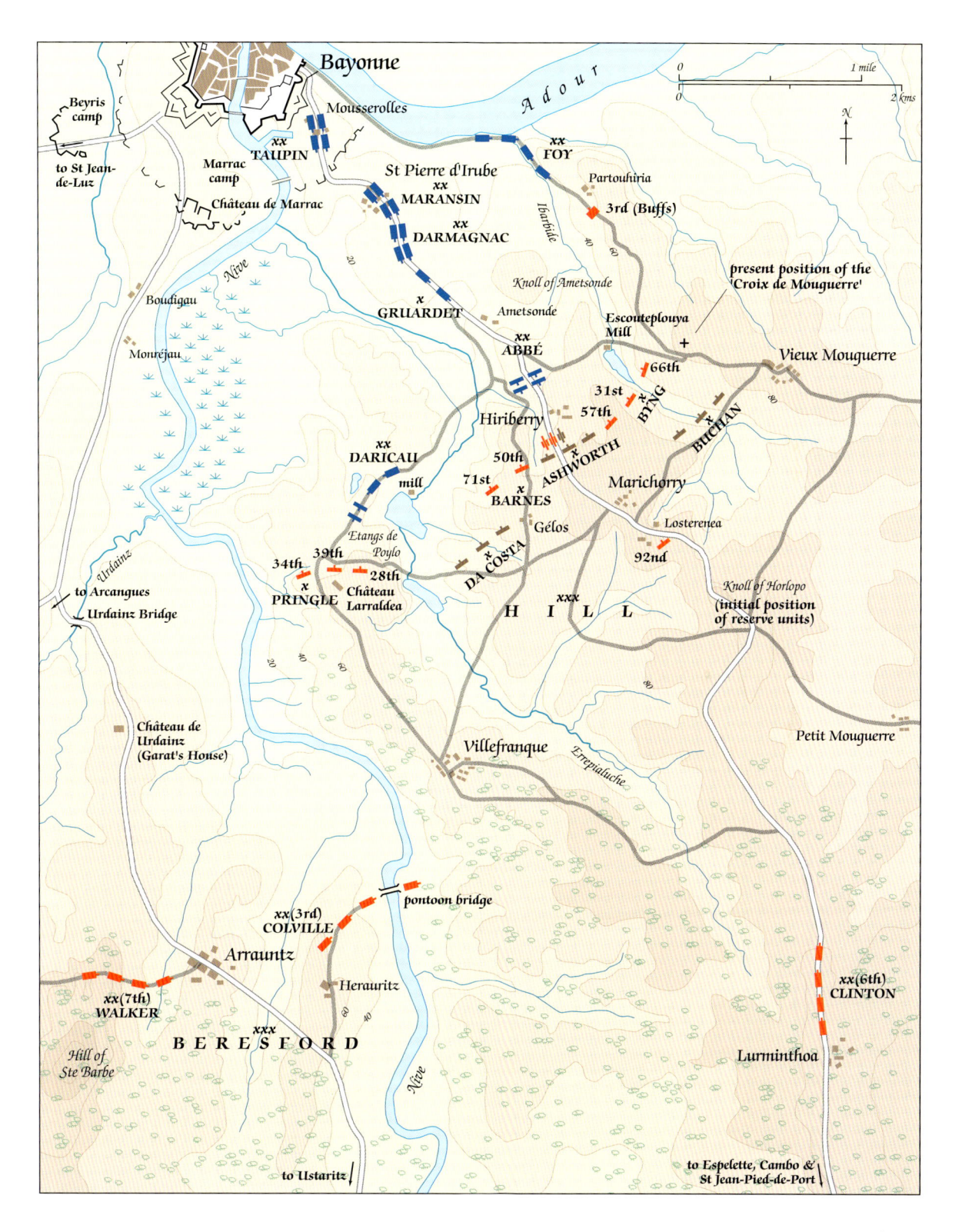

48 Bayonne: the Investment; and the Sortie (14 April 1814)

Mid December 1813 to 14 April, 1814

It was now Wellington's plan to isolate Bayonne, already quite closely invested, but it was hazardous to attempt any crossing of the Adour while Soult's forces remained concentrated in its vicinity. It was essential to lure the majority of them to the east by threatening to cut them off from the hinterland. He could then cross the Adour near its mouth in order to encircle the fortress.[1] Henry Sturgeon of the Engineers was entrusted with the design of a form of 'bridge of boats', taking into account the strong currents and heavy tides in the lower reaches of the river.[2] The passage of the Adour did not take place until the 23 February, when Stopford's brigade was ferried across on skiffs, rafts, and pontoons; the bridge was laid by the 26th, and the investment of Bayonne completed next day.

Wellington was aware also that Soult had a problem of logistics, for both the civilian population and the garrison of Bayonne (commanded by Gen. Thouvenot) had to be kept supplied with food.[3] If his field army of 60,000 remained in the vicinity for even a week, it would reduce for almost two months the length of time the garrison could hold out.

Meanwhile, by placing some of his artillery east along the south bank of the Adour, Wellington could stop any barges – even if defended by gun-boats – from entering the town, except possibly during the night.

In the event, on 14 December Soult had started moving inland, setting up his headquarters at Peyrehorade, some 20 miles upstream.[4]

***

It was at Bayonne, still with a garrison of 12,000 (to which it had been reduced by sickness and desertion) and, encircled by Hope's troops,[5] that the last action of the Peninsular War took place. Thouvenot stubbornly held out, his swivel guns on the citadel's walls keeping the Allies at arms' length, and even when receiving the extraordinary news late at night on 11 April of Napoleon's abdication, he refused to credit it, not having received official confirmation from Soult. Two nights later, Hope was warned by a deserter that a sortie might take place, so was not entirely surprised at 3am in the morning of the 14th, when a feint was made from the southern line of fortifications, but he did not expect that the sortie from the north side of citadel by 3,000 men in two columns would be in such strength.

Edmund Wheatley, *Sketch of the damaged church of St Etienne, seen from the Jewish Cemetery.*

Breaking through his picquet line, one column overran the suburb of St Etienne, where Gen. Hay was killed. Both Hope and Gen. Stopford were wounded in the confused night fighting, and command devolved on Gen. Colville. The serious situation was not resolved until Gen. Hinüber's KGL units counter-attacked from the suburb of St Esprit, and the second column was repulsed by the 1st Guards Brigade. The Allies suffered some 600 unnecessary casualties in this pointless action, for which there was no military justification, while those of the French were about 900. Thouvenot did not formally surrender until the 27th, on receiving Soult's copy of the armistice.[6]

1 Major John Burgoyne of the Engineers had already cursorily surveyed the area after traversing the pine-woods north of Biarritz.
2 Its preparation, construction, and the actual crossing, are described briefly in the present author's *Wellington invades France*, and in more detail by Robert Burnham in *Inside Wellington's Peninsular Army*.
3 The civilian population at this time was approximately 13,000.
4 Reille, with four divisions, remained in the vicinity of Bayonne; three others manned the intervening right bank, while those of Daricau and Harispe stayed on the left to attack the Allied flank, should it attempt to cross. Soult still had 77 field-guns and a cavalry division to hand.
5 Outposts of the 1st Division were stationed on the right bank of the Adour, with the 5th on the south, supported by three brigades of infantry and one of cavalry.
6 The cordon of blockade was not withdrawn until 4 May.

BAYONNE: THE INVESTMENT; AND THE SORTIE | 117

49 THE ADVANCE ON ORTHEZ, AND THE COMBAT AT GARRIS

12–27 February 1814

It was not until 10 January 1814 that Wellington was aware that the armies of Russia, Prussia, and Austria had crossed the Rhine late in December and that the general invasion of France was in progress. To combat this, Napoleon requisitioned half Soult's cavalry, which were making their way north on 16 January, followed three days' later by three infantry divisions: altogether some 14,000 veteran troops.[1] He was assured that reinforcements would reach him in the form of reserve battalions and recruits being assembled at Toulouse, which was little compensation.

On 12 February, after a week of fine weather, having left Hope with 18,000 men south of Bayonne ready to tighten the blockade (reinforced by several thousand Spaniards not yet repatriated), the first of seven Allied divisions commenced their march east.[2] Hill's column (with Picton's 3rd in echelon with him) formed the right wing, with Morillo's Spaniards on his flank. Beresford's column (initially the 4th and 7th Divisions, followed later by the Light and 6th) advanced further north, with heavy cavalry brigades on their left flank, parallel to the Adour. Although Soult attempted to hold that river line, his front extended from Peyrehorade (his HQ) to the old fortress of Navarrenx,[3] a distance of over 30 miles, impossible to defend with only four divisions against the overwhelming numbers pressing on him. He was forced to withdraw additional troops from near Bayonne,[4] which was precisely what Wellington had intended.

In the face of Hill's thrust, Gen. Harispe had abandoned the line of the Joyeuse, but on the 15th, with 7,000 men at hand, he briefly put up a stout resistance to Hill's attack on the ridge-sited village of Garris before retreating over the Bidouze at St Palais and blowing up the bridge behind him.[5]

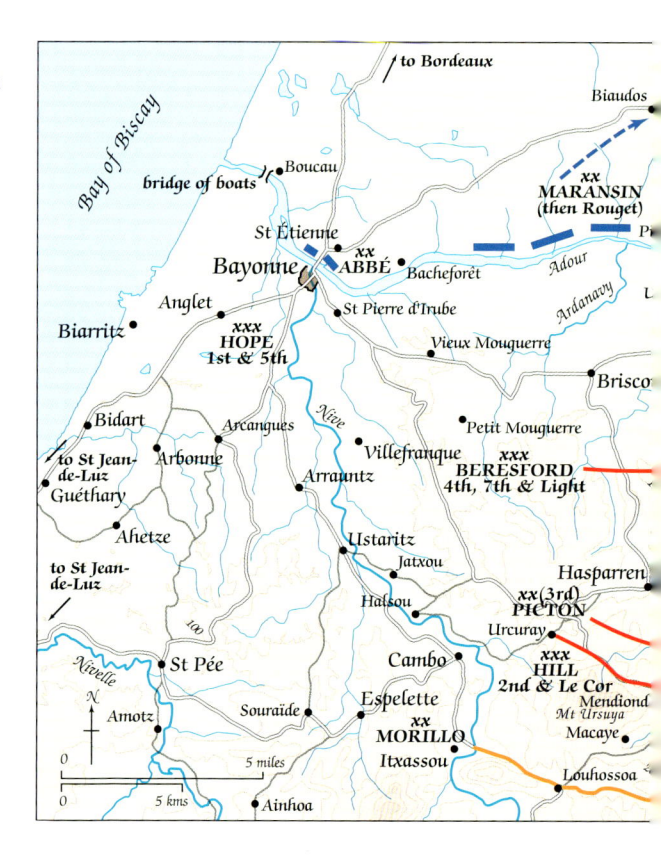

---

1 Suchet, in Catalonia, had received similar orders, and 8,000 infantry and 2,000 cavalry had started north on the road from Perpignan to Lyon by 24 January.
2 These were the 2nd, 3rd, 4th, 6th, 7th, Light, and Le Cor's Portuguese, together with Morillo's Spaniards, and three light cavalry brigades: a total of some 43,000 infantry and 2,500 cavalry. Their progress is described in detail in Oman's *History*, vol. VII, pp. 315–29, and 341–50.
3 Later invested by Morillo's units.
4 One division only (Abbé's) was left to reinforce the garrison.
5 The bridge was soon repaired. Much of the skirmishing here took place south-west of Garris, between the hill of Tourouna and the farm of Duronia, further west. Allied casualties amounted to some 170, but Harispe's were heavy: some 500, including 200 taken prisoner.

While demonstrations in force by the 4th and 7th Divisions were made against both Peyrehorade and Sauveterre (near the confluence of the Saison with the Gave d'Oloron), the 6th and Light Divisions marched south-east from Hasparren and La Bastide-Clarence respectively to strengthen Hill's column. On the 24th, Picton's 3rd Division forded the Saison near Rivareyte and Osserain and, after suffering some losses, traversed the Gave d'Oloron and the bridge at Sauveterre next day. Meanwhile, the river had been crossed at fords further upstream, enabling the rest of Hill's column to swing north and approach the transpontine suburb of Orthez.

Meanwhile, the 4th and 7th Divisions, having forded the Gave de Pau near Lahontan, converged with the 3rd, which was crossing the Gave downstream from the broken bridge at Bérenx. The Light Division followed in their wake, and by dawn on the 27th Wellington had five divisions and two cavalry brigades on the north bank of the Gave de Pau: Soult's defensive line had been completely turned.

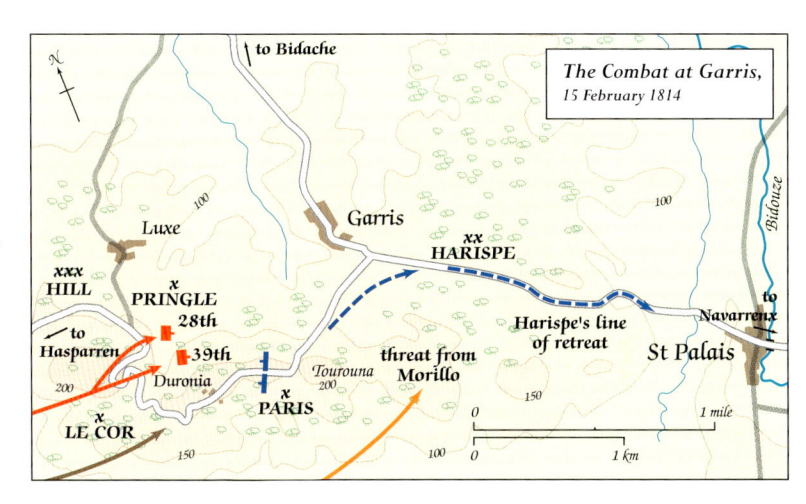

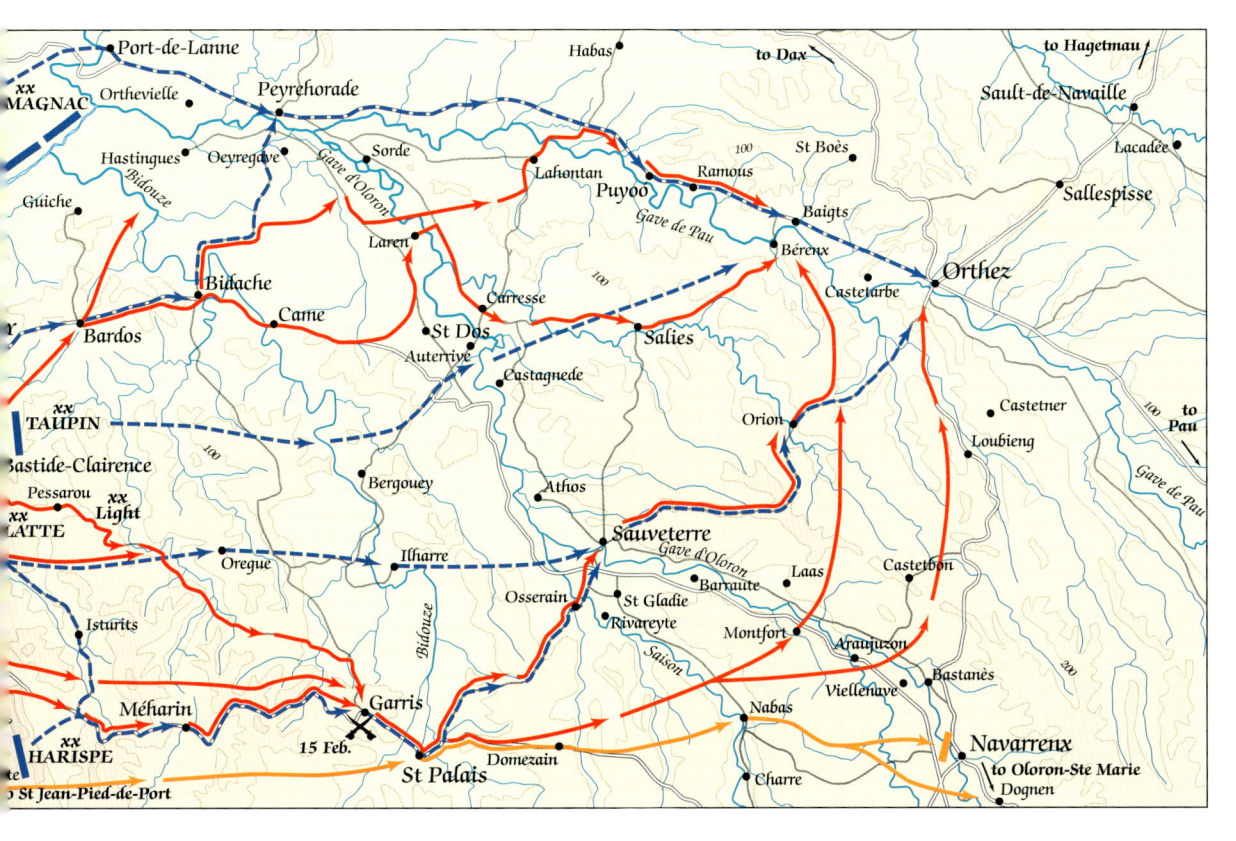

The Combat at Garris, 15 February 1814

THE ADVANCE ON ORTHEZ | 119

50 The Battle of Orthez

27 February 1814

Hill, with the 2nd and Le Cor's Divisions, plus some light cavalry (some 13,000 men altogether), remained on the south bank of the Gave de Pau, with orders to demonstrate only, but blatantly, against Orthez for the time being.[1] At about 11am Hill's Corps started to cross by the upstream fords of Souars to turn the French left flank, a successful operation meeting comparatively slight resistance.

Meanwhile, Wellington, with some 31,000 men,[2] approached Soult's four divisions (those of Taupin, Rouget, Darmagnac, and Foy) deployed along an L-shaped ridge rising north of the town, from which several spurs

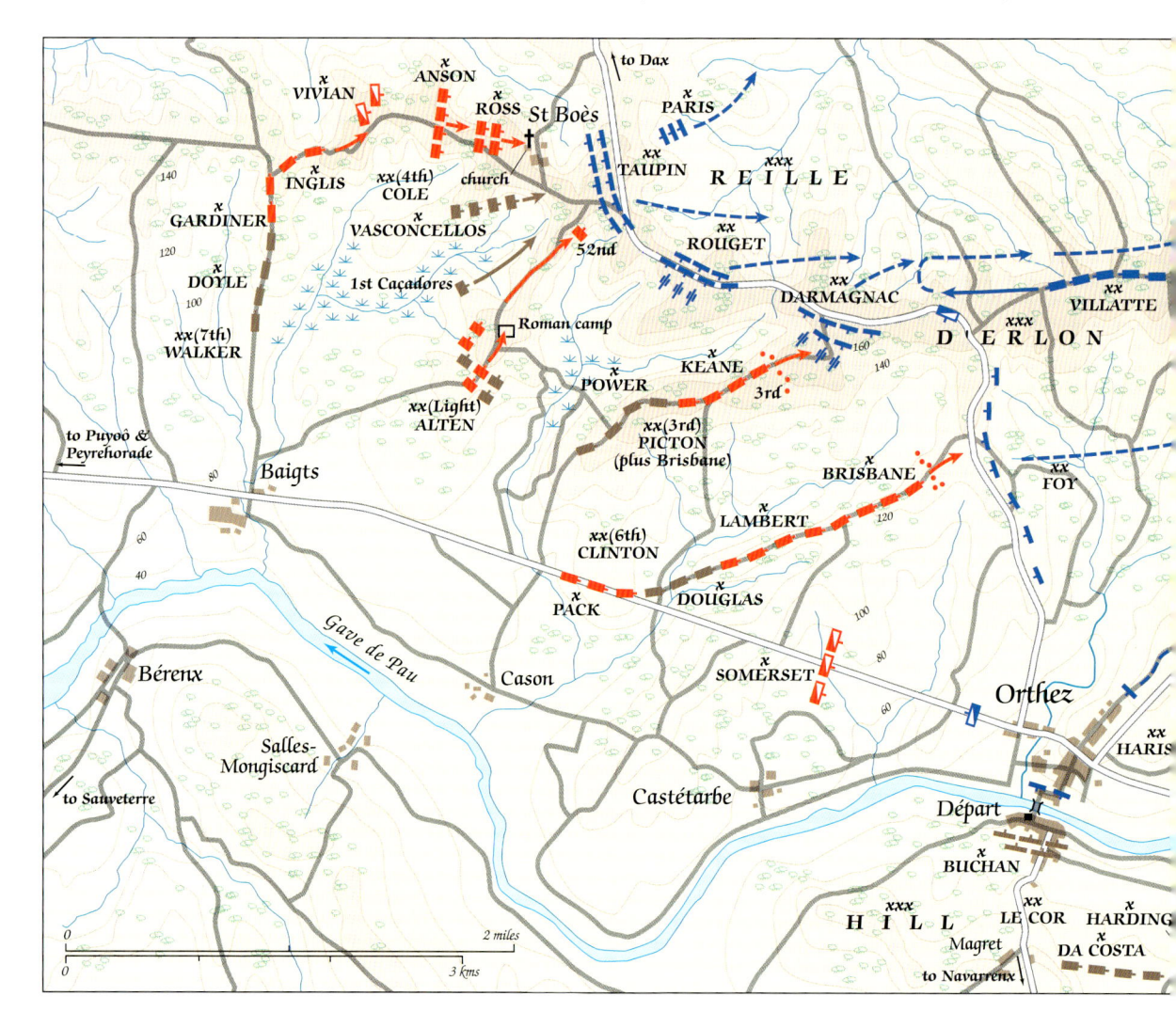

120   AN ATLAS OF THE PENINSULAR WAR

descended. Harispe's Division was posted further east, with Villatte's in reserve, altogether some 36,000.[3] On the western extremity of the main ridge stood the village church of St Boès, not far south of which rose a hill on which were remains of a Roman camp.

The action commenced soon after 8.30am with the 4th Division ascending from the village of Baigts, the 7th in support, attacking St Boès; but Ross's Brigade, although clearing the churchyard, was unable to occupy the strongly defended village, and a second attempt also failed. The Light Division now occupied the hill on which stood the Roman camp, from which Wellington directed operations further east, where the 3rd and 6th Divisions started to ascend two parallel spurs, the intervening valleys being waterlogged and impassable for artillery. With the 3rd being forced to halt out of range of Soult's guns, a lull in the fighting took place, during which several units were redeployed, among them Brisbane's Brigade of the 3rd, the 6th in its wake, advancing up the easternmost spur towards Foy's Division.

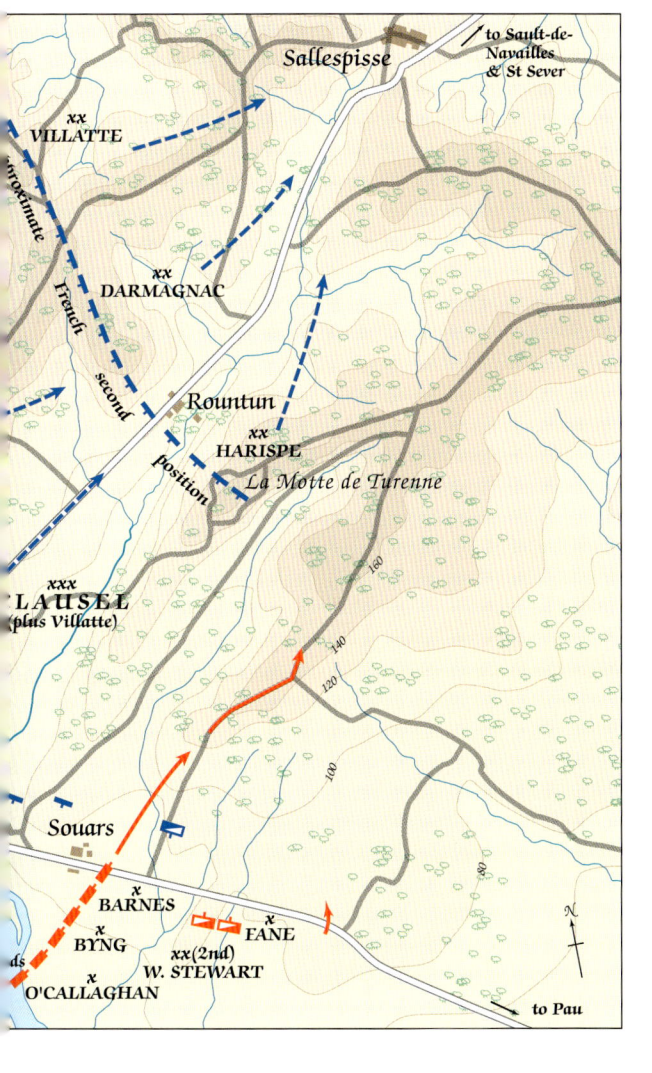

When Foy himself was severely wounded in the ensuing action and carried to the rear, his troops began to give way, exposing other units which began to retreat in disorder, while Harispe's two battalions, nearer Orthez, retired in haste to avoid being cut off. After putting up a strong resistance, Darmagnac's men in the French centre now gave way. They were able to form a defensive line facing west between Villatte's and Harispe's redeployed units, only to sustain destructive artillery fire from batteries by then brought forward, while Taupin's troops on the right flank were now forced out of St Boès.

What had been a reasonably orderly withdrawal now became a confused flight, as the French streamed north-east, after a rearguard action at Sallespisse, to converge on the bridge over the Luy de Béarn at Sault-de-Navailles,[4] from which their retreat continued towards Hagetmau. Soult's casualties at Orthez had been over 4,000 (including numerous prisoners), double those of the Allies.

1 The river was – and is still – spanned here by an imposing medieval bridge, the approach to which was blocked.
2 An additional 7,500 under Freire, ordered forward from before Bayonne, did not catch up with the Allied army until 4 March.
3 The Allies had the superiority in both men and guns.
4 It was here that Wellington – having on this rare occasion been wounded during a battle, when a bullet had forced his sword hilt against his thigh, seriously bruising it – established his Headquarters that night.

THE BATTLE OF ORTHEZ

51 The Advance on Bordeaux, Tarbes, and Toulouse

27 February to 26 March 1814

Soult's communications with Bayonne were severed by his defeat at Orthez. On 1 March, Beresford, with the Light Division, pushed north to capture extensive enemy magazines at Mont-de-Marsan; and on the same day Wellington reached and crossed the Adour at St Sever, which remained his Headquarters until 10 March. Meanwhile, he received a communication from the mayor of Bordeaux that, if supported by Allied troops, he would declare against Napoleon. Beresford, with the 4th and 7th Divisions, was immediately ordered to march north via Bazas and Langon, entering the city unopposed on the 12th.[1] On the 18th, Beresford proceeded south-east to rejoin the main army, leaving Dalhousie (with the 7th) in charge at Bordeaux until the cessation of hostilities.[2] Meanwhile, Adm. Penrose had entered the Gironde with a naval force, swept the estuary of French men-of-war, and destroyed defensive batteries along its banks.

Hill's Corps, marching east from St Sever along the south bank of the river, found no opposition until approaching Aire-sur-Adour. However, the 3rd and 6th Divisions, on the far bank, after traversing Grenade, encountered D'Erlon's two Divisions at Cazères-sur-Adour, from which they were forced back towards Reille's two, also north of Aire. But Soult, assuming the whole Allied army was approaching, prudently gave way, withdrawing his troops north of the river towards Barcelonne, unaware of Hill's threatening thrust further south. For the ensuing action at Aire, see Map 52.

By now reinforced by Freire's Spaniards from Bayonne and Morillo's from Navarrenx, Wellington divided his army into three 'Corps', with the intention of pinning Soult against the Pyrenees.[3] Units under Beresford, now forming Wellington's left wing, had swung round via Plaisance to Rabastens by the 20th, cutting two of Soult's lines of retreat north-east. Wellington, with the central column, advanced through St Mont, Viella (HQ on 18 March), Madiran, Maubourguet (19th), and Vic-en-Bigorre, towards Tarbes, while Hill, forming his right wing,[4] was approaching Tarbes rapidly from the north-west via Conchez and Lembeye: for the combat at Tarbes, see Map 52.

The Allies, dragging their siege guns and pontoon trains across country along poor roads and over a series of ridges fanning out from the Pyrenees, were to take seven days to cover a distance the French marched in four. Hill's Corps, following on the heels of Soult's main force, entered and descended the Garonne valley to approach Muret. From Tarbes, and then Tournay, Headquarters progressed north-east through Galan (22nd), Boulogne-sur-Gesse (23rd), L'Isle-en-Dodon (24th), and Samatan (25th), to enter St Lys next day. The left flank was guarded by Beresford's units, while squadrons of cavalry rode ahead as far as Auch and Gimont, searching in vain for any trace of enemy troops in that general direction

1 Vandeleur's dragoons, progressing directly across the desolate Landes from Dax, would also be converging on the city.
2 Troops marching south in an attempt to recapture the city, were defeated by Dalhousie in a minor action on 7 April at Etauliers, north-east of Blaye on the Garonne estuary.
3 By retiring south towards Tarbes, Soult had intended to lure the Allies away from the main road east via Auch, which might give more time to strengthen the defences of Toulouse, and then attack their most advanced and isolated columns. In the event, Wellington kept his columns closely linked, and Soult was to find himself threatened by not only a concentrated frontal attack, but also a wide turning movement against his right flank.
4 Hill commanded some 13,000; Beresford 12,000; the central column was about 25,000 strong.

THE ADVANCE ON BORDEAUX, TARBES, AND TOULOUSE | 123

52 | The Combats at Aire, and Tarbes

2 March, and 20 March 1814

Soult was under the impression that Hill had crossed to the right bank of the Adour near Grenade, and thus Clausel's troops, deployed along a wooded ridge rising at right-angles immediately west of the small town of Aire, with his right (Villatte) close to the river,[1] and extended by Harispe's brigades, were taken by surprise. The position overlooked a rivulet flowing north into the Adour, towards which two minor roads converged.

Suddenly, in the early afternoon of 2 March, Villatte found his position being assaulted by Barnes's Brigade, with Byng's in its wake, followed by Harding's Portuguese, while Harispe, about a mile further south, was attacked by Da Costa's Brigade of Le Cor's Division. Villatte's troops were forced back towards the town, with the 71st hard on their heels; but when charged by Dauture's brigade, Da Costa's men were forced back downhill. Seeing this temporary reverse, Stewart detached the 50th and 92nd of Barnes's brigade to advance south along the saddle of the ridge to take Dauture in flank, a movement which forced Clausel's two divisions apart, with Harispe's Brigade retreating south, and Villatte's to the south-east.[2]

Although a spirited rear-guard action was fought at Vic-Bigorre on 19 March,[3] D'Erlon, once aware that the advancing Light Division threatened to turn his right flank, withdrew south towards Tarbes as darkness fell. During that night, the rest of Soult's army started to cross the one bridge spanning the Adour at Tarbes, to take up a defensive position along the first of several ridge of hills to the east. Clausel's divisions were then deployed to guard Soult's right flank and the road leading north-east towards Trie-sur-Baïse. Reille's would cover the subsequent withdrawal of D'Erlon's Corps, and together they would retire up the road ascending steeply south-east to Tournay, along which Soult's convoys of equipment, artillery, and wounded were already in motion towards Toulouse.

At dawn on the 20th, the two Allied columns were advancing south along roads from Vic-en-Bigorre and Rabastens, converging on Tarbes. At about noon, on passing

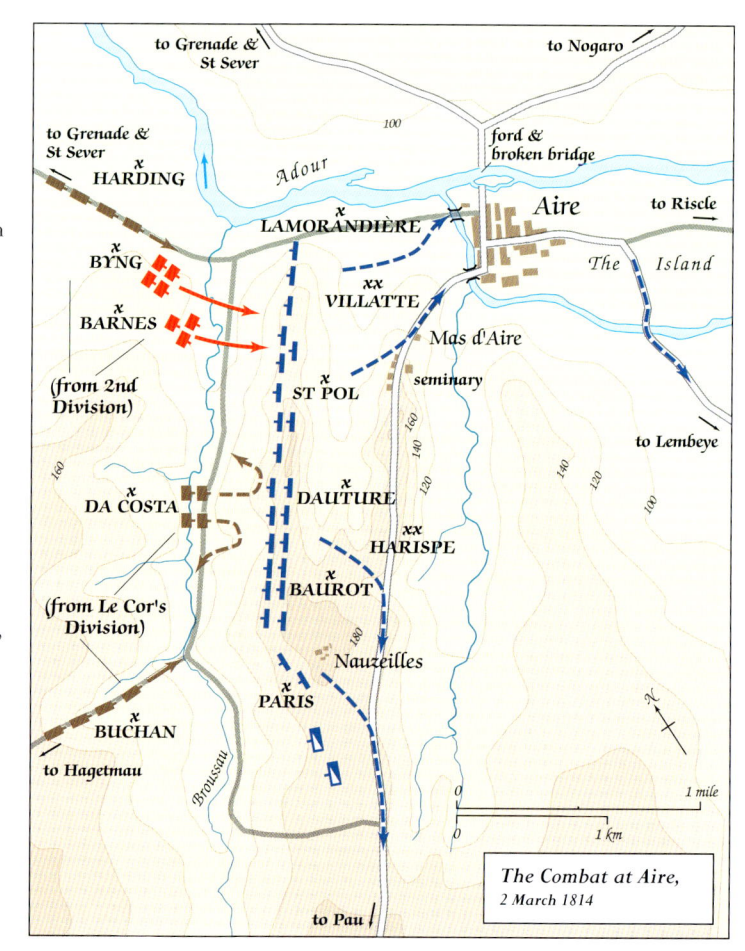

The Combat at Aire, 2 March 1814

the village of Orleix to their left, the 95th Rifles at the head of the left column turned to wade across the Canal d'Alaric to make an uphill attack on part of Harispe's Division deployed on a wooded ridge.[4] After a strongly contested action, the crest was taken, but their counter-attack being repulsed, the French withdrew towards the hamlet of Boulin on the Trie road, on which Villatte's Division was also converging, forced south by Clinton's units thrusting along the parallel ridge and past the telegraph tower and hamlet of Oléac.[5]

With the Trie road cut, and with Hill's column occupying Tarbes, and crossing the Adour by the still intact bridge, Clausel's Corps had little alternative but to retreat rapidly across country south-east through Galan and then towards St Gaudens,[6] on the highway from Tarbes to Toulouse. It was along this, after his artillery had briefly delayed the Allied advance on Tournay, that Taupin's rearguard of Reille's Corps now retired to avoid being cut off.

At dusk, Wellington called a halt: any pursuit through the intricate country further east would be a hazardous operation.

1 Aire itself stood on an island site, but the bridge over the Adour, swept away by a flood some time previously, remained unrepaired.
2 Allied casualties (c. 250) were about equal to those of the French, partly due to losses suffered by Da Costa, who was relieved of his command after the action; but the French lost 100 prisoners in addition, and very many conscripts then took the opportunity to desert.
3 In which Col. Sturgeon of the Engineers was unfortunately killed.
4 As Michael Ayrton has explained in *The Sharpest Fight*, Oman's description of the action was incorrect.
5 The telegraph tower has often been referred to in error as that of a windmill.
6 On the 22nd, Galan briefly became Wellington's Headquarters, as the Allies continued their advance north-east.

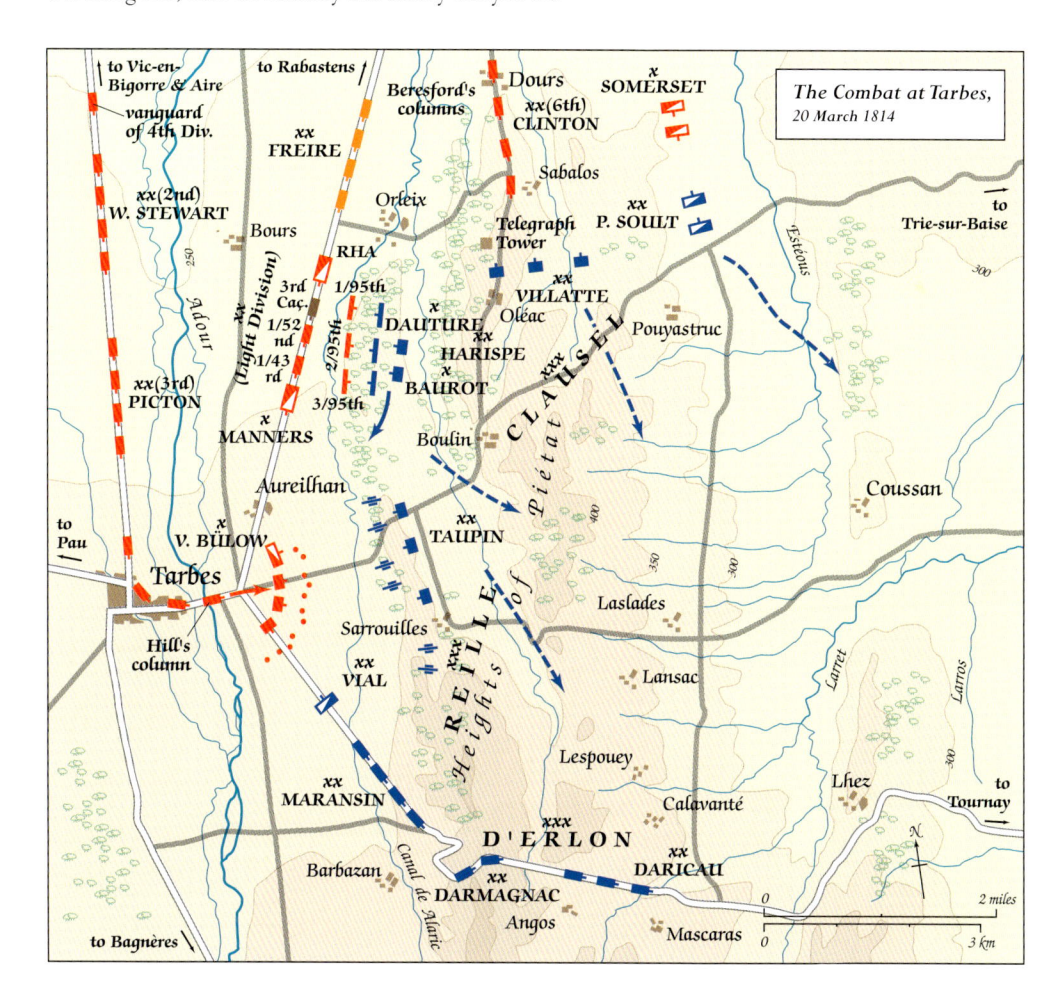

53. Manoeuvres on the Garonne, and the Battle of Toulouse

27 March to 10 April, 1814

The first attempt to cross the Garonne was made from Portet on the 27th, but Wellington had not enough pontoons at hand. Three nights later, the river was spanned successfully further upstream at Pinsaguel, at its junction with the Ariège. Hill crossed with 13,000 men, but on finding no convenient roads leading towards Toulouse, his troops returned to the west bank,[1] and the pontoons were taken downstream past the heavily fortified transpontine suburb of St Cyprien to a point east of Merville, where the river narrowed.[2] Here, on 4 April, the pontoon bridge was re-laid, and Beresford, with 19,000 men, cavalry and artillery, crossed, only to be isolated within hours when one pontoon was swept away by the river in flood. The pontoon was recovered and, by the afternoon of the 8th, the bridge replaced a short distance south near the village of Seilh. On the following day the whole Allied army apart from Hill's Corps, left to invest and demonstrate against St Cyprien, had crossed and was proceeding south, with the river Hers protecting its left flank. Ahead of them rose the Calvinet or Mount Rave, commanding the eastern suburbs of Toulouse, the possession of which was essential.[3]

Wellington was preoccupied by the fact that 20,000 of Suchet's veterans might be marching from Catalonia to join Soult: it was vital to take Toulouse before this occurred.[4] The Calvinet ridge had been fortified by several redoubts, and the city walls lined with artillery. Picton, with the 3rd Division, and Alten's Light Division approached and menaced the 2-mile stretch of walls flanking the canal between the Ponts Jumeaux redoubt, abutting the Garonne, and the northern extremity of the Calvinet and the adjacent knoll of La Pujade.

The main Allied offensive was made further east, with Freire's Spaniards attacking the northernmost redoubt once Beresford, with the 4th and 6th Divisions (forming the left flank), pushing south between the Calvinet and the bank of the Hers from the suburban hamlet of Croix d'Aurade,[5] had reached their first objective, the south-eastern slope of the ridge. They then swung north-west to ascend and capture the redoubt of La Sypière. But the progress of Beresford's artillery was delayed by waterlogged ground near the river bank. Assuming that the sound of their gunfire against the flank of the Clavinet ridge was the signal to attack, the Spaniards advanced prematurely – not simultaneously – up a sunken road south of the Pujade knoll to find themselves raked by canister, and in a cul-de-sac. On scrambling out,

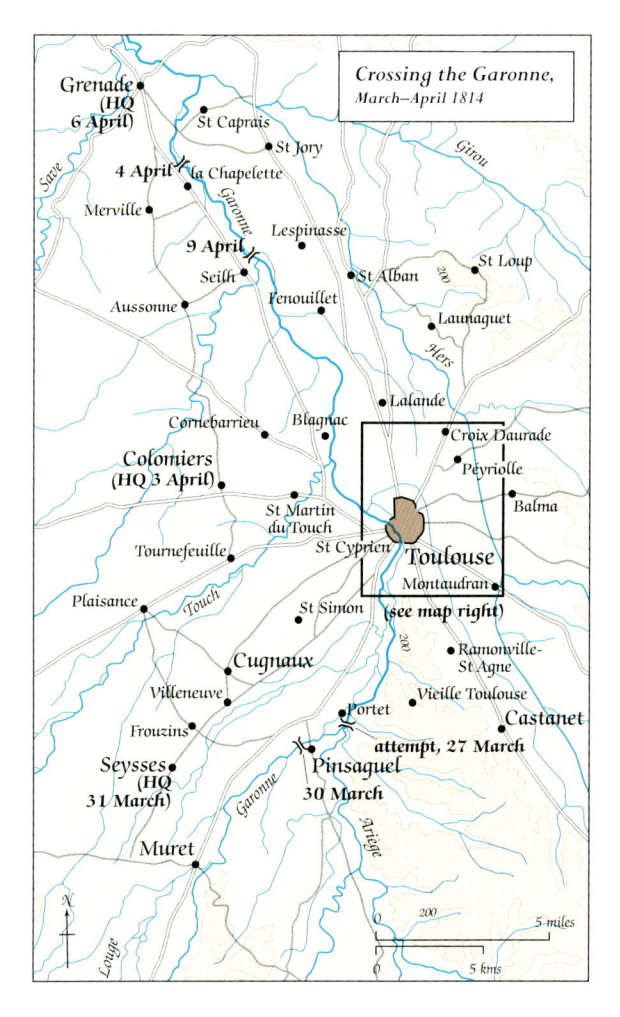

Crossing the Garonne, March–April 1814

126 | An Atlas of the Peninsular War

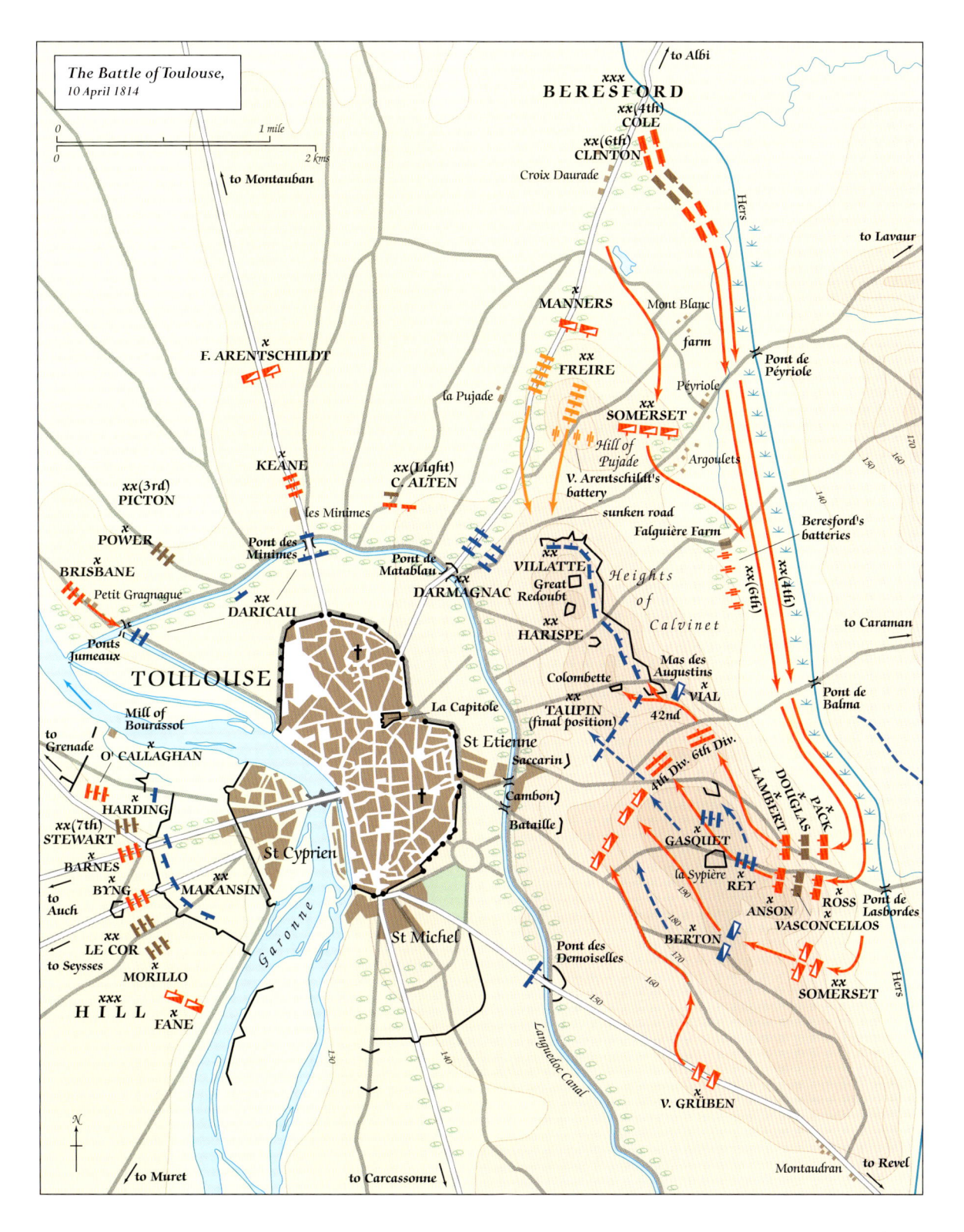

MANOEUVRES ON THE GARONNE, AND THE BATTLE OF TOULOUSE | 127

Anon. *Contemporary sketch of the battlefield of Toulouse from east of the Hers.*

they were counter-attacked by troops emerging from adjacent redoubts, and turned tail, their only way of escape.[6] On observing this reverse, Beresford wheeled right immediately, rather than further south, in anticipation of Wellington's urgent order to do just that.

Meanwhile, Picton, impatient, and contrary to orders, had attempted to capture the Ponts Jumeaux position and had been repulsed.[7]

On approaching the summit, Beresford's columns were met by Taupin's two massed brigades, but in the ensuing engagement (in which Taupin was killed) the latter were powerless to stem the Allies' implacable advance and, unable to redeploy, poured back past the Sypière redoubt, where they were joined by other demoralised units. Beresford stormed ahead to occupy the entire southern half of the ridge, from which the 4th then descended towards the suburb of St Etienne, while his artillery, belatedly hauled to the crest, was able to play on any defences still resisting; the town walls were also coming within range. Almost all Soult's troops now retired behind the encircling canal, but the fighting petered out as dusk fell.

The ensuing day was spent attending to the wounded and burying the dead.[8] Wellington realigned his divisions, and brought further supplies and ammunition across the Garonne in expectation of a counter-attack; but that never took place, Soult preferring to abandoned the city during the following night rather than be trapped within it. Leaving behind some 1,600 of the more severely wounded, including three generals, his depleted army discretely withdrew south-east. By 6am next morning Wellington was receiving invitations to enter the city from its Royalist citizens. Hill's brigades were now able to traverse the main Garonne bridge from their position facing the suburb of St Cyprien, and from the Pont des Demoiselles (spanning the canal south-east of the walls) they followed in Soult's wake as far as Villefranche-de-Lauragais.

It had been a very bloody encounter which need not have taken place if news of Napoleon's abdication, signed four days earlier, had arrived beforehand. But the emissaries from Paris only reached Toulouse on the evening of the 12th. Wellington had entered the city in triumph earlier that day. The emissaries sent on to Soult were disbelieved by him, and it was not until the 17th, on receiving a formal notice of the cessation of hostilities from Berthier, that he reluctantly agreed to an armistice.

But the battle of Toulouse was not the last action in the Peninsular War: that would to take place on 14 April, at Bayonne: see Map 48.

1 Toulouse was partly encircled to the north by the Canal Royal (later, du Midi), which additional obstacle might be avoided if the city was approached from the south. Wellington then concurred with Hill that it was impractical to attack in force from this direction, which they had no chance of reconnoitring: a rare occasion on which he was thwarted by inadequate topographical information.
2 Near the farm of La Capellette, close to the wooded left bank of the Garonne.
3 The population of Toulouse at this time was about 51,000.
4 He may not yet have been aware of the antipathy between the two marshals.
5 This low-lying area – now playing-fields – lies between the present motor-way and the river.
6 They were rallied in time to distract a French counter-attack on the 6th Division, and were later supported by the Light Division.
7 Later, a fruitless attack was made on this sector by Brisbane's Brigade, in which Brisbane was wounded.
8 French casualties were around 3,200; those of the Allies were 4,570, of which 1,900 were among the 7,800 of Freire's Spaniards present.

Dispersal, and Epilogue

The next few weeks were occupied in the dispersal of the Allied troops. Some regretted having to leave France, where they were largely accepted as deliverers rather than conquerors, for both food and wine were good and cheap. It was not always easy to disengage after such a long war. One Commissary, whose duty it was to pay off public and private debts and claims as promptly as possible, found it 'a thankless and disgusting task', due to 'the various attempts at fraud and imposition' made by some of the French, for 'Enormous demands were made (but very properly rejected) even for marks left by encampments, whereas in almost every instance, and always when possible, the troops encamped on heaths and uncultivated ground', and so many 'were enriched in every direction we moved'.

The majority of the British infantry marched from their encampments near Toulouse towards Bordeaux. Several brigades followed the road west from Montauban via Lectoure and Condom before veering north-west through Nérac, Casteljaloux, Bazas, and Langon. Most of them embarked for home from Pauillac, on the west bank of the Garonne estuary, although a battalion each from several regiments were unlucky enough to be sent across the Atlantic, for the war with America was not to end until December.

On the 14 June, Wellington paid his formal farewell to his forces near Bordeaux. Although it has been recorded that some officers and men displayed their disappointment, sensing a lack of gratitude, expecting him to be more emphatically complimentary to his troops – which would have been totally out of character – Jonathan Leach, for one, witnessed him riding off 'amidst loud cheers of men and officers, many of whom had followed him through seven successive campaigns in the Peninsula and the south of France'. Nine days later, after a continuous absence from the shores of Britain of five years and two months, the forty-five-year-old Duke of Wellington disembarked at Dover to a hero's welcome.

The cavalry had made their way at a leisurely pace towards the Channel ports, although not always welcome en route. They had been divided into two columns, each of four groups, with their departure being staggered over a period of days, and were accompanied by the horse artillery batteries. Together with those of the Waggon Train, the total number of horses amounted to over 11,000. As the weather was exceedingly sultry, they usually started at 4am each morning, according to Lieut George Woodberry. The first column, under Fane, set off from Grisolles, not far north of Toulouse, on 1 June, the van reaching Calais on 14 July. Their cross-country route traversed Montauban, Cahors, Brive, Limoges, Châteauroux, Vierzon, and Orléans, before passing west of Paris (visited briefly by a number of officers), and continued via Mantes and Abbeville. The second column, under Vandeleur, starting further to the west, followed the highway north from Bordeaux via Angoulême, Poitiers, and Tours, to approach Boulogne, where they were obliged to wait impatiently for days before transports could put into port. Wellington, who had passed them at Tours, was apparently satisfied with their conduct, although the columns had not always been hospitably received, depending on whether or not the town through which they rode favoured the new regime. Occasional disputes had been reported, for the highways were frequently obstructed, not only by French troops and conscripts making their way home, but also by 'immense numbers' of prisoners of war just landed from England where they had been confined in camps or hulks, some of them for years.

Spanish units had been ordered back across the Pyrenees several weeks earlier. Some Portuguese infantry had also marched to Bordeaux to embark for Lisbon; others remained there until the Commissaries could dispense with their transport. They then separated, taking their mules and muleteers with them, and set out through Spain for Portugal, a good three months' trip. Gen. D'Urban had the invidious task of commanding the contingent, which reached Lisbon on 30 August. Also making the trek home were several hundred 'Soldier's wives', those who had never been formally married to their companions in arms.

An officer in the Portuguese service later described how these women, once separated from their 'husbands' at Bazas, had 'formed a column of 800 or 900 strong; that they were told off in regular companies; and that the commanding-officer, a major, and all the captains, were married men, who had their families with them – all excellent arrangements; but that they were the most unmanageable set of animals that ever marched across a country. The officers had to draw rations for them all the way; but many of them … left the column and went wherever they pleased. Few reached Portugal in the order in which they started.'

Dalhousie was left in charge of any troops still in and around Bordeaux. Larpent, writing in mid July, remarked that among those regretting the end of the British occupation were the tradesmen of Bordeaux: 'They had made a famous time of it these last three months, for the army has in that time received six months' pay, and most of it had found its way into the pockets of the … restauranteurs, the hotels, &c. Bordeaux has had its full share of the spoils of the *milords*.' Larpent went on to state that depredations made by the troops were largely confined to helping themselves from local allotments, although this had been exaggerated, much of it being done 'by the French peasantry and country servants, who, if a soldier takes six cabbages, immediately take a dozen more themselves, sell them in the camp, and swear to the owners that the soldiers are the culprits', moreover those with vineyards had 'their full revenge in the price of their wines, which was immediately doubled, by the arrival of the troops … it is fortunate for the inhabitants that we shall be off before the grapes begin to ripen, and for our own soldiers likewise … [for] the temptations would be irresistible …'

The Guards at Bayonne, the last units to leave, remained under Colville's command. Gradually, accumulated stores, together with the wounded, once sufficiently recuperated to endure the passage, were shipped home. Among them, after a period of convalescence at Pasajes, was Private Wheeler (wounded at the Nivelle). Although discharged from a 'General hospital' at Fuenterrabía in early July, it was not until 9 September that he embarked in the last convoy, setting sail for Portsmouth.

***

On 7 March 1815, news of Napoleon's escape from Elba reached Wellington at the Congress of Vienna, and he was called again to command Allied armies; but it was not until his decisive defeat of Napoleon at Waterloo on 18 June 1815 that peace was temporarily restored to Europe. But in Spain, regrettably, the aftermath of the Peninsular War was possibly even more calamitous than the long-drawn-out contest itself. Fernando VII, after his release from captivity at Valençay – kept in ignorance meanwhile of the sufferings of his subjects – neglected the opportunity of exploiting their enthusiasm and good-will to set his wasted kingdom back on its feet. As king, he chose to follow a rigidly conservative rather than a more liberal course: repressive absolutism was reinstated, with deplorable results. Indeed, in 1823, to support his tottering regime, he invited another French army of 100,000 men into Spain, commanded by the Duc d'Angoulême.

Michael Quin, a British journalist in Madrid at the time, remarked that the inhabitants could hardly believe that the French had the temerity to cross the Pyrenees yet again, in the face of the heroic Spanish people, who only a decade earlier had 'destroyed the flower of their veteran army'. It was sad, but true, that whilst they were thus vaingloriously reassuring themselves, whenever they alluded to the events of their War of Independence, as they called the Peninsular War, 'the British army was never mentioned, or thought of, no more than if such a force had never been in the Peninsula'.

And yet, in the resounding words of William Napier, the first great historian of the war, it was this inconsequential force, which – just prior to the advance on Vitoria – had eventually grown to almost 53,000 British troops (although Portuguese and, later, Spanish units formed a substantial proportion of the Anglo-Allied army) that had 'fought and won nineteen pitched battles and innumerable combats; had made or sustained ten sieges, and taken four great fortresses; had twice expelled the French from Portugal, and once from Spain; had penetrated France, and killed, wounded, or captured two hundred thousand enemies, leaving of their own number forty thousand dead, whose bones whiten the plains and mountains of the Peninsula.' These figures are largely confirmed by Wellington himself in conversation with Stanhope some twenty years later, when stating that he had 'made a computation of all the men I lost in Spain – killed, prisoners, deserters, everything – it amounted to 36,000 men in six years'. It is of some interest that he added: 'It would have been infinitely greater, but for the attention to regular subsistence. The French armies were made to take their chance and to live as they could, and their loss was immense. It is very singular that in relating Napoleon's campaigns this has never been clearly shown in anything like its full extent.'

One may presume that Moore's losses were not included in his total. Nor is there any mention there of the wounded, many crippled for life. An inspection of some surviving officers after their return from the Peninsula – but only referring to those who had commanded companies of the 95th – has been wryly described by John Kincaid. There was

> Beckwith with a cork leg – Pemberton and Manners with a shot each in the knee, making them as stiff as the other's tree one – Loftus Gray with a gash in the lip, and minus a portion of one heel, which made him march to the tune of dot and go one – Smith with a shot in the ankle – Eeles minus a thumb – Johnstone, in addition to other shot holes, a stiff elbow, which deprived him of the power of disturbing friends as a scratcher of Scotch reels upon the violin – Percival with a shot through his lungs. Hope with a grape-shot lacerated leg – and George Simmons with his riddled body held together by a pair of stays …

And, of the rank and file, how many thousand scarred and maimed veterans – many impoverished if not destitute – were left adrift: that, we shall never know.

Glossary

This concise glossary may be found of help, even if only a proportion of the terms are referred to in the text of the atlas. Those requiring further information on the administration of the army in the Peninsula should refer in particular to the following titles in the Bibliography: Glover, *Peninsular Preparation; Inside Wellington's Peninsular Army*; Oman, *Wellington's Army*; and Ward, *Wellington's Headquarters*.

abatis or **abattis**, a defensive work formed of felled trees with their branches facing outwards, usually placed a short distance in front of field-works.

Adjutant-General, one of the two great heads of departments at Headquarters. He was responsible for the supervision of discipline, providing statistical information (returns of men and mounts, 'morning states', etc.), and numerous miscellaneous duties; he had several assistant-adjutant-generals and their deputies to aid him. In the Peninsula, the position was held until April 1813 by Maj.-Gen. the Hon. Charles Stewart (later Lord Londonderry), who was succeeded by Maj.-Gen. Edward Pakenham. *See* Quartermaster-General.

afrancesados (lit. 'frenchified'), either Spaniards sympathising with the French and their Revolutionary tenets (among the more prominent of whom were many cultured and liberal-minded persons anticipating the end of the malign influence of the Roman Catholic Church and the parasitic nobility), or merely collaborators.

aldea, an hamlet

arroyo, a water-course

Artillery, Royal (RA), of which the Officer Commanding, representing the Ordnance Department, was responsible for providing all arms and ammunition, and acted as artillery advisor to the Commander-in-Chief. A civilian subordinate acted as Inspector of the Field Train Department.

A British field artillery 'brigade' or horse artillery 'troop' (akin to what was later known as a 'field battery'), usually consisted of five guns and one 5.5-inch howitzer, the caliber (or 'nature') of the gun usually defining the unit. Early in the war, these guns were usually light 6-pounders, with some longer-ranged heavy (or 'long') 6-pounders: 3-pounders composed a single brigade in 1809 and were also employed as mountain guns, while 9-pounders became the principal field piece later in the war. The light 6-pounders were an efficient and easily-handled arm, weighing almost 1,650 lb including the carriage, while the heavy version weighed 2,000 lb, and the 9-pounders weighed 2,884 lb; meanwhile, the heavy 5.5-inch howitzer, at 2,550 lb. was generally replaced in the field by the light 5.5-inch, weighing 1,680 lb, by the mid-point of the war. Their common shot was a solid round iron ball. Common case or case-shot (canister) consisted of a number of smaller cast-iron balls within a tin can, which disintegrated on discharge and spread the shot evenly over a large area. Howitzers, capable of firing a large, explosive shell, were particularly effective at close range with case-shot, which projected a greater number of heavy bullets than field guns. While guns could not fire shells, British guns alone carried 'spherical case shot' (the '**shrapnel**', named after its inventor, Henry Shrapnell, RA, 1761–1842), adopted by the army *c*.1804. This was a projectile consisting of a hollow iron ball filled with carbine balls – later by musket-balls – mixed with gunpowder and fused to explode approximately 50 yards above and 100 yards in front of a target, over which the shot would shower. It was effective up to a range of 1,000 yards. The French had no equivalent to it. *See also* under Congreve rocket.

It was not until 1811 that Col Alexander Dickson, often in charge of Wellington's siege-artillery, was able to command an adequate battering-train of modern iron guns, shipped out from England, with which to replace the obsolete Portuguese brass 24-pounders, no two of which had the same bore. At Ciudad Rodrigo, 2,754 rounds of 24-pound shot were fired in two days, which – as a mule could only carry eight rounds – was, according to Dickson, almost 360 mule loads. At Badajoz, 2,523

132 | An Atlas of the Peninsular War

barrels of powder weighing 90 lb each (requiring some 1,200 mules), 18,832 rounds of solid shot for 24-pounders and 13,029 rounds for the 18-pounders (some 3,590 mule loads) – not taking into account grape and case shot or howitzer shells – were expended.

Additional transport was required also to supply huge amounts of fodder daily in order to keep these working mules on their feet.

banquette, an earthen platform, raised behind a parapet, from which men could stand and fire.

bastion, a section of fortifications formed at the angle of two walls, and extending beyond the main defences.

battering train, the guns, ammunition and equipment required to besiege a place.

bivouac, a temporary improvised shelter against the elements, or camping in the open, without tents, also referred to as hutting; *see* cantonments, and woods.

breach, a gap made in a rampart or wall by gunfire or an exploded mine to allow troops to break in: 'practicable' meaning that it was by then in a state to be entered without an undue amount of climbing.

breastwork or *faussebraie*, a 4-5 foot high protective wall.

bridgehead or *tête de pont*, fortifications designed to defend the far end of a bridge or pontoon; sometimes on both banks.

bridges, of which there was a variety, among them floating, flying, and pontoon, or 'of boats'. The floating bridge might be formed by a pontoon, barge, or raft or two moored to both banks by cables, and which would be hauled across or, with a strong current and properly steered, would be swept to either side of the river. At the 'bridge' of Vila Velha, a vital crossing-point of the Tagus, only a company or two, or up to twenty horses, could be ferried over at a time. *See* pontoons.

caçadores (hunters), Portuguese light infantrymen, an increasing proportion of whom were armed with rifles as the war progressed.

caisson, a chest containing explosives or, more usually, a wagon conveying ammunition.

caltraps (cavalry traps), metal spikes set in pyramidal form, which were strewn in the path of cavalry to impale hooves (and men falling on them).

canister or **case shot**, a projectile formed by a thin metal tube filled with lead musket balls, fired from guns at short range and at a low trajectory over attacking troops, scattering over a wide area and often causing widespread casualties. It is frequently confused with grapeshot; *see* below.

cantonments, lodgings or quarters assigned to troops, or in which they were billeted; more permanent than a bivouac.

carcass, a perforated projectile filled with incendiary

Robert Batty, *Bridge of boats across the Adour at Bayonne.*

material, lighted before firing, intended to ignite inflammable defences, etc.

casemate, a bomb-proof vault built below a rampart to protect men and ammunition. Usually, it had embrasures or was loop-holed.

casualties, an indiscriminate reckoning of the total number of dead, wounded, and missing in an action, and frequently misleading. Many were mortally wounded, while a proportion referred to in returns as 'missing' might either be dead but not found, or have strayed from the scene of action and might later have reported for duty, while some of the wounded might have been either malingerers or slightly wounded and soon back among the 'effectives'.

chaussée, a paved highway or trunk-road, of which at this period there were few and those far between; almost all others were furrowed, knee-deep in mud, and well-nigh impassable during wet weather and throughout the winter.

chevaux-de-frise, literally 'horses of Friesland', because this form of barrier was invented by the Frisians, who had no cavalry. These were usually constructed by setting large nails, swords, bayonets, and other sharp objects into heavy beams, which, when placed within a breach, provided an additional hazard to assaulting troops.

Commissariat. A civilian department responsible to the Treasury, and headed in the Peninsula by a Commissary-General. The Store Department was responsible for depots, and provisioning the Army: the regular supply of food and liquor to troops, and of forage to the cavalry, the transport and issue or distribution of which (together with clothing and necessaries), were regulated by Commissaries (later entitled Deputies, Assistants, Deputy-assistants, and Commissary Clerks). There was a separate Accounts Department. Each infantry brigade and cavalry regiment had their own commissariat officers. See Ordnance Department.

Congreve Rocket, an inaccurate projectile, invented in 1805 by Col. Sir William Congreve (1772–1828), in which Wellington had little confidence, for its trajectory was unpredictable, although the loud hiss effectively frightened troops encountering them for the first time, notably at the crossing of the Adour late in January 1814. The 32-pounders had a range of 3,000 yards, while the more portable 12-pounders out-ranged field artillery.

counterscarp, the abrupt nearer side to the glacis of an excavated ditch, often of brick or stone construction, to make its descent more difficult.

covertway, an area between the glacis and ditch surrounding fortifications, along which troops could pass from one position to another while being protected by a palisade, not actually 'covered'.

curtain wall, a wall joining two projecting bastions.

dehesa, rough pasture or grazing land, without scrub undergrowth, often with sparsely scattered groves of stone- or umbrella pines, *alcornoques* (cork-oaks), *encinas* (holm-oaks or ilex), providing food and shelter for cattle and sheep, but mainly herds of pigs, which thrive on the acorns. Both gave some sustenance to troops during the last phase of the retreat from Burgos.

demilune; *see* ravelin.

depot, in the Peninsula there were both base and forward depots, established by the Commissariat, where provisions, clothing, candles, and a variety of other stores were assembled prior to onward transmission to military units.

diseases, etc. Among those prevalent in the Peninsula were typhoid (bacterial infection causing fever), typhus (spread by body louse), dysentery (bacterial infection affecting bowels), and malaria (fever caused by mosquito bite); 'Walcheren fever', from which many men who had taken part in the expedition off the Dutch coast in 1809 suffered, was a relapsing fever, probably caused by a combination of the above. 'Hospital gangrene' was another virulent epidemic.

ditch, a deep trench (about 16 feet), usually at least five times as wide, encircling defensive works, its outer supporting wall being designated a counterscarp. The excavated earth could be used to make a parapet. If filled with water, the ditch formed a moat.

earthworks or **fieldworks**, any form of temporary fortifications (or a trench) providing shelter from enemy fire, direct or enfilading.

embrasures, openings in the flank of fortifications through which guns might fire and enfilade.

enfilade, gunfire from a position directed against the flank of approaching troops or their earthworks.

Engineers, Royal (RE), of which the Officer Commanding, who acted as consultant on matters of siegecraft and defence, was the storekeeper of engineering equipment for bridge-building and construction of pontoons, etc. In 1812 the department changed its title from the 'Royal Military Artificers' to the Royal Sappers and Miners. In the Peninsula, the position was held by Col.

Richard Fletcher until his death at San Sebastian; and then by Lieut.-Col. Howard Elphinstone. In his *Narrative*, Londonderry remarked:

> Ours was, perhaps, the only army in Europe which possessed no corps of sappers or miners, nor any body of men peculiarly trained to carry on the more intricate details of a siege. We had, it is true, what was termed the regiment of the royal military artificers; that is to say, a battalion of carpenters, blacksmiths, stonemasons, and other handicraftsmen; but not one of these had ever seen a mine; and as to a sap, they were probably incapable of understanding the very meaning of the word … We had no pontoons or pontooners … and our intrenching tools consisted simply of the most common description of spades, bill-hooks, and pick-axes.

At Badajoz, however competent Col. Richard Fletcher, the chief engineer, and his officers may have been, there were still only 169 men of the line attached to the department to act as overseers, 48 carpenters, 48 miners, and 25 rank and file of the corps of artificers.

escalade, to assault fortifications by means of ladders rather than by making a breach in the walls.

fascines, bundles of brushwood or small branches, roped together, to revet and support the earthen walls of trenches, or when constructing a battery.

fire-balls, phosphorous projectiles or flares fired after dark, to hover over and illuminate any threatening enemy movements.

'Forlorn Hope', a group of volunteers formed to assault a breach, who would advance ahead of the main body of troops.

frise, a line of sharpened stakes set into the lower slope of a rampart, partly to ensure that the outworks are not taken by surprise.

fuente, a spring or fountain.

gabions, cylindrical, open-ended, wickerwork baskets, about 3 feet high, filled with earth, placed above ground to provide cover for men approaching siege-works.

glacis, the gentle exterior slope of defensive works, extending beyond a parapet and/or ditch, constructed to ensure an uncluttered target area over which approaching troops had to cross.

grapeshot, often confused with that of canister, is a heavier shot (usually nine golf-ball-sized projectiles) tightly encased in a canvas cylinder and fired from cannon, designed to break spars and foul rigging in naval engagements, and comparatively infrequently used on land.

grenade, a 2½ inch hollow iron ball charged with powder with a short fuse, lit and thrown to explode near an enemy.

grenadiers, historically, men throwing grenades; usually the heavier-weight company in a battalion, often forming assault troops.

guerrilla (lit. 'little war'), a partisan or member of a band of irregular troops (a *partida*) acting independently of formal armies.

horn-work, an outwork of two demi-bastions connected to the main work by parallel wings. That at Burgos was a notable example.

Horse Guards, the building in Whitehall, London, housing the offices of the Commander-in-Chief and his staff, the Military Secretary throughout much of the Peninsular War period being Col. Henry Torrens.

Hospitals, the Inspector-General of these, as representing the Medical Board, was in overall charge of the physicians, surgeons, and their assistants in the Peninsula, a position first held by James Frank, and from 1812 by Sir James McGrigor. A separate department, that of the Purveyors, was responsible for the equipping of hospitals, supplying drugs, etc.

howitzer, a short-barrelled field artillery piece projecting a common (explosive) shell at a low velocity, and capable of a higher angle of fire than a gun; unlike a mortar, it was supported by trunnions and pivoted from the middle of its barrel.

huerta, an area of well-cultivated market-gardens and orchards in the immediate vicinity of most towns

invest, to; a preliminary action to isolate a town to be besieged from receiving any reinforcements or supplies.

Judge-Advocate-General, a civilian lawyer responsible for the legal control of Courts Martial. It was not until the latter part of the war that Francis Larpent, as Deputy JAG, reached the Peninsula to supervise such proceedings.

junta, in the Peninsula, an administrative committee set up in emergencies on a municipal, provincial or national level.

KGL, the King's German Legion, a formation of largely Hanoverian-officered troops serving with the British army after Napoleon's invasion of Hanover in 1803.

GLOSSARY | 135

league, an imprecise measure of distance, varying in different countries from 3 to 4 miles.
lunette, works on either side of a ravelin, larger than a redan, and with two faces and two flanks.
magazine, a bomb-proof arsenal storing arms, powder and ammunition; also a store for provisions.
matorral, heath or scrubland, often covered with *Cistus*.
meseta, the high-lying central plateau of the Iberian peninsula.
Military Secretary, the confidential assistant to the Commander-in-Chief in the Peninsula, partly concerned with financial business and officers' appointments, but junior in rank to heads of departments. The position was first held by Lieut.-Col. James Bathurst, until late 1810, and then by Capt. Lord Fitzroy Somerset, a colonel by the end of the war and, later, Lord Raglan.
miqueletes, Spanish (or rather Catalan) term for their irregular 'home guard', sometimes spelt *migueletes*; also known as *somatenes*.
mine, an aperture or tunnel excavated below fortifications, in which gunpowder was placed to explode, weakening or destroying the walls.
mortar, a large–, but short-bore – cannon on a fixed mounting, able to fire shot, explosive shells, or carcass (combustible material) at a high trajectory.
musket. The great majority of the British infantry in the Peninsula were armed with the Tower or Brown Bess flint-lock. This ranged from 9lb 11oz to 10lb 8oz in weight and with a 39- or 42-inch smooth-bore barrel, on the muzzle of which a bayonet might be mounted. The ammunition for one shot – a round leaden bullet – was contained in a paper cartridge (60 of which, in a waterproof pouch, were normally carried per man, plus another 60 in his knapsack), and its highest practical rate of fire was three times in a minute (if already loaded). 200 yards was about the limit at which it could kill or seriously wound, but it was most effective when at a range of less than 160 yards, or in volleys at massed troops at 100 yards, but its accuracy when aimed at a single target was limited to 75 yards. Much of its effect depended on the care and correctness with which it was loaded, but it could not be relied on to fire in damp or wet weather.
ordenança, irregular forces called out to supplement the uniformed militia in the defence of Portugal.
ordnance, piece of; any gun, mortar or howitzer. They were classified by the weight of the solid shot they fired: i.e. a 24-pounder howitzer threw a shot weighing 24 lb.
Ordnance Department, responsible for the storage and distribution of all forms of arms, ammunition, gunpowder, etc.; regrettably, their storekeepers in the Peninsula were often close-fisted and reluctant to supply any material unless the requisite order was made by the appropriate officer.
palisade, a fence of stakes, about 9 feet long, set into the ground, often close to the crest of a glacis, and protecting the covered way between that point of the counterscarp of a defensive ditch.
parallel/s, a deep and wide trench or trenches dug at the approaches to a besieged place, from which troops excavating a sap could be supported. They were usually zig-zag in plan, partly to evade enfilading fire, and two or three (or more) in number.
parapet, a thick protective wall of earth raised above the crest of a rampart, usually with a ledge behind it to prevent the earth – if hit by enemy fire – from falling into and filling the adjacent ditch.
Paymaster-general, or rather his Deputy, acted as the army's banker and was ostensibly responsible for the Military Chest.
picquets, piquets, or pickets, a small outposts of troops – infantry or cavalry – placed to guard against surprise attack, by day or night, from which a vedette might be advanced.
pontoons were, ideally, 21 feet in length, 3 feet 11 inch wide, and 2 feet 1 inch thick, and were usually carried on a two-wheeled carriage (but with another two wheels supplied by a limber, making the vehicle, when in motion, four wheeled) and with its equipment weighted approximately 1,200 lb. A serious flaw in their construction was that their top was open, not enclosed, allowing them occasionally to fill with water and sink. For details, see pp. 262-70 in Robert Burnham's chapter on Bridge Building in *Inside Wellington's Peninsular Army*. Occasionally, empty wine-casks served the purpose when there was no other material at hand with which a bridge might be constructed.
Provinces, former Portuguese. While these are indicated on individual maps, those more frequently referred to during the war are situated as follows: the *Alentejo* (formerly Alemtejo, and sometimes so spelt) lying south of the Tagus and abutting Spanish Extremadura (anglice Estremadura). Portuguese **Estremadura** ran north

along the Atlantic coast from Lisbon (but also extended south of the estuary to include Setúbal). Between that and the Alentejo was the ***Ribatejo*** (banks of the Tejo), through which ran the lower reaches of the Tagus. Little action took place in the southern half of the Alentejo, a large province divided into the Alto and Baixa (Upper and Lower). The province of ***Beira***, likewise divided, extended north of the Tagus on the eastern half of the country between that river and (roughly) the Douro. Further north-east stood the ***Tras-os-Montes***, while the Douro ran west through the ***Douro Litoral*** to Oporto, this being abutted to the north by the province of ***Minho***.

Provost marshal, head of the military police, assisted by his provost guard. He was also in temporary charge of prisoners of war.

pueblo, a village; but may also refer to the People of Spain in general.

puente, a bridge, sometimes also the name of an adjacent town, as in Puente de Arzobispo.

puerto, a door, harbour, or mountain pass.

Quartermaster-General (QMG), senior officer responsible for overseeing the embarkation and disembarkation, movement, quartering, equipping, and supplying of troops, aided by his deputies (DQMG), assistants (AQMG), and deputy-assistants (DAQMG). Headquarters usually had their separate quartermaster. His department was also responsible for making topographical surveys, reporting on the condition of roads, bridges, and fords, and the resources of areas through which the army might be advancing, etc. In the Peninsula, George Murray held the post until late May 1812, and again from mid March 1813, in the intervening period being replaced (unsatisfactorily) by Col. James Willoughby Gordon.

rambla, the dry sandy bed of a river or rivulet, which, during several seasons, being less rutted than most roads, often provided a more convenient and smoother line of march. Wellington stated that he had 'been obliged more than once to give orders at the [adjacent] villages that the large stones and fragments might be picked out of the [dry] rivulets, so that the troops might march on these roads'.

ravelin; also demi-lune, a work beyond a curtain wall, usually of two walls set at an angle, or triangular in construction, providing a position from which the approaching enemy would receive flanking fire.

redan, a simple form of field-work of two faces forming a salient angle.

redoubt, a defensive work detached from the main fortifications of a town.

revetment, a wall of brick or stone supporting the side of a rampart or ditch.

ricochet fire, round shot fired at a low angle, the bounding trajectory of which on hard ground, or off a hard surface, would cause havoc among massed troops.

rifle, a firearm whose barrel's interior was slightly spiraled, rather than smooth-faced, so as to impart a spin to the bullet, increasing its stability and, thus, accuracy. Modestly used by most armies, it was generally regarded as too costly and slow-firing for general issue, but the London

The *rambla*, or dry river bed of the river Ponsul at Idanha-a-Velha.

gunsmith Ezekiel Baker's design, *c*. 1800, was to become famous in the hands of the specialised British, KGL, and Portuguese light-infantrymen.

At 9½lb, it was slightly lighter in weight than a musket (see above), and was extremely accurate up to 150 yards, still dangerous between 200 and 300 yards, and could hit a massed target such as a square of infantry or cause casualties among troops on the march at a range of 500 yards. However, the grooving in the 30-inch barrel made the ramming down of the bullet a stiffer operation and thus it took longer to load and fire: approximately one minute. It could fire a 'carbine' size cartridge also, and at a faster rate. The Baker rifle was first issued with a triangular bayonet 18 inches in length, later replaced by a 24-inch long, flat, single-edged, sword bayonet.

The British infantrymen were the only troops which regularly practised firing at targets using live ammunition, and thus were far more accurate than the French; nor did the French *tirailleurs* have rifles, merely smooth bore weapons, as Napoleon had withdrawn rifles from the Republican army, and they were thus at a distinct disadvantage when it came to making an accurate shot at longer range. The three light infantry regiments trained in the use of the rifle by Moore at Shorncliffe in 1803–4 were the 43rd, 52nd, and 95th. It was not until February 1816 that three battalions of the latter regiment were formally styled The Rifle Brigade. Some other light infantry regiments later contained rifle-armed battalions.

rio, a river.

rockets; *see* Congreve Rocket.

round-shot, a solid metal ball between 3 and 4¼ inches in diameter. Cannon were categorised by the weight of shot they fired, which in the Napoleonic period ranged from 6-, 8- or 9-pounders to the 12-pounders, the heaviest used in the field.

sap, a trench, approached by parallels, and usually covered to protect the sappers from the garrison's fire, excavated close to defensive walls, from which they could be undermined or mined. The insidious burrowing operations of sappers were usually directed by an engineer.

saucisson, a long sausage-like waterproof canvas tube, packed with powder, used for firing a mine.

semaphore; *see* telegraph.

shrapnel, a projectile composed of 1-oz lead carbine balls and later by musket-balls mixed with gunpowder, fired from cannon as well as from howitzers, with the length of fuse calculated to explode in mid air just short of a target, over which the shot would shower. This type of shell, invented by Henry Shrapnell (1761–1842) of the Royal Artillery, was improved and adopted by the army in about 1804.

sierra, a mountain range (*serra* in Portuguese), a *serranía* being a mountainous district.

spherical case shot, the official name for shrapnel.

squares, forming, the deployment of infantry into a square (or oblong) formation in expectation of a cavalry charge.

As a generalisation, its frontage was approximately 100 feet (though the frontage of its different faces varied from perhaps 50 to 275 feet, depending upon the drill used to form it), while each side might be anything from four to six ranks in depth, of which those on the outer would be kneeling, holding their muskets (butts on the ground) at an angle, making a bristling hedge of sharp bayonets against which attacking cavalry would steer clear rather than collide, usually swerving round the sides of the square. In the hollow centre of the tightly-packed formation stood sergeants and officers, exhorting their men to hold their fire and keep steady.

Well-disciplined troops – even those without experience of battle – could thus hold the enemy at bay, their inner ranks keeping up regular fire, once the cavalry were within effective range. The closer the range, the more devastating the result. Although the sight of massed cavalry bearing down on a square was one that was likely to make the bravest man flinch, rarely did one break in the face of a charge, although if a horse was mortally wounded in close proximity to such a formation, there was the danger that it might collapse into its ranks and cause confusion, of which advantage could be taken. This happened at Garcihernández, when the KGL Dragoons scattered a square of the 6th Léger.

A square – or squares, in which case they formed at some distance from each other – was vulnerable to artillery, both from round-shot and more so from canister, being a dense target; and if remaining so formed, should a line of infantry be supporting the cavalry attack, only a comparatively small proportion of their muskets would be able to reply, but this dangerous situation was not one in which they found themselves very frequently.

Staff Corps, Royal (RSC), a separate organisation from the Royal Engineers, and controlled by the QMG, it was largely responsible for the construction and repair of temporary bridges, but its officers also surveyed extensive areas and provided maps, while they were frequently landed with a variety of other tasks not undertaken by the Engineers. There was a certain amount of rivalry between the two bodies.

telegraph, a system of visual communication from one area to another made by varying the position of flags or balls on the yard-arms of masts placed on conspicuous heights.

terreplein, a level emplacement for a battery of guns, behind a protective rampart.

vedette, a mounted sentry usually placed on high ground beyond an outpost to observe and give notice of enemy movements; *see* picquet.

wagons, or waggons, were four-wheeled vehicles, not to be confused with the two-wheeled 'car': thus bullock cars are not wagons, but two-wheeled cars. The Royal Wagon Train, formed in 1799, consisted largely of *spring wagons*, which, being unsuitable for carrying heavy loads on the execrable roads of the Peninsula, were increasingly employed for transporting the wounded. By 1810, only three were attached to each regiment, which was ridiculously inadequate. Although their springs were strong, this caused them, in the words of George Simmons, to 'dance up and down in an awful manner,' and worse than the fitful movement of the bullock cars. The French ambulance system was far superior.

woods. In the Peninsula, at least until the Basque provinces were entered later in the Vitoria campaign, with their forests of both coniferous and a variety of deciduous trees, the occasional woods encountered were mostly of evergreen ilex or holm oak (*Quercus ilex*), umbrella or stone-pines (a *pinal* being a pine wood), cork-oaks (*Quercus suber*, Sp. *alcornoques*). Frequently, they took the form of *dehesas*, sparsely wooded pastures with scant scrub undergrowth (*matorral*). Olive groves proliferated in certain regions, but the troops, when bivouacking, were not permitted to cut these down to protect them from the elements or as fuel. Sherer well described the scene, when troops, tired by a long march, reached the edge of a wood near a river or stream. Here

> they halted, in open columns, arms piled, picquets and guards paraded and posted, and, in two minutes, all appear at home. Some fetch large stones to form fire-places; others hurry off with canteens and kettles for water, while the wood resounds with the blows of the bill-hook. Dispersed, under the more distant trees, you see the officers; some dressing, some arranging a few boughs to shelter them by night; others kindling their own fires; while the most active are seen returning from the village, laden with bread, or, from some flocks of goats, feeding near us, with a supply of new milk. How often, under some spreading cork-tree, which offered shade, shelter, and fuel, have I taken up my lodging for the night … The inconveniences of one camp taught me to enjoy the next; and I learned … that wood and water, shade and grass, were luxuries.

Selective Bibliography

This is an idiosyncratic selection of books covering several aspects of the war, including contemporary memoirs and narratives of particular interest and value, many of which contain bibliographies. Articles in the *Journal of the Society for Army Historical Research,* a fertile field of study, should not be overlooked. Several rare texts have been and are still being reissued by Leonaur, Naval & Military Press, and Ken Trotman, among other publishers, although the cartography and illustrations are not always of the quality of those in original editions.

Aitchison, John (ed. W.F.K. Thompson), *An Ensign in the Peninsular War: The Letters of J. Aitchison* (1981)

Ayrton, Michael and John Taylor, *The Sharpest Fight: the 95th Rifles at Tarbes, 20th March 1814* (2007)

Batty, Robert, *Campaign of the Left Wing of the Allied Army, in the Western Pyrenees and South of France …* (1823)

Beamish, North Ludlow, *History of the King's German Legion* (1832; 1837)

Belmas, J., *Journaux de sièges faits ou soutenus par les français dans la Péninsule, de 1807 à 1814* (1856)

Bingham, George (ed. Gareth Glover), *Wellington's Lieutenant, Napoleon's Gaoler: the Peninsula Letters and St Helena Diaries of Sir George Ridout Bingham, 1809–21* (2005)

Blakeney, Robert (ed. Julian Sturgis), *A Boy in the Peninsular War* (1899)

Bragge (ed. Simon A.C. Cassels), *Peninsular Portrait, 1811–14: The Letters of Captain William Bragge* (1963)

Brett-James, Antony, *Life in Wellington's Army* (1972)

Bridgeman, Orlando (ed. Gareth Glover), *A Young Gentleman at War: the Letters of Captain Orlando Bridgeman* (2008)

Browne, T. (ed. Roger Norman Buckley), *The Napoleonic Journal of Captain Thomas Henry Browne* (1987)

[Buckham, E.W.], *Personal Narrative of Adventures … during the War in 1812–1813* (1827)

Burgoyne (ed. Hon. George Wrottesley), *The Life and Correspondence of F.M. Sir John Burgoyne, Bart.* (1873)

Burnham, Robert; *see Inside Wellington's Peninsular Army;*

Burnham, Robert, and with Ron McGuigan (foreword by Rory Muir), *The British Army Against Napoleon: Facts, Lists, and Trivia, 1805–1815* (2010)

Cartografía de la Guerra de la Independencia (Ministerio de Defensa & Ollero y Ramos Editores, 2008)

Cassini, *Carte géométrique de la France* (revised between 1798 and 1812) [copies of individual sections are available from the Cartothèque de L'I.G.N. at St-Mandé, France.]

Chambers, George L., *Bussaco 1810* (1910)

[Cocks] Page, Julia, *Intelligence Officer in the Peninsula* (1986), devoted to Major the Hon. Edward Charles Cocks

Cooke, John Henry, *Memoirs of the Late War …* (1831); and *A Narrative of Events in the South of France …* (1835). The first volume, ed. Eileen Hathaway, was re-titled *A True Soldier Gentleman* (2000); the chapters describing the Peninsular War have been published as *With the Light Division* (2007)

Costello, Edward, *Adventures of a Soldier* (1841), ed. Eileen Hathaway as *Costello, The True Story of a Peninsular War Rifleman* (1997)

Crowe, Charles (ed. Gareth Glover), *An Eloquent Soldier: the Peninsular War Journals of Lieut. Charles Crowe of the Inniskillings, 1812–14* (2010)

Crumplin, Michael, *Men of Steel: Surgery in the Napoleonic Wars* (2007)

[Daniel, John Edgecombe], *Journal of an Officer in the Commissariat …* (1820)

Dempsey, Guy, *Albuera 1811* (2008)

[Dickson] (ed. John H. Leslie), *The Dickson Manuscripts: being Diaries, etc. of Sir Alexander Dickson* (1908–12)

Documentos cartográficos históricos de Gipuzkoa (two series, San Sebastian 1994, and 1999)

Dumouriez, Gen. Charles-François, *An Account of Portugal, as it appeared in 1766 …* (1797)

D'Urban, B. (ed. I.J. Rousseau), *Peninsular Journal of Major-Gen. Sir Benjamin D'Urban* (1930)

Eliot, William Granville, *Treatise on the Defence of Portugal* (3rd edn, 1811)

Fletcher, Ian, *Galloping at Everything: the British Cavalry in the Peninsular War… : A Reappraisal* (1999)

Fortescue, the Hon. Sir John, *A History of the British Army* (1899–1930), vols VI–X and corresponding map volumes; and with R.H. Beadon, *The Royal Army Service Corps, a History of Transport and Supply in the British Army* (1930–2)

Frazer (ed. Edward Sabine), *Letters of Col Sir Augustus Simon Frazer… commanding the Royal Horse Artillery …* (1859)

Gleig, George Robert, *The Subaltern* (1825); ed. with an Introduction by Ian Robertson (2001)

Glover, Gareth (ed.) *From Corunna to Waterloo: The Letters and Journals of Two … Hussars, 1808–1816* (2007), being those of Major Edwin Griffiths and Captain Frederick Philips

Glover, Richard, *Peninsular Preparation: The Reform of the British Army, 1795–1809* (1963)

Gómez de Arteche, *Atlas de la Guerra de la Independencia* (1869–1901)

Gordon (ed. Rory Muir), *At Wellington's Right Hand: The Letters of Lt-Col Sir Alexander Gordon, 1808–1815* (2003)

Grattan, William (ed. Sir Charles Oman), *Adventures with the Connaught Rangers, 1809–14* (1902)

Griffith, Paddy (ed.), *Modern Studies of the War in Spain and Portugal, 1808–1814* (1999), the complementary vol. IX to Greenhill's reprint of Oman's *History*: pertinent essays and a bibliography of works published since 1930, etc.

Hall, John A., *The Biographical Dictionary of British Officers Killed and Wounded 1808–1814, together with non-combat casualties* (1998), the complementary vol. VIII to Greenhill's reprint of Oman's *History*.

Hamilton, Thomas, revised and augmented by Frederick Hardman, *Annals of the Peninsular Campaigns* (1849)

[Hill], Gordon L. Teffeteller, *The Surpriser: the Life of Rowland, Lord Hill* (1983)

Hennegan, Sir Richard D., *Seven Years' Campaigning in the Peninsula …* (1846)

Hennell, George (ed. Michael Glover), *A Gentleman Volunteer: … Letters … from the Peninsula, 1812–13* (1979)

Henry, Walter, *Events of a Military Life …* (1843); ed. by Pat Hayward as *Surgeon Henry's Trifles …* (1970)

Holland (ed. Earl of Ilchester), *The Spanish Journal of Elizabeth Lady Holland* (1910)

Horward, Donald D., *The Battle of Bussaco: Masséna versus Wellington* (1965); *Napoleon and Iberia – the twin sieges of Ciudad Rodrigo and Almeida, 1810* (1984)

Houlding, J.A., *Fit for Service: The Training of the British Army, 1715–1795* (1981)

Howard, Martin, *Wellington's Doctors* (2002)

Inside Wellington's Peninsular Army …; articles by Robert Burnham, Ron McGuigan, Howie Muir, and Rory Muir (2006)

Jones, John Thomas, *Journals of Sieges … in Spain ,…* (1814; preferably the 3rd edn., ed. Harry D. Jones, 1846), including his *Memoranda Relative to the Lines thrown up to cover Lisbon in 1810*

Jones, Rice (ed. the Hon. Henry Shore), *An Engineer Officer under Wellington in the Peninsula: The Diary and War Correspondence of Lieut. Rice Jones* (1986)

Kincaid, John, *Adventures in the Rifle Brigade …* (1830)

Laborde, Alexander de, *A View of Spain, comprising a Descriptive Itinerary and a General Statistical Account of the Country* (5 vols; translated from the French, 1809)

Landmann, George Thomas, *Historical, Military and Picturesque Observations on Portugal* (1818); *Recollections of my Military Life* (1854)

Larpent, Francis Seymour (ed. Sir George Larpent, Bart.), *The Private Journal of Judge-Advocate Larpent …* (3rd edn. 1854); with an Introduction by Ian Robertson (2000)

Leach, Jonathan, *Rough Sketches of the Life of an Old Soldier* (1831)

Link, Henry Frederick, *Travels in Portugal, and through France and Spain* (1801)

Londonderry, Robert Stewart, Marquess, *Narrative of the Peninsular War* (1828)

López, Tomás, *Atlas Geográfico de España* (1804), which includes maps of Portugal

McGuigan, Ron: see *Inside Wellington's Peninsular Army*, and under Burnham

Maxwell, W.H. (ed.), *Peninsular Sketches, by Actors on the Scene* (1845)

Mitchell, Thomas Livingston (cartographer): see Wyld

Mollo, John, *The Prince's Dolls: Scandals, Skirmishes and Splendours of the first British Hussars, 1793–1815* (1997)

Muir, Howie; see *Inside Wellington's Peninsular Army*

Muir, Rory, *Britain and the Defeat of Napoleon, 1807–1815* (1996); *Tactics and the Experience of Battle in the Age of Napoleon* (1998); *Salamanca, 1812* (2001); *Inside Wellington's Peninsular Army*

Murray, Sir George; *see* Wyld

Napier, Sir William, *History of the War in the Peninsula and the South of France* (1828–40); *English Battles and Sieges in the Peninsula* (1852)

National Archives (formerly Public Record Office), Map Room, WO 78/1004, etc.

Naval Intelligence Division Geographical Handbook, Spain, and to *Portugal* (1942–4), despite outdated information.

Neale, Adam, *Letters from Portugal and Spain … from Mondego Bay to the Battle of Corunna* (1809)

Oman, Sir Charles, *Wellington's Army, 1809–1814* (1912); *History of the Peninsular War* (1902–30)

Public Record Office; *see* National Archives

Robertson, Ian C, *Wellington Invades France: the Final Phase of the Peninsular War, 1813–1814* (2003); *A Commanding Presence: Wellington in the Peninsula: Logistics · Strategy · Survival* (2008)

Sánchez Rubio, Carlos and Rocío, and Isabel Testón Núñez, *Cartografía de un espacio en Guerra: Extremadura, 1808–1812* (2008)

Schaumann, August (trans. and ed. Anthony M. Ludovici), *On the Road with Wellington. The Diary of a War Commissary …* (1924)

[Sherer, Moyle], *Recollections of the Peninsula* (1824)

Simmons, George (ed. Willoughby Verner), *A British Rifle Man. The Journals and Correspondence of Major George Simmons …* (1899)

Stothert, William, *A Narrative of the Principal Events … in Spain and Portugal* (1812)

Suchet, Marshal, *Memoirs of the War in Spain 1808–1814* (1829)

Tofiño de San Miguel, Vicente, *España Marítima or Spanish Coasting Pilot: containing directions for navigating the coasts and harbours of Spain … and Portugal* (1812)

Tomkinson, William (ed. James Tomkinson), *The Diary of a Cavalry Officer … 1809–1815* (1894)

Uffindell, Andrew (ed.), *Wellington's Armies: Britain's Campaigns in the Peninsula and at Waterloo* (2003)

Ward, Stephen George Peregrine, *Wellington's Headquarters: A Study of the Administrative Problems …* (1957)

Weller, Jac [John Allen Claude] (ed. Ian Robertson), *Wellington in the Peninsula* (1962)

[Wellington, 1st Duke of] (ed. John Gurwood), *General Orders of … Wellington* (1839); *Selections from the Dispatches and General Orders …* (1841); (ed. John Gurwood); *The Dispatches of … Wellington* (1834–9; 1844; 1852); (ed. 2nd Duke); *Supplementary Despatches, Correspondence and Memoranda of … Wellington* (1858–72)

Wheatley, Edmund (ed. Christopher Hibbert), *The Wheatley Diary* (1964)

Wheeler, William (ed. Basil H. Liddell-Hart), *The Letters of Private Wheeler, 1809–1828* (1951)

Whittingham, Samuel Ford, *A Memoir of the Services of Samuel Ford Whittingham* (1868)

[Wyld, James, publisher], *Maps and Plans of the Principle Movements, Battles and Sieges … 1808–1814* (1840), together with the *Memoir Annexed to the Atlas*, by Sir George Murray (1841)

Index to Actions

Maps and plans of the major campaigns and actions will be found on the following pages.

To describe and draw additional plans of every comparatively minor cavalry or infantry skirmish, would considerably over-extend the intended scope of this atlas: thus, those taking place at Benavente, Fuengirola, Maguilla, Majadahonda, Ordal, Osma, San Millán, Usagre, and Villagarcía for example, are neither detailed in the text, nor drawn, although their position is indicated on the map concerned. Those for the rearguard actions which took place at Casal Novo, Condeixa, Foz de Arouce, and Redinha may be found in Oman's *History*.

Plans of battles and sieges in which the Spanish fought alone against the French (printed below in roman, not bold type), are not included, but their sites may be found on the page indexed.

Agueda, combats on the, 46–7
Aire, combat at, 124
Albuera, battle of (La), 64–7
Alcañiz (south-west of Zaragoza), 23
Alcolea (just north-east of Córdoba), 25
Almaraz, expedition to, 74–5
Almeida, besieged, 46–8
Almonacid (south-west of Madrid), 83
Andalucia, 24–5
Arcangues, action at, 112–13
Arroyomolinos, combat at, 68–9
Astorga, siege of 83
Azuaga, action at, 62–3

Badajoz, the final siege of, 72–3
Bailén (east of Córdoba), 25
Barba del Puerco, action at, 46–7
Barrosa, battle of, 56–7
Barrouillet, action at, 112–13
Bayonne, the investment of, 116
Bayonne, the Sortie from, 117
Benavente, action near, 33
Beunza, combat near, 100
Bidasoa, Passage of the, 108–9
Bodón, El, combat at, 68
Bordeaux, the advance on, 122–3
Burgos, the advance on, 82–3
Burgos, retreat from, to Portugal, 82–3
Burgos, siege of, 84–5
Busaco, battle of, 50–1

Cacabelos, action at, 33
Cadiz under siege, 24–5
Cadiz to Gibraltar, 56
Campo Maior, action at, 62–3
Cardadeu (north-east of Barcelona), 23
Casal Novo, action at, 55–6

Castalla, battle of, 22–3
Castrejón, action at, 77
Castrillo, action at, 77
Catalonia and eastern Spain, 22
Ciudad Rodrigo, siege of, 70–1
Côa, combats on the, 46–7
Condeixa, action at, 54–5
Corunna, battle of, 4–5
Corunna, the retreat to, 32–3

Douro, the Passage of, at Oporto, 38–9

Echalar, action at, 38
Esla, the Passage of the, 89–90
Espinosa de los Monteros (between Burgos and Santander), 33

Figueras (north-east of Barcelona), siege of, 23
Foz de Arouce, action at, 54–5
Fuengirola (south-west of Málaga), 25
Fuentes de Oñoro, battle of, 20–1

Gamonal (just east of Burgos), 33
Garcihernández, action at, 81
Garonne, manoeuvres on the, 126
Gebora (north-west of Badajoz), 63
Gerona (north-east of Barcelona), sieges of, 23
Gibraltar to Cadiz, 56

La Rhune, ascent of, 108–9
Lérida (east of Zaragoza), siege of, 23
Lines of Torres Vedras, 52–3
Lisbon, the advance on, 26–7
Lizaso, combat near, 100

Madrid, the advance on, 82–3
Maguilla (north-east of Llerena), 63
Majadahonda (north-west of Madrid), 83

María (south-west of Zaragoza), 23
Masséna's invasion of Portugal, 48–9
Masséna's retreat, 54–5
Maya, combat at, 98–9
Mayorga, action at, 32–3
Medellín (east of Merida), 33
Medina de Rio Seco (north-west of Valladolid), 33
Miserela bridge, action at the, 36–7
Molins de Rei (west of Barcelona), 23
Mondego valley, 48–9, 54–5
Moore's advance into Spain, 32–3
Moore's retreat to Corunna, 32–3
Morales de Toro, action at, 90

Nive, battle of the, 112–3
Nivelle, battle of the, 110–1

Ocaña (south of Madrid), 83
Olivenza (south-west of Badajoz), 63
Oporto, advance on, 36–7
Oporto, the Passage of the Douro at, 38–9
Ordal (west of Barcelona), 23
Orthez, advance on, 118–9
Orthez, battle of, 120–1
Osma (west of Vitoria), 89

Passage of the Bidasoa, 108–9
Passage of the Douro, 38–9
Passage of the Esla, 89–90
Peninsula, physical map of the, 20–1
Peñíscola (south of Tortosa), 23
Pombal, action at, 54–5
Pyrenean quadrilateral, 94–5
Pyrenees, battles of the, 99–102

Redinha, action at, 54–5
Rhune, the ascent of La, 108–9
Roliça, combat at, 28–9
Roncesvalles, combat at, 98–9
Rosas (north-east of Gerona), siege of, 23

Sabugal, combat at, 54–5
Sagunto (north of Valencia), sieges of 23
Sahagún, combat at, 32
St Pierre, battle of, 114–15
Salamanca, battle of, 78–82
Salamanca, forts of, 76
Salamanca, manoeuvring prior to, 76–7

San Marcial, combat at, 106–7
San Millán (south-west of Osma), 89
San Muñoz, on the Huebra, at, 82–3
San Sebastian, advance on, 94–5
San Sebastian, siege of, 102–3
Sobral, action at, 52
Somosierra (north of Madrid), 33
Sorauren, battles of, 100–1
Soult's advance on Pamplona, 96–7
Soult's retreat from Sorauren, 96–7
Spain, south-west, 62–3

Tagus valley, advance up the, 40–1
Talavera, battle of, 42–5
Talavera, retreat from, 40–1
Tarbes, action at, 125
Tarbes, advance on, 124
Tarifa, siege of, 56
Tarragona, siege of, 22–3
Tolosa, action at, 94
Torres Vedras, Lines of, 52–3
Tortosa (south-west of Tarragona), siege of, 23
Toulouse, advance on, 122–3
Toulouse, battle of, 126–8
Tudela (north-west of Zaragoza), 23

Ucles (east of Ocaña), 83
Usagre, 63

Valencia, sieges of, 23
Vals (north of Tarragona), 23
Venta del Pozo, action at, 82–3
Vera, combats near, 106–9
Villagarcía (north-west of Llerena), 63
Villamuriel, action at, 82–3
Vimeiro, battle of, 30–1
Vitoria, advance on, 88–90
Vitoria, battle of, 91–3
Vitoria, the pursuit after, 94–5
Vouga, action on the, 36

Winter cantonments, 1811–12, 68–9
Winter cantonments, 1812–13, 86–7

Yanci, action at, 96–7

Zaragoza, sieges of 23
Zornoza (east of Bilbao), 21